ULTIMATE MUSIC THEORY
GLORY ST. GERMAIN ARCT RMT MYCC UMTC

Edited by Shelagh McKibbon-U'Ren RMT UMTC

PREP 2 RUDIMENTS ANSWER BOOK

UltimateMusicTheory.com

Enriching Lives Through Music Education - *The Way To Score Success!*

ISBN: 978-0-9813101-0-7

Ultimate Music Theory Ltd. © COPYRIGHT 2021 Gloryland Publishing. All Rights Reserved.

ULTIMATE MUSIC THEORY: *The Way to Score Success!*

The Ultimate Music Theory workbooks are for all Musicians.

The more we understand the universal language of music, the more we are capable of communicating our ideas through performing and writing music, interpreting musical compositions of others, and developing a deeper appreciation of music. It is through music education that we progress from student to musician and are able to enjoy and understand music at a more comprehensive level.

Respect Copyright 2021 Glory St. Germain
All rights reserved. No part of this publication may be reproduced or transmitted in any form or by any means, electronic or mechanical, including photocopying, recording, or any information storage and retrieval system, without permission in writing from the author/publisher.

Published in 2021 by Gloryland Publishing

GlorylandPublishing.com

UltimateMusicTheory.com

Library and Archives Canada Cataloguing in Publication St. Germain, Glory 1953-
Ultimate Music Theory Series / Glory St. Germain

Gloryland Publishing - Ultimate Music Theory Series:
GP - UP1   ISBN: 978-0-9809556-6-8   Ultimate Prep 1 Rudiments
GP - UP1A   ISBN: 978-0-9809556-9-9   Ultimate Prep 1 Rudiments Answer Book
GP - UP2   ISBN: 978-0-9809556-7-5   Ultimate Prep 2 Rudiments
GP - UP2A   ISBN: 978-0-9813101-0-7   Ultimate Prep 2 Rudiments Answer Book
GP - UBR   ISBN: 978-0-9813101-3-8   Ultimate Basic Rudiments
GP - UBRA   ISBN: 978-0-9813101-4-5   Ultimate Basic Answer Book
GP - UIR   ISBN: 978-0-9813101-5-2   Ultimate Intermediate Rudiments
GP - UIRA   ISBN: 978-0-9813101-6-9   Ultimate Intermediate Answer Book
GP - UAR   ISBN: 978-0-9813101-7-6   Ultimate Advanced Rudiments
GP - UARA   ISBN: 978-0-9813101-8-3   Ultimate Advanced Answer Book
GP - UCR   ISBN: 978-0-9813101-1-4   Ultimate Complete Rudiments
GP - UCRA   ISBN: 978-0-9813101-2-1   Ultimate Complete Answer Book

♪ **Note:** The Ultimate Music Theory Program includes the UMT Workbook Series, Exam Series & Supplemental Series to help students successfully prepare for international theory exams.

Ultimate Music Theory Prep 2 Rudiments
Table of Contents

Lesson 1	The Grand Staff, Landmarks and Ledger Lines	5
	Lesson 1 Review Test - Score: _____ / 100%	14
Lesson 2	Note and Rest Values, Melodic and Harmonic Intervals	17
	Lesson 2 Review Test - Score: _____ / 100%	26
Lesson 3	Simple Time	29
	Lesson 3 Review Test - Score: _____ / 100%	38
Lesson 4	Semitones, Whole Tones and Accidentals	42
	Lesson 4 Review Test - Score: _____ / 100%	47
Lesson 5	Major Pentascales - Major Scales - Outside the Circle of Fifths	51
	Lesson 5 Review Test - Score: _____ / 100%	60
Lesson 6	Minor Pentascales - Natural Minor Scales - Inside the Circle of Fifths	64
	Lesson 6 Review Test - Score: _____ / 100%	74
Lesson 7	Key Signature	78
	Lesson 7 Review Test - Score: _____ / 100%	82
Lesson 8	Key Signatures on the Grand Staff	86
	Lesson 8 Review Test - Score: _____ / 100%	90
Lesson 9	Major Triads - Solid and Broken	94
	Lesson 9 Review Test - Score: _____ / 100%	98
Lesson 10	Harmonic Minor Scales	102
	Lesson 10 Review Test - Score: _____ / 100%	105
Lesson 11	Melodic Minor Scales	109
	Lesson 11 Review Test - Score: _____ / 100%	112
Lesson 12	Analysis and Musical Terms	116
	Lesson 12 Final Prep 2 Exam - Score: _____ / 100%	118
Guide & Chart	UMT Guide & Chart - Prep 2 Rudiments Flashcards	122

Score: 60 - 69 Pass; **70 - 79** Honors; **80 - 89** First Class Honors; **90 - 100** First Class Honors with Distinction

Ultimate Music Theory: *The Way to Score Success!*

ULTIMATE MUSIC THEORY: *The Way to Score Success!*

The focus of the **Ultimate Music Theory** Series is to simplify complex concepts and show the relativity of these concepts with practical application. These workbooks are designed to help teachers and students discover the excitement and benefits of a music theory education.

Ultimate Music Theory workbooks are based on a proven approach to the study of music theory that follows these **4 Ultimate Music Theory Learning Principles**:

- ♪ **Simplicity of Learning** - easy to understand instructions, examples and exercises.

- ♪ **Memory Joggers** - tips for all learning styles including visual, auditory, and kinaesthetic.

- ♪ **Tie it All Together** - helping musicians understand the universal language of music.

- ♪ **Make it Relevant** - applying theoretical concepts to pedagogical studies.

The **Ultimate Music Theory**™ Rudiments Workbooks, Supplemental Workbooks and Exams help students prepare for successful completion of internationally recognized theory examinations.

BONUS - Convenient and easy to use Ultimate Music Theory Answer Books - Identical to the student workbooks for quick, easy & accurate marking. UMT Answer Books available for all levels.

♫ **Note:** Each Ultimate Music Theory Rudiments Workbook has a corresponding Supplemental Workbook Level to enhance knowledge of analysis, develop a deeper understanding of music history, provide a proven step-by-step system in melody writing, and much more!

The Ultimate Music Theory Series includes these EXCLUSIVE BONUS features:

Ultimate Music Theory Guide & Chart - a convenient summarization to review concepts.

12 Comprehensive Review Tests & Final Exam - retention of concepts learned in previous lessons.

♫ **Notes:** point out important information and handy memory tips.

80 Music Theory Flashcards - Musical Terms & Signs, Rhythms, Key Signatures, Time Signatures, Note Naming, Dynamics, Tempos, Articulation, Triads, Chords, etc. (each workbook is different).

Ultimate Music Theory FREE Resources - Music History Videos, Worksheets, Music Theory Blogs, Free Ultimate Music Theory Teachers Guide & Free Teach Basic Rudiments Online Mini-Course.

Go To: **UltimateMusicTheory.com** Today!

Enriching Lives Through Music Education

Lesson 1   The Grand Staff, Landmarks and Ledger Lines

The **GRAND STAFF** is made up of the Treble Staff (on the top) and the Bass Staff (on the bottom) joined together by a BRACE and a bar line. Middle C can be written in both the Treble Staff and the Bass Staff.

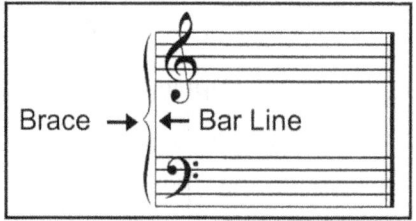

♪ **Note:** The Treble Staff is also called the Treble Clef.
            The Bass Staff is also called the Bass Clef.

A **NOTE** written on the **GRAND STAFF** corresponds to a specific **PITCH** (sound) on the keyboard.
The lower the note on the Grand Staff (to the left on the keyboard) the lower the pitch.
As notes move higher up the Grand Staff (to the right on the keyboard) the sound gets higher in pitch.

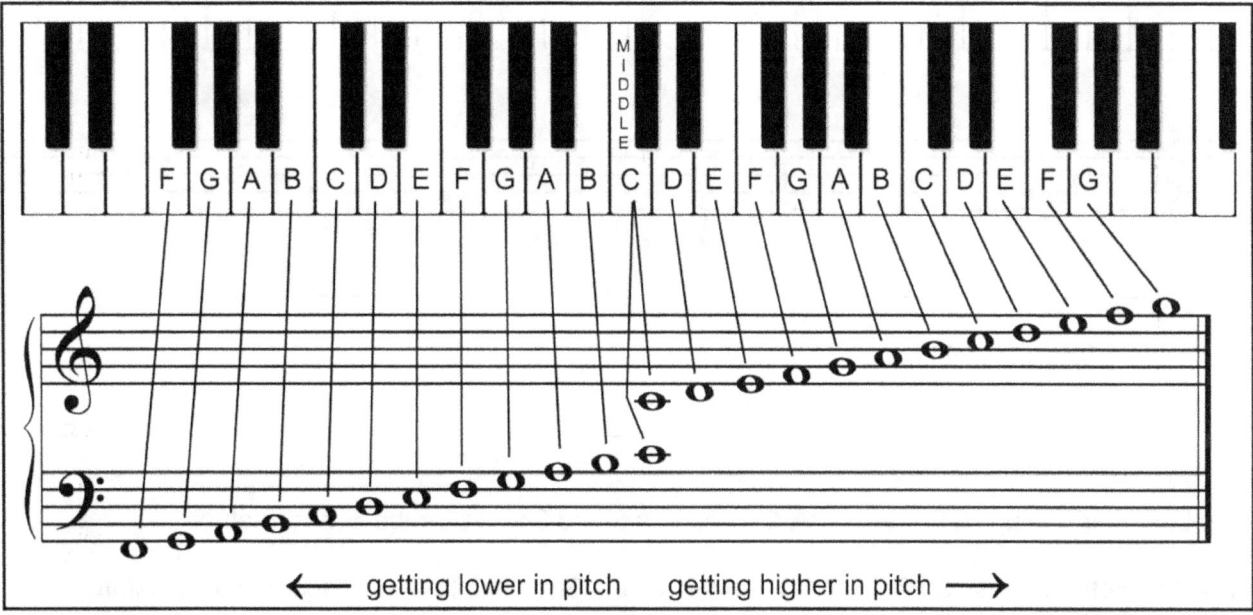

← getting lower in pitch   getting higher in pitch →

1. a) Name the following notes on the Grand Staff.
   b) Draw a line from each note to the corresponding key on the keyboard (at the correct pitch).

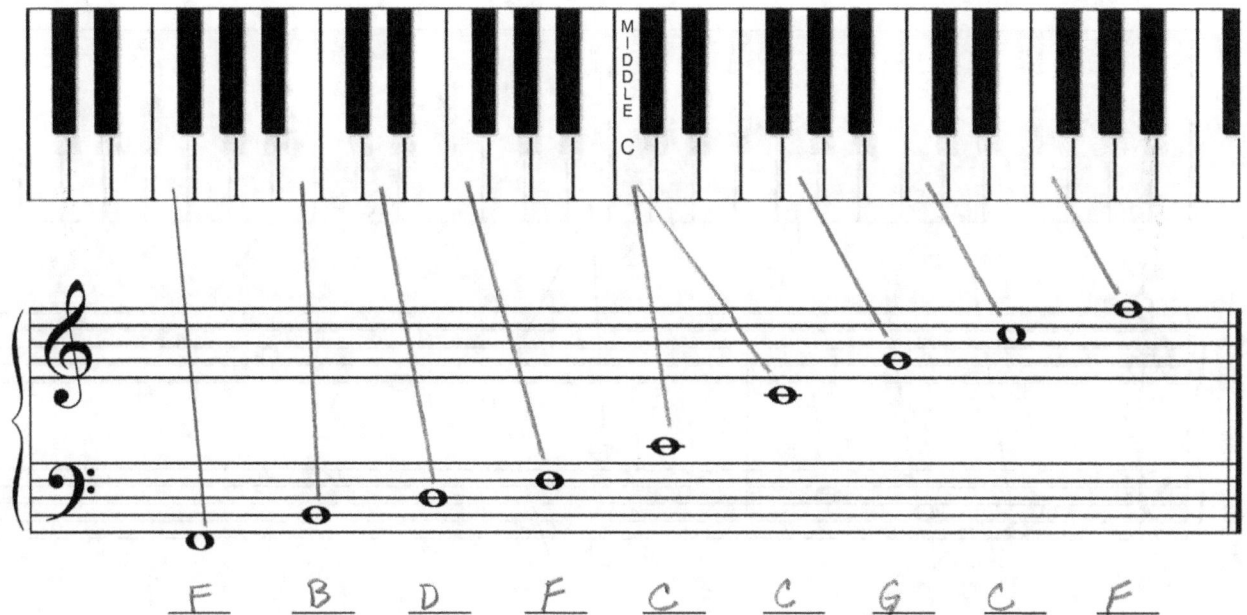

F   B   D   F   C   C   G   C   F

LANDMARK NOTES

LANDMARK NOTES are used to quickly identify notes on the Grand Staff. They are defined by their PITCH and by their PLACEMENT ON THE GRAND STAFF.

The Landmark Skipping Pattern of "**G B D F**" can be found 3 times on the Grand Staff.

1. a) Name the following Landmark notes on the Grand Staff.
   b) Draw a line from each note to the corresponding key on the keyboard (at the correct pitch).

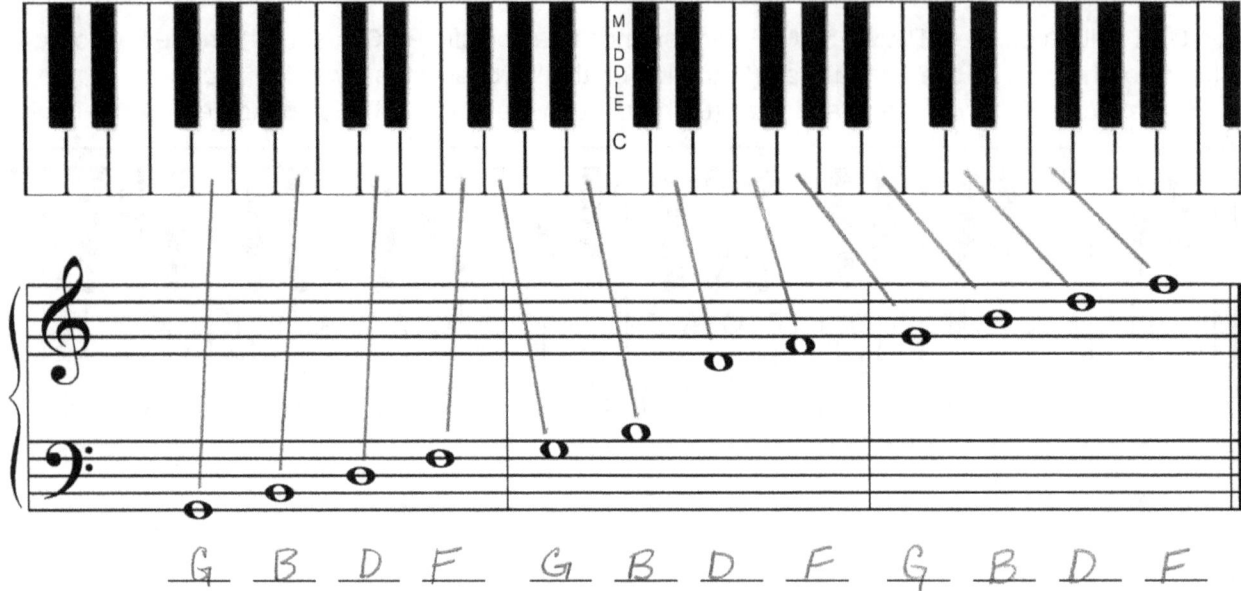

G B D F   G B D F   G B D F

The Landmark Skipping Pattern of "**A C E**" can be found 3 times on the Grand Staff.

♪ **Note:** Both the Bass Staff Middle C and the Treble Staff Middle C correspond to the **SAME MIDDLE C** on the keyboard.

2. a) Name the following Landmark notes on the Grand Staff.
   b) Draw a line from each note to the corresponding key on the keyboard (at the correct pitch).

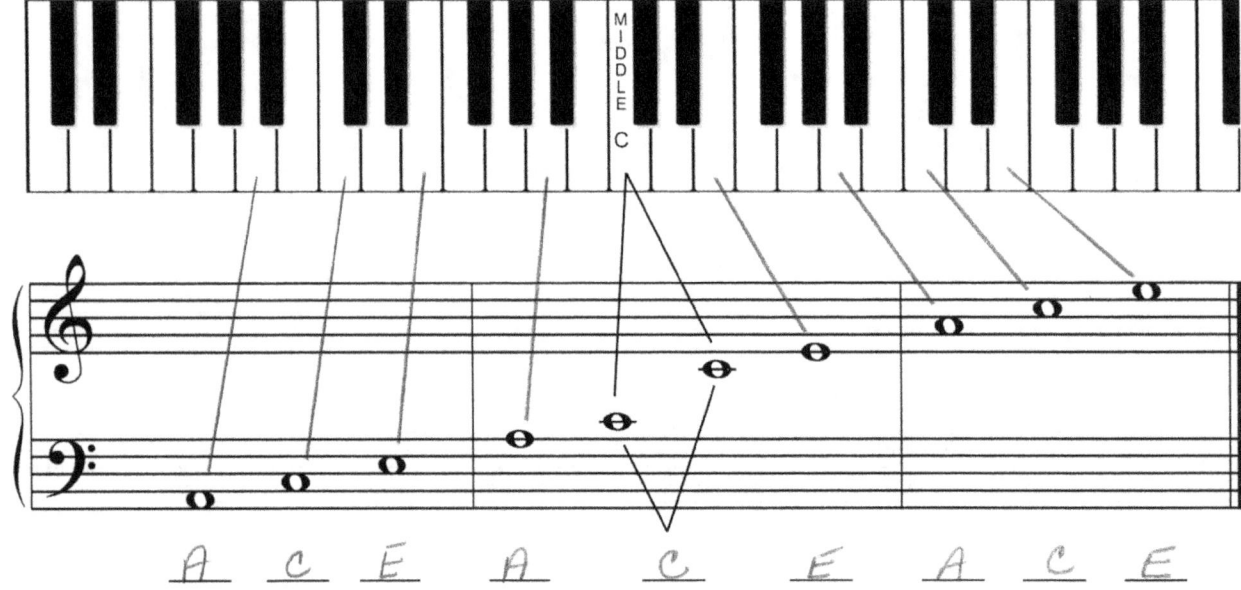

A C E   A C E   A C E

PITCHES on the KEYBOARD

When matching a note on the staff to the corresponding key on the keyboard, notes are to be placed at the correct PITCH on the KEYBOARD. The pitch is the high or low sound.

♪ **Note:** Start with the note Middle C on the Grand Staff; as notes move higher on the staff, they will move up (to the right) on the keyboard. As notes move lower on the staff, they will move down (to the left) on the keyboard.

1. a) Name the following notes on the Grand Staff.
   b) Draw a line from each note to the corresponding key on the keyboard (at the correct pitch).

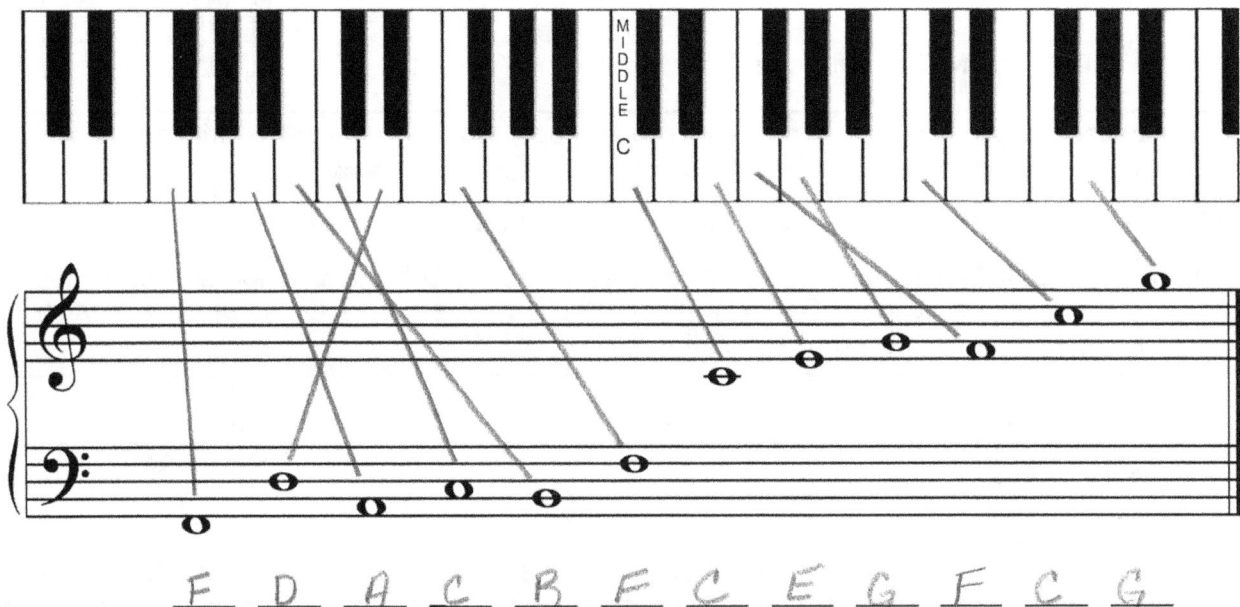

F D A C B F C E G F C G

2. a) Draw a Treble Clef ("G" Clef) and a Bass Clef ("F" Clef) on the staff to complete the Grand Staff.
   b) Write the notes on the Grand Staff for the keys marked with a ☺. Use whole notes.
   c) Name the notes.
   d) Draw a line from each note to the corresponding key on the keyboard (at the correct pitch).

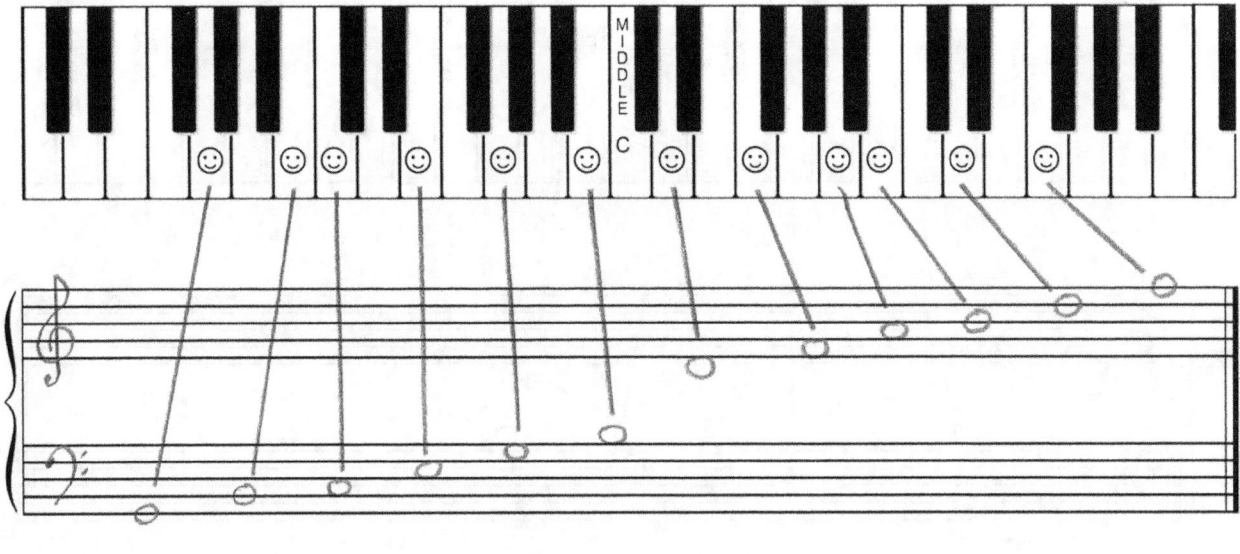

G B C E G B D F A B D F

ACCIDENTALS

An **ACCIDENTAL** is a sign that lowers or raises the pitch one semitone (half step).

A **SEMITONE** or **half step** is the shortest distance between two neighbouring (next door) notes on the keyboard, black or white, no key in between.

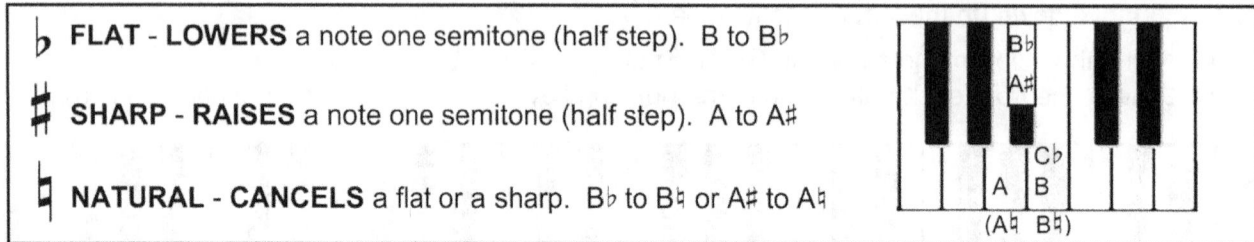

When an accidental appears on a line or in a space, it applies to any note that is written on that line or in that space until it is cancelled by either another accidental or by a bar line.

BAR LINES divide the music into **MEASURES**. A measure is a unit of musical time.

♪ **Note:** An **ACCIDENTAL** only applies to the notes on the line or in the space where it is written in that measure. It does **NOT** apply to notes that have the same letter name but appear at a higher or lower position on the staff.

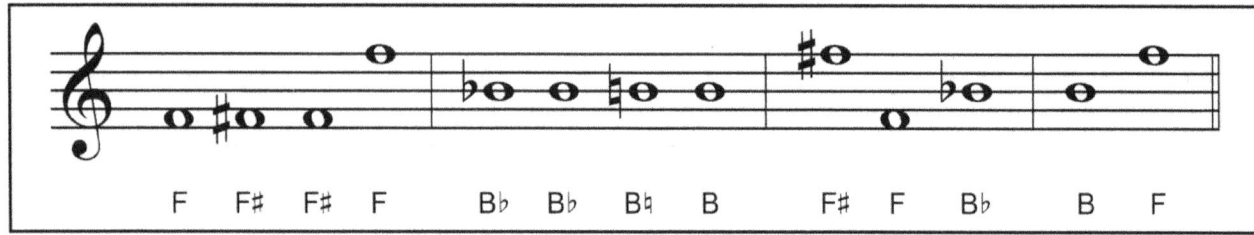

♪ **Note:** An **ACCIDENTAL** is written in front of the note and after the letter name.

1. a) Name the following notes on the Grand Staff.
   b) Draw a line from each note to the corresponding key on the keyboard (at the correct pitch).

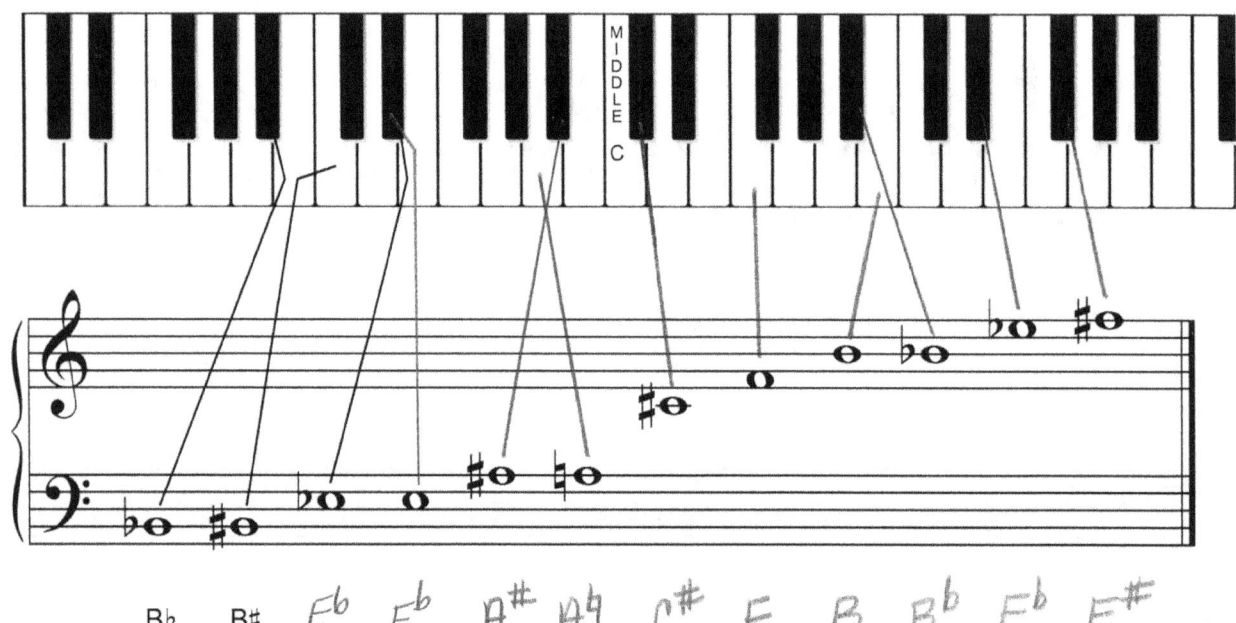

Bb B♯ E♭ E♭ A♯ A♮ C♯ F B B♭ E♭ F♯

8

ACCIDENTALS on the KEYBOARD

1. a) Name the following notes on the Grand Staff.
   b) Draw a line from each note to the corresponding key on the keyboard (at the correct pitch).

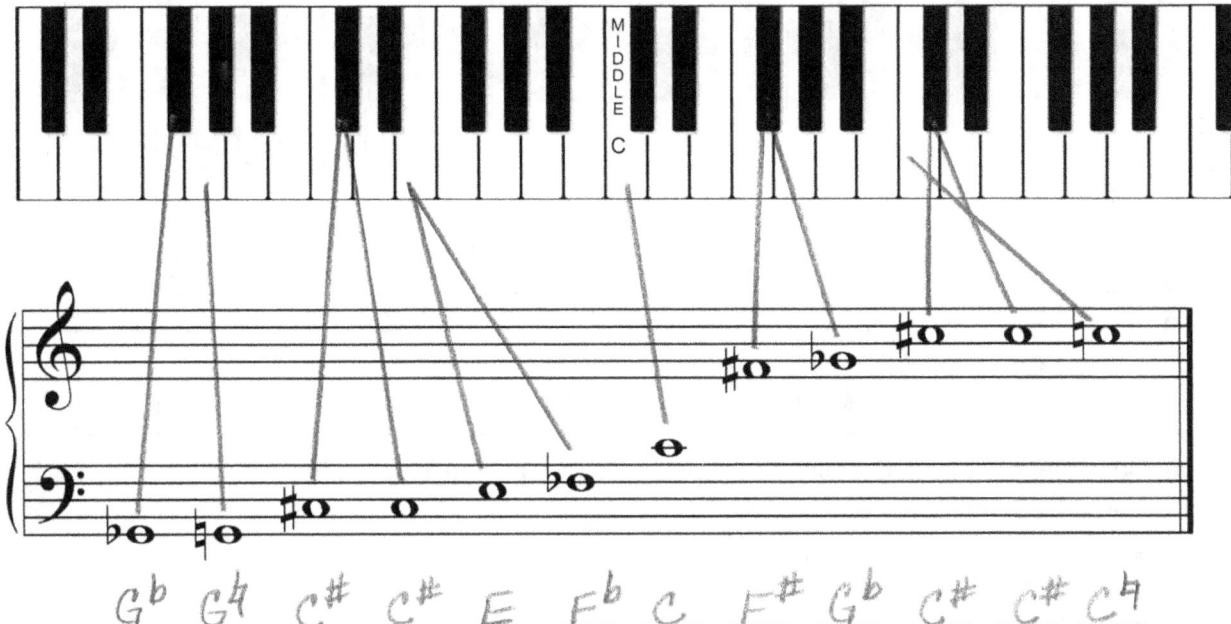

G♭ G♮ C♯ C♯ E F♭ C F♯ G♭ C♯ C♯ C♮

♪ **Note:** Each black key has 2 names - a sharp name and a flat name. The white keys D, G and A have only one name. All other white keys have 2 names: C (B♯), B (C♭), E (F♭) and F (E♯).

2. a) Write the notes on the Grand Staff for the keys marked with a ☺. Use whole notes.
      Use notes with accidentals (sharps or flats) or without accidentals.
   b) Name the notes.
   c) Draw a line from each note to the corresponding key on the keyboard (at the correct pitch).

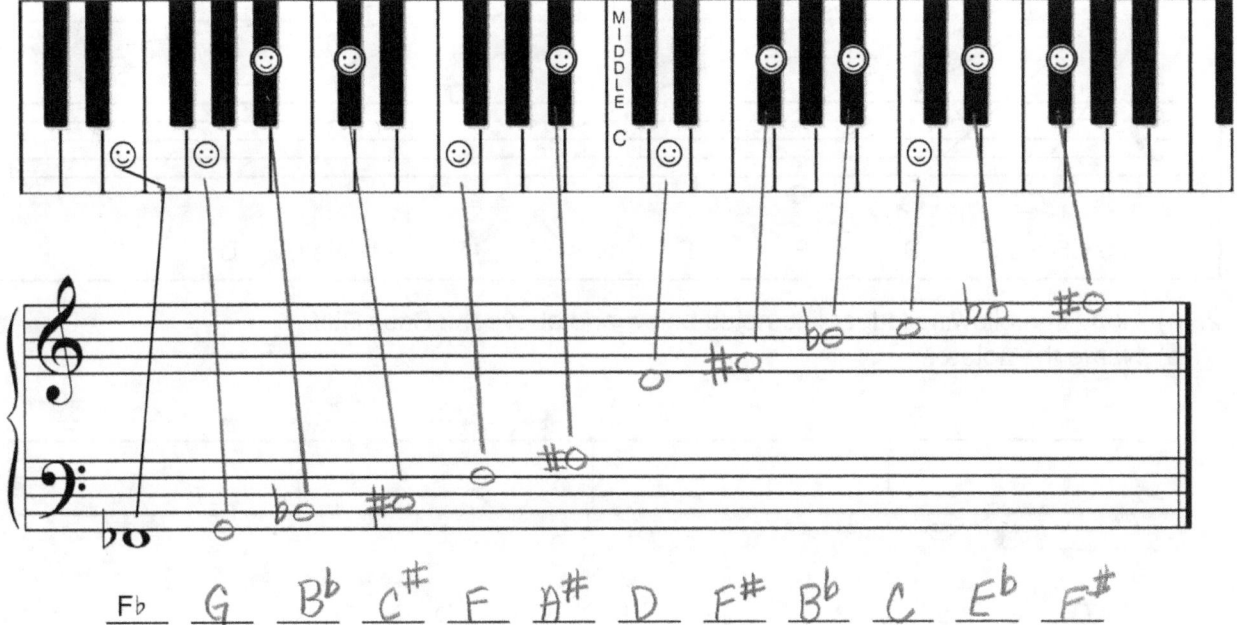

F♭ G B♭ C♯ F A♯ D F♯ B♭ C E♭ F♯

9

LEDGER LINES

LEDGER LINES are short lines used to extend the staff as needed for notes written above or below the Treble Clef and Bass Clef. Ledger lines must be equal distance from the staff.

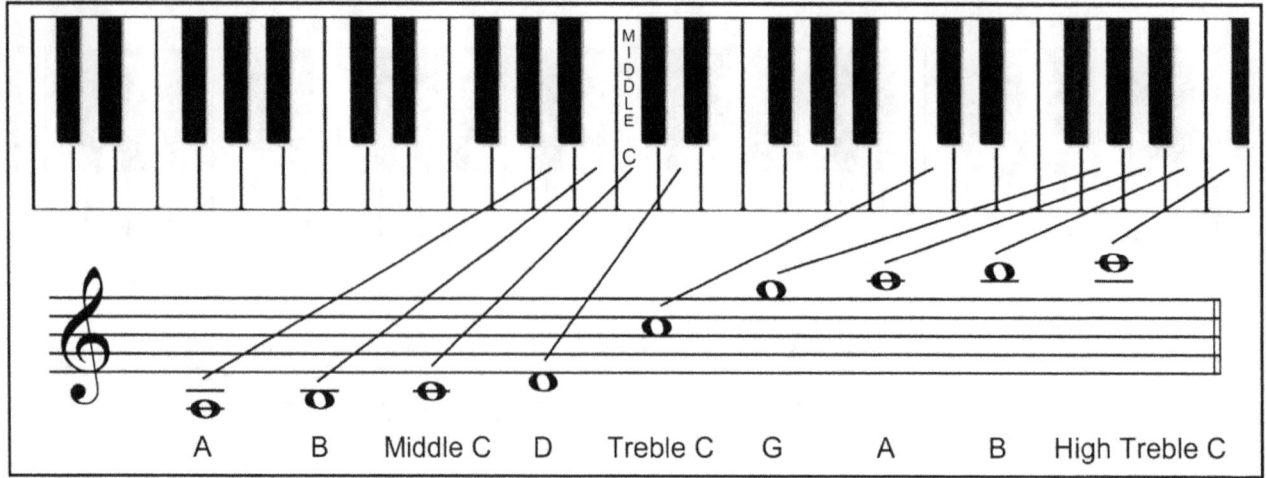

1. a) Copy the following ledger line notes below and above the Treble Clef.
   b) Name the notes.

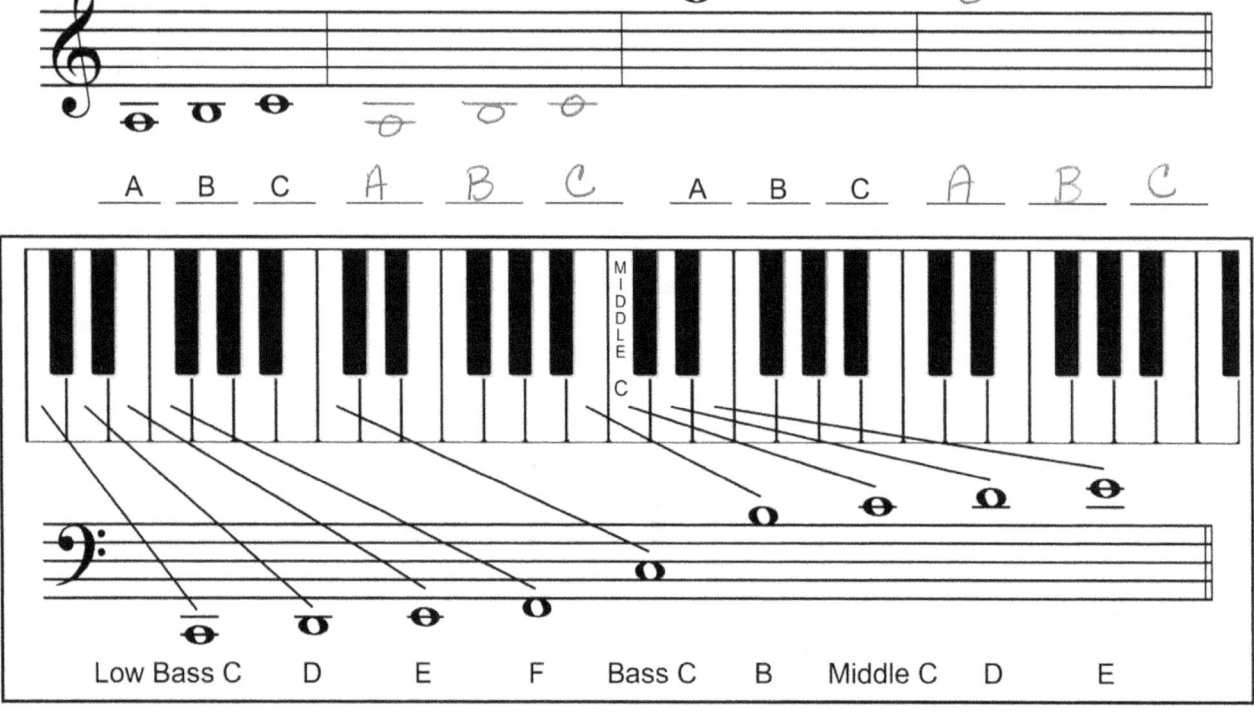

2. a) Copy the following ledger line notes below and above the Bass Clef.
   b) Name the notes.

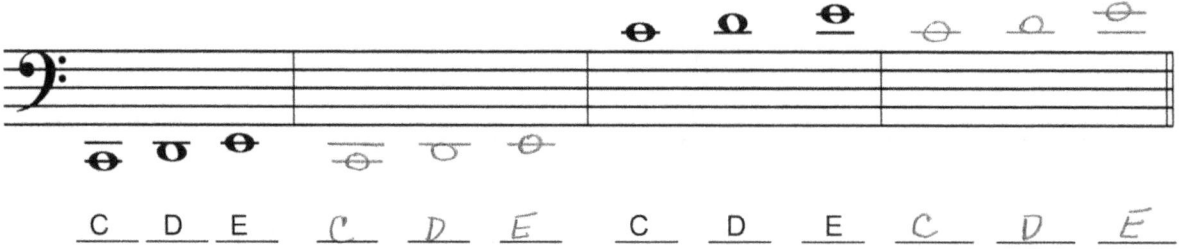

LEDGER LINE NOTES in the TREBLE CLEF and BASS CLEF

1. Write the following notes. Use ledger lines. Use whole notes.

   a) ABOVE the Treble Clef.

   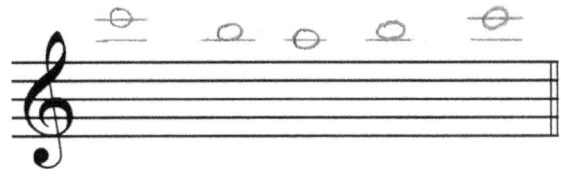

   High C   B   A   B   High C

   b) BELOW the Treble Clef.

   Middle C   B   A   B   Middle C

2. Write the following notes. Use ledger lines. Use whole notes.

   a) ABOVE the Bass Clef.

   Middle C   D   E   D   Middle C

   b) BELOW the Bass Clef.

   Low C   D   E   D   Low C

3. Name the following notes in the Treble Clef.

   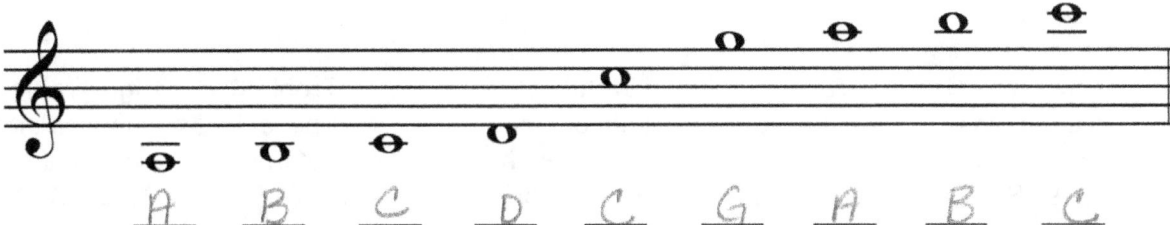

   A   B   C   D   C   G   A   B   C

4. Name the following notes in the Bass Clef.

   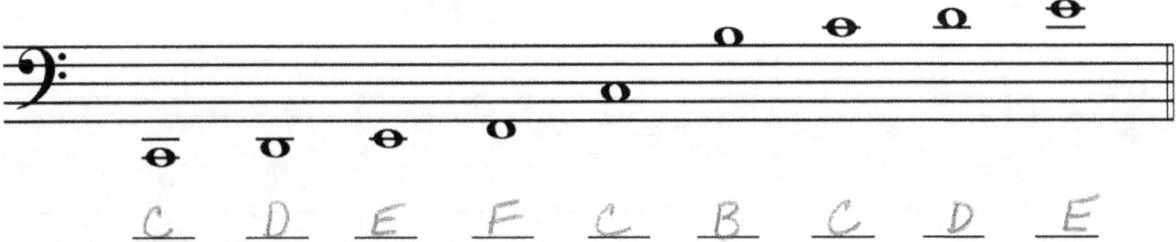

   C   D   E   F   C   B   C   D   E

5. Name the following notes in the Bass Clef.

   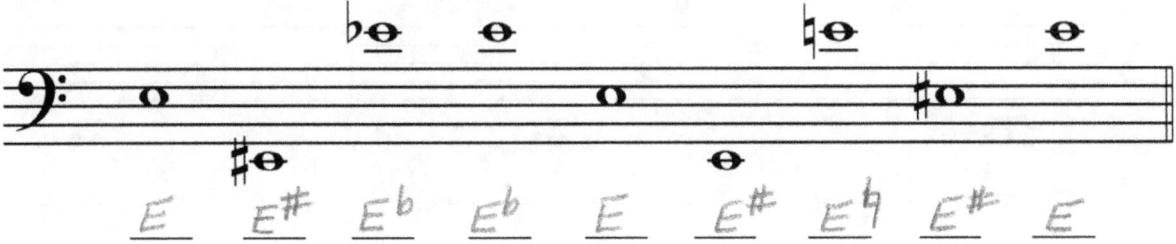

   E   E#   Eb   Eb   E   E#   E♮   E#   E

C on the GRAND STAFF

The **NOTE** "**C**" appears 5 times on the **GRAND STAFF** at 5 different pitches.

♪ **Note:** Two ledger lines **ABOVE** the Treble Clef is High Treble C and two ledger lines **BELOW** the Bass Clef is Low Bass C. Middle C is the ledger line in the **MIDDLE** between the Treble Clef and the Bass Clef.

1. a) Copy the following C's on the Grand Staff at each of the 5 different pitches.
   b) Draw a line from each note to the corresponding key on the keyboard (at the correct pitch).

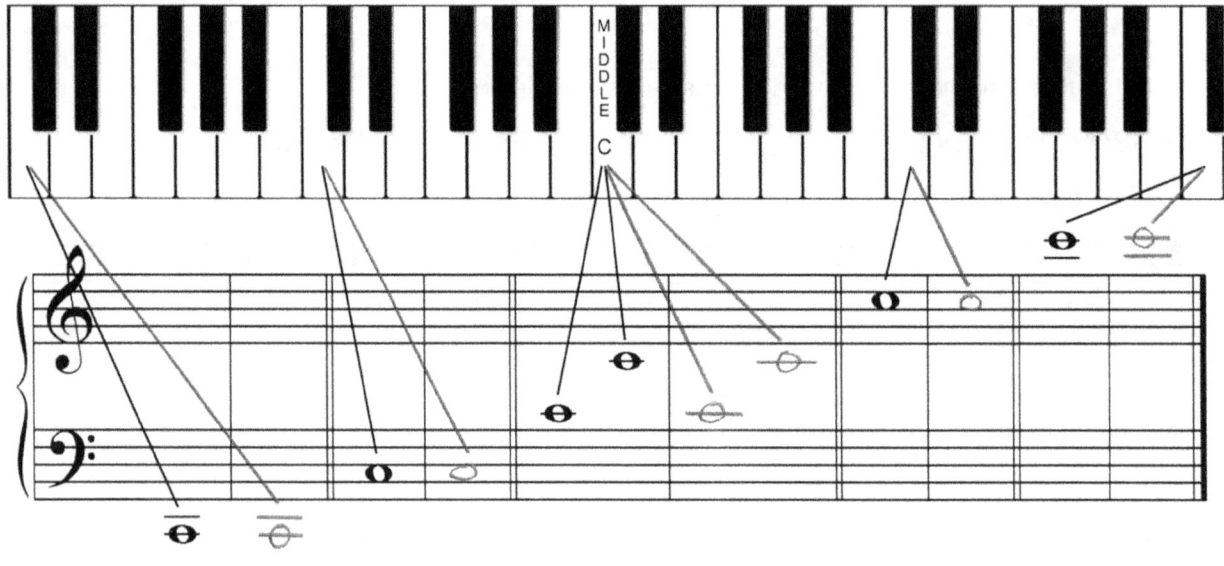

| **Low Bass C** | **Bass C** | **Middle C** | **Treble C** | **High Treble C** |
| 2 ledger lines below the Bass Staff | Space 2 of the Bass Staff | Ledger Line in between the Grand Staff | Space 3 of the Treble Staff | 2 ledger lines above the Treble Staff |

2. Name the following notes. Observe the accidentals.

C# C C# C♭ C♭ C C♭ C♭ C♮

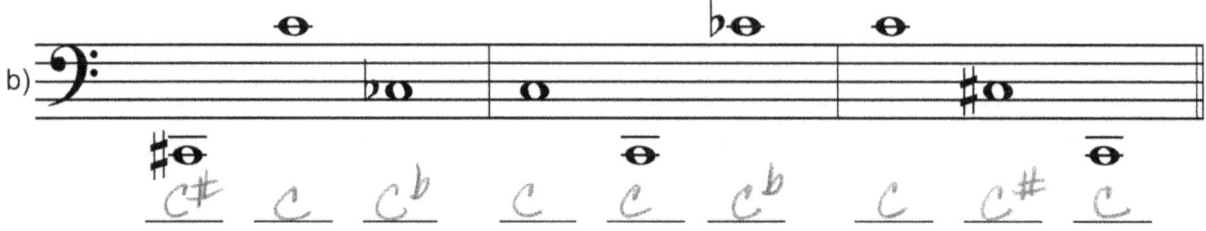

C# C C♭ C C C♭ C C# C

LEDGER LINE NOTES on the GRAND STAFF

The notes written with ledger lines **BELOW** the Treble Clef are at the **SAME PITCH** as the corresponding notes in the Bass Clef (the alternate clef). The notes written with ledger lines **ABOVE** the Bass Clef are at the **SAME PITCH** as the corresponding notes in the Treble Clef (the alternate clef).

1. a) Name the following notes.
   b) Rewrite the given notes at the same pitch in the alternate clef (either above the Bass Clef or below the Treble Clef). Use ledger lines. Use whole notes.

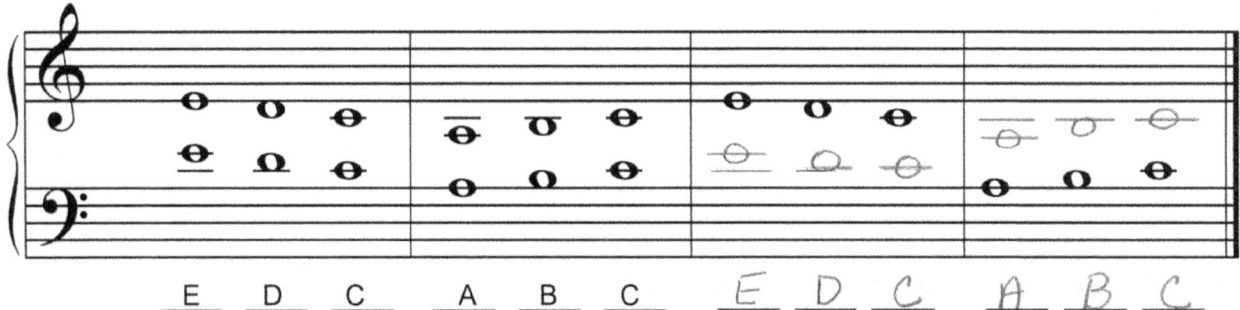

E D C   A B C   E D C   A B C

2. Name the following notes on the Grand Staff.

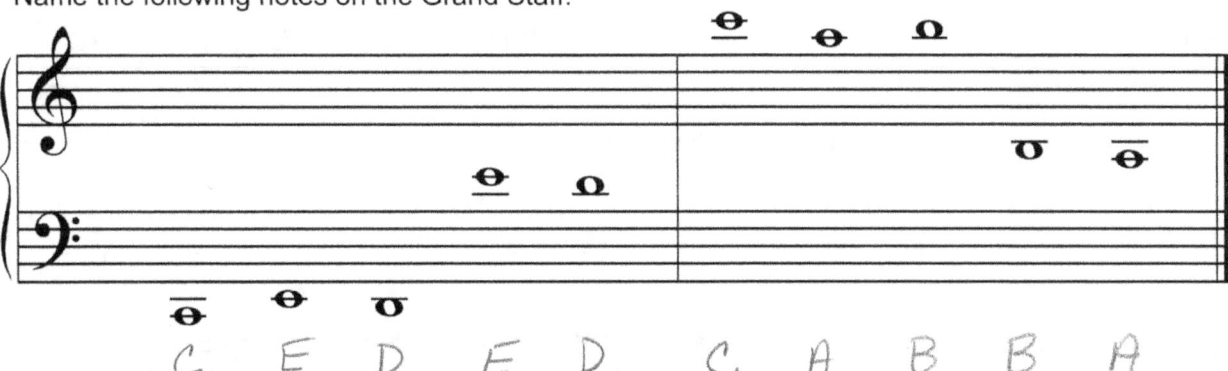

C E D E D   C A B B A

3. a) Write the following notes indicated on the keyboard with a ☺ directly on the Grand Staff below. Use whole notes.
   b) Name the notes.
   c) Draw a line from each note to the corresponding key on the keyboard (at the correct pitch).

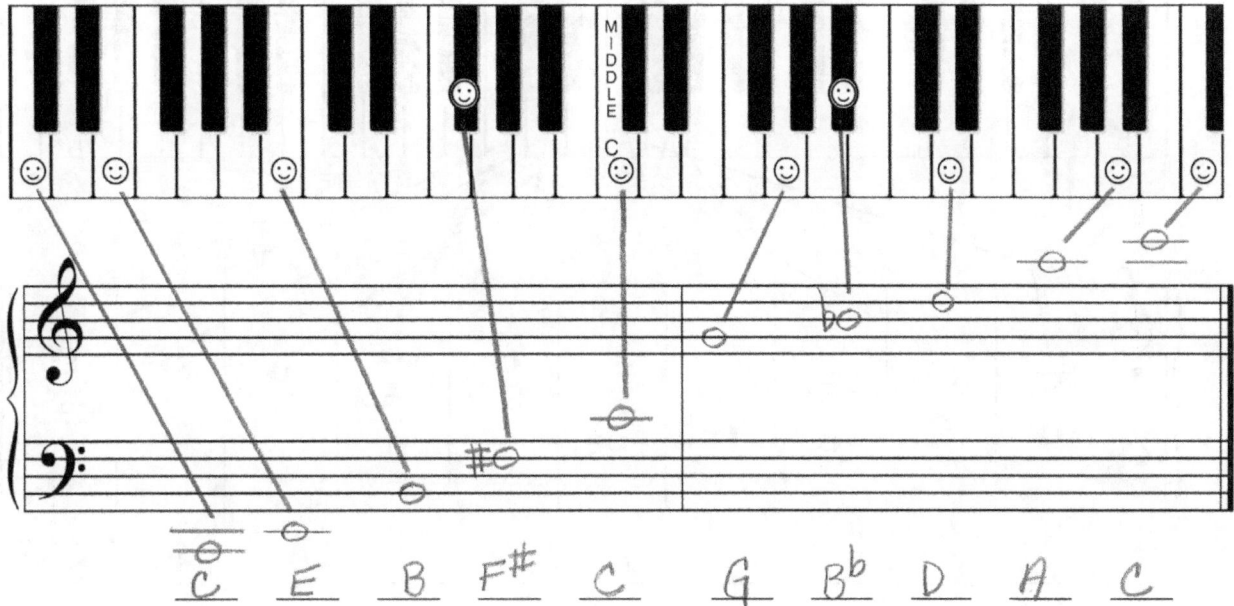

C E B F# C   G Bb D A C

Lesson 1   Review Test

Total Score: ____ / 100

1. a) Draw a **Treble Clef** ("G" Clef) on the staff below.
   b) Name the notes

   /10

D B C G A C A B C G

2. a) Draw a **Bass Clef** ("F" Clef) on the staff below.
   b) Name the notes.

   /10

F C G# G♮ D D♭ C E F D♭

3. a) Rewrite the given notes at the **SAME PITCH** in the alternate clef (either ABOVE the Bass Clef or BELOW the Treble Clef). Use LEDGER lines. Use whole notes.
   b) Name the notes.
   c) Draw a line from each note to the corresponding key on the keyboard (at the correct pitch).

   /10

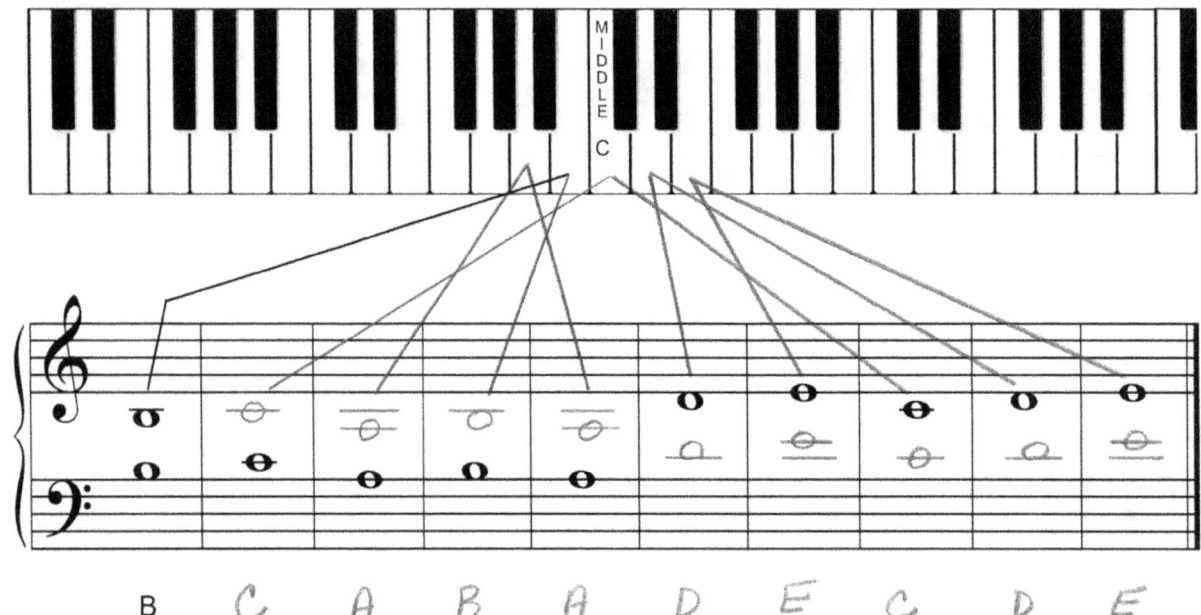

B C A B A D E C D E

14

4. Following the examples, add an accidental (♯, ♭ or ♮) in front of the note to write each of the following notes in the Treble Clef.

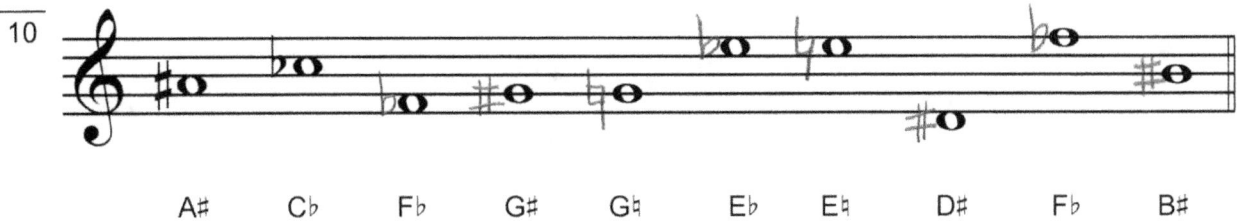

A♯   C♭   F♭   G♯   G♮   E♭   E♮   D♯   F♭   B♯

5. Write the following notes. Use ledger lines. Use whole notes.

a) **ABOVE** the Treble Clef.   b) **BELOW** the Treble Clef.

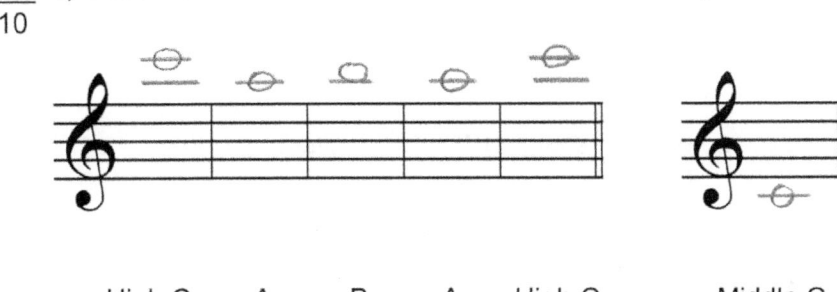 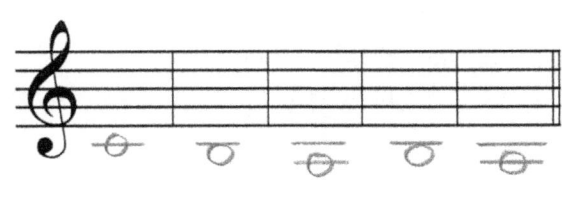

High C   A   B   A   High C   Middle C   B   A   B   A

6. Write the following notes. Use ledger lines. Use whole notes.

a) **ABOVE** the Bass Clef.   b) **BELOW** the Bass Clef.

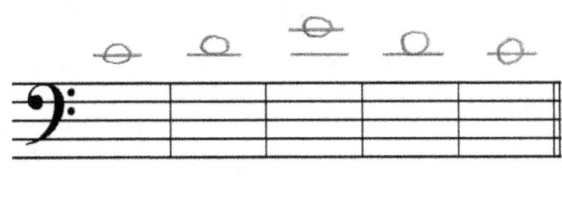 

Middle C   D   E   D   Middle C   Low C   D   Low C   E   D

7. Write the following notes in the Bass Clef. Use whole notes.

B   D♯   F   A♭   C   G♯   G♮   E♯   E♮   B♭

8. a) Name the following notes.
b) For each pair of notes, circle the note which sounds **LOWER** in pitch.

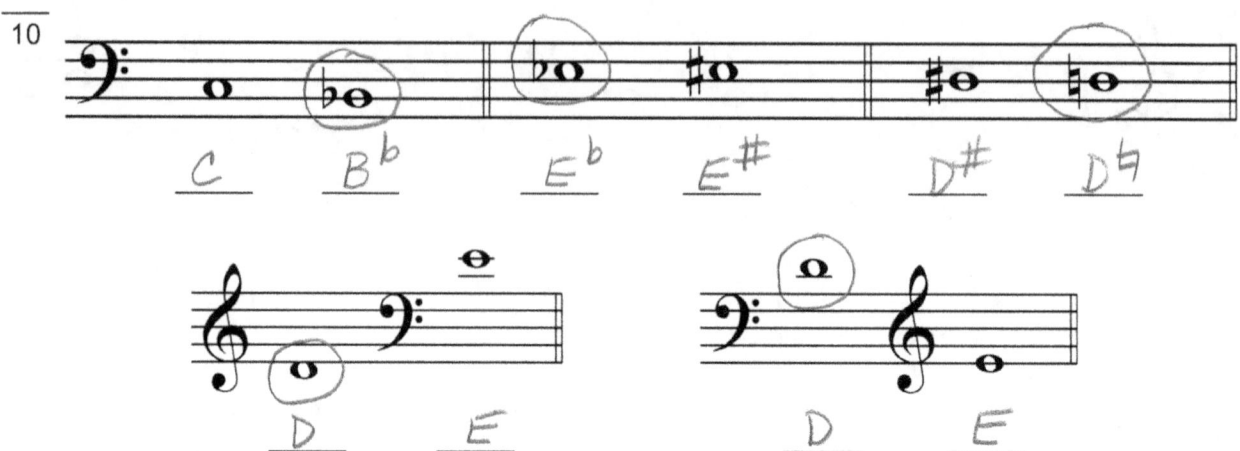

9. a) Name the following notes.
b) For each pair of notes, circle the note which sounds **HIGHER** in pitch.

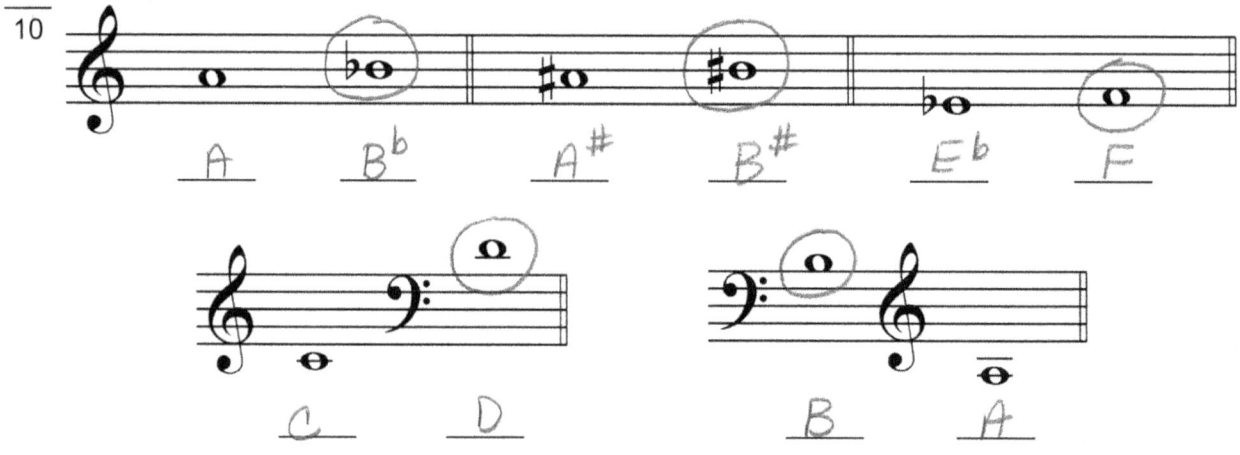

10. a) Name the following notes.
b) Identify the melodic pattern in each measure as either:
same line, same space, step up, step down, skip up or skip down.

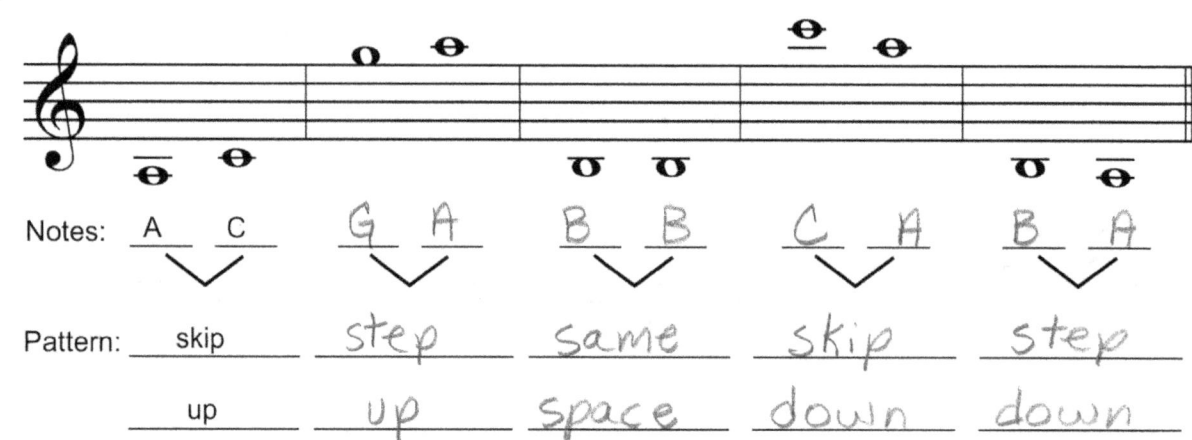

Lesson 2

Note and Rest Values, Melodic and Harmonic Intervals

Each **NOTE** has a specific time value of sound and each **REST** has a specific time value of silence.

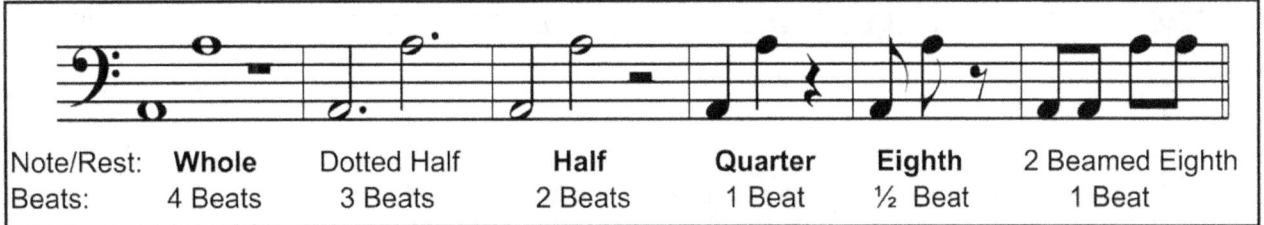

Note/Rest:	Whole	Dotted Half	Half	Quarter	Eighth	2 Beamed Eighth
Beats:	4 Beats	3 Beats	2 Beats	1 Beat	½ Beat	1 Beat

FLAGS: For an eighth note, the **FLAG** always goes to the **RIGHT**.
When writing a single eighth note, the end of the flag does not touch the notehead.

DOTS: For a dotted half note, the **DOT** always goes to the **RIGHT** of the notehead. The dot is placed in the same space for a space note and in the space above the line for a line note.

RESTS: ― hangs from line 4. ▬ sits on line 3. ❼ starts in space 3.

STEM RULES: When the notehead is:

ABOVE the middle line, stem DOWN on the left: 'ρ' like 'p' in → ρizza
ON the middle line, stem DOWN on the left or UP on the right:
BELOW the middle line, stem UP on the right: 'd' like 'd' in → ᗪonuts

A Stem is approximately one octave in length.

---

1. a) Following the example at the top of the page, copy the notes and rests in the Bass Clef.
   b) Write the number of beats each note/rest receives.

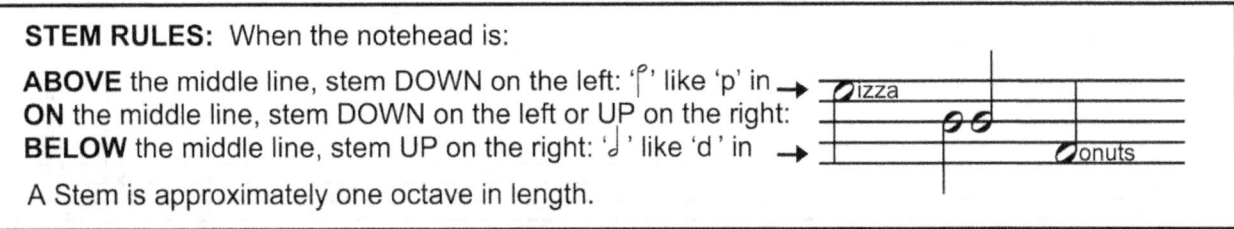

Note/Rest:	Whole	Dotted Half	Half	Quarter	Eighth	2 Beamed Eighth
Beats:	_4_ Beats	_3_ Beats	_2_ Beats	_1_ Beat	_½_ Beat	_1_ Beat

2. Complete the following Note Value Chart.

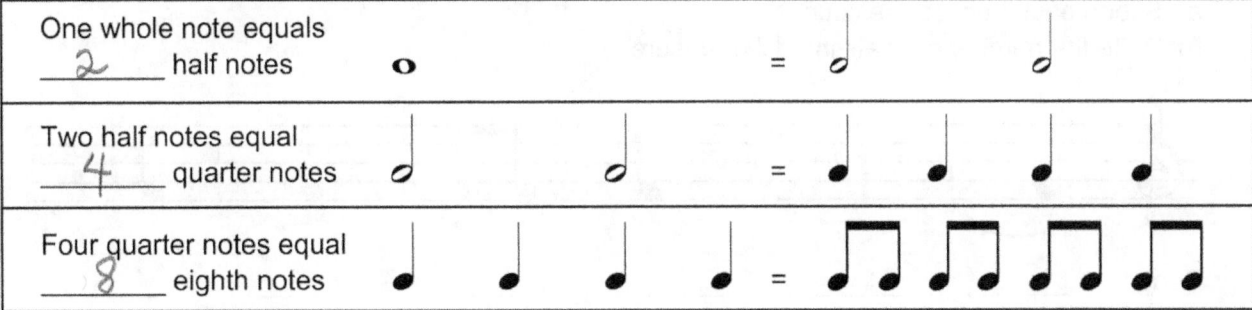

One whole note equals _2_ half notes	o		=	♩	♩
Two half notes equal _4_ quarter notes	♩	♩	=	♩ ♩ ♩ ♩	
Four quarter notes equal _8_ eighth notes	♩ ♩ ♩ ♩	=	♫ ♫ ♫ ♫		

17

NOTE and REST VALUES

1. Write the number of beats each note and each rest receives.

Beats: 2, 1, 4, ½, 4, 3, ½, 1, 2, 1

2. a) Write the total number of beats found in each measure.
   b) Name the type of note in each measure.

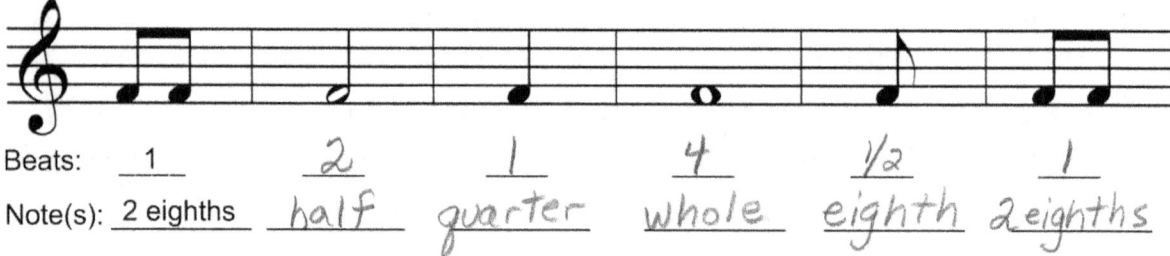

Beats: 1, 2, 1, 4, ½, 1
Note(s): 2 eighths, half, quarter, whole, eighth, 2 eighths

3. a) Write the number of beats for the rest in each measure.
   b) Name the type of rest in each measure.

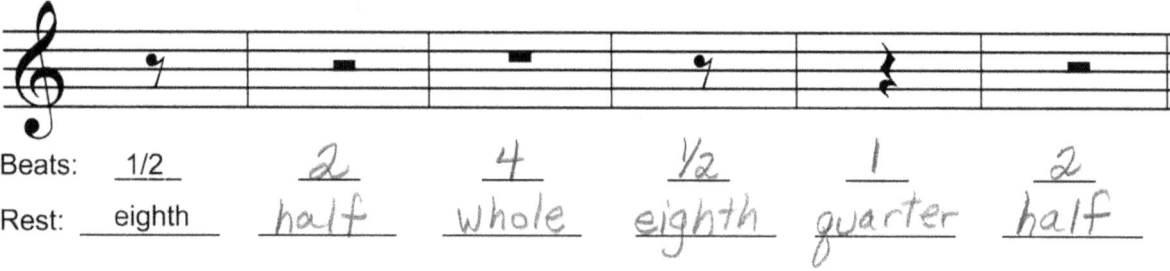

Beats: ½, 2, 4, ½, 1, 2
Rest: eighth, half, whole, eighth, quarter, half

♪ **Note:** 2 Eighth notes or 1 Eighth note and 1 Eighth rest = 1 Quarter note = 1 Beat

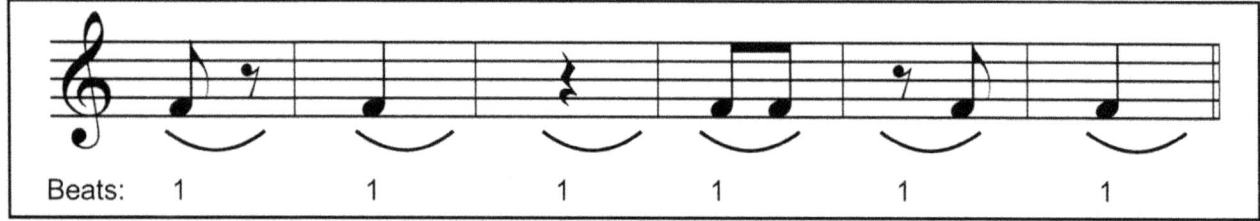

Beats: 1, 1, 1, 1, 1, 1

4. a) Scoop each beat of one count.
   b) Write the number of beats in each measure.

Beats: 1, 1, 1, 1, 1, 1

TIES and DOTTED NOTES

A **TIE** (curved line) connects two or more notes of the **SAME PITCH**. The first note is played and held for the value of both (or all) tied notes. A tie is written close to the notehead and away from the stems.

♪ **Note:** Ties usually occur between notes in neighbouring measures.

1. a) Add a tie (curved line) or ties in each measure.
   b) Write the number of beats that each note receives.
   c) Write the total beats for the value of the tied notes.

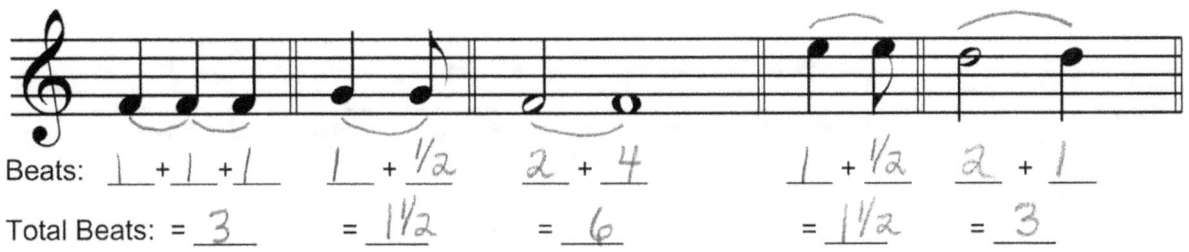

A **DOT** placed after a note **ADDS HALF** the **VALUE** of the note.

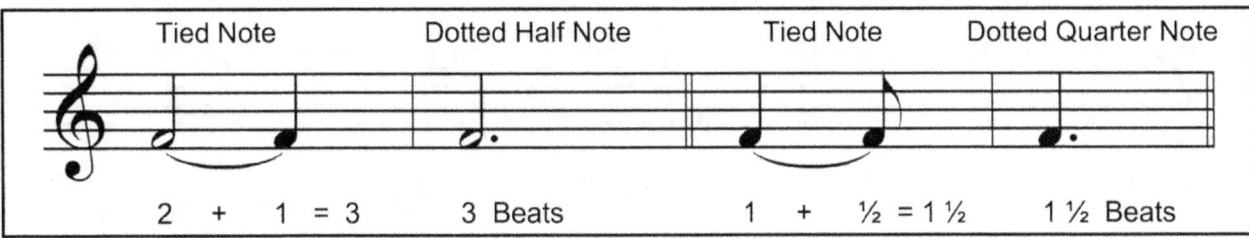

2. a) Write the note and the note value of the dot.
   b) Write the total number of beats in each measure.

3. Add a stem and dot to each notehead to create a dotted half note or a dotted quarter note. Follow the Stem Rules.

TRIPLET

A **TRIPLET** is a group of three notes played in the time of two notes of the same value. The number 3 (the "triplet *3*") is written above or below the middle of the group of three notes.

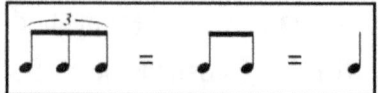

♪ **Note:** A Triplet may be written WITH or WITHOUT a curved line or a square bracket.
It will ALWAYS be written with the number *"3"* ABOVE or BELOW the group of three notes.

Correct

Incorrect

1. a) Write the total number of beats for the note or group of notes in each measure.
   b) Name the type of note as: triplet 8ths, quarter, or eighths.

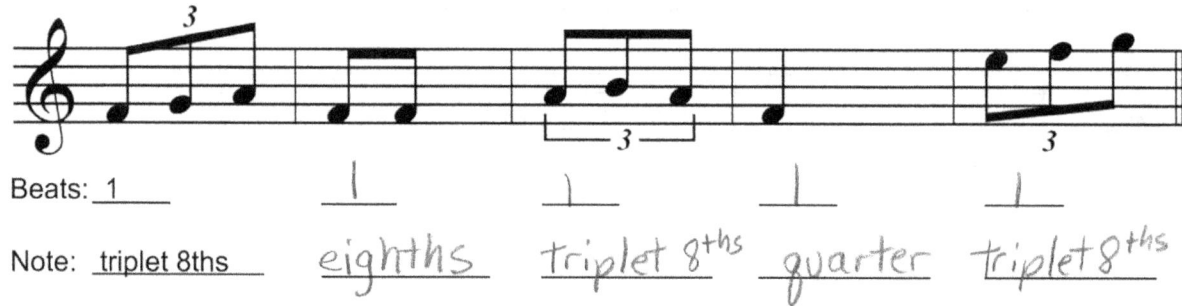

Beats: __1__   __1__   __1__   __1__   __1__

Note: __triplet 8ths__   __eighths__   __triplet 8ths__   __quarter__   __triplet 8ths__

2. Name the following notes as: whole, dotted half, half, dotted quarter, quarter, eighth or triplet 8ths.

__dotted half__   __eighth__   __whole__   __triplet 8ths__

__triplet 8ths__   __half__   __dotted quarter__   __quarter__

ARTICULATION

ARTICULATION refers to the way that a note can be played. Different types of sound are created by using different articulation (touch). **Articulation marks** are used in music to indicate different sounds.

Term	Definition	Articulation Mark
accent	a stressed note	
fermata	pause, hold for longer than its written value	
staccato	detached	
slur	play notes legato (smooth)	
tenuto	held, sustained (hold for the full value of the note)	

1. Write the term above each articulation definition.

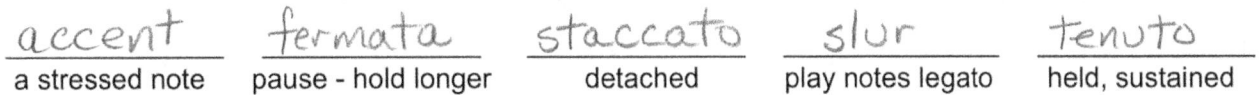

accent	fermata	staccato	slur	tenuto
a stressed note	pause - hold longer	detached	play notes legato	held, sustained

🎵 **Note:** An **ACCENT**, **STACCATO**, **SLUR** and **TENUTO** are all placed close to the notehead and away from the stems. Depending on the stem direction, the articulation is placed above or below the note. A **FERMATA** always goes above the staff.

2. Write the articulation mark in the appropriate location (either above or below each note).

accent   tenuto   staccato   slur   fermata

3. Copy the music below, adding the articulation markings.

21

MELODIC INTERVALS

An **INTERVAL** is the distance in pitch between two notes. Numbers (1, 2, 3, etc.) are used to identify the numerical size of the interval.

To identify the **INTERVAL** number: count each line and each space from the lower (bottom) note to the higher (top) note, or count each letter name from the lower (bottom) note to the higher (top) note.

♪ **Note:** A **MELODIC** interval is two notes written one note **AFTER** the other. Melodic intervals are played separately, one note after the other.

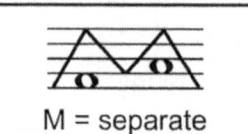
M = separate

Arrows are used to indicate direction. An "up" arrow (↑) indicates that the second note of the interval is higher (going up). A "down" arrow (↓) indicates that the second note is lower (going down).

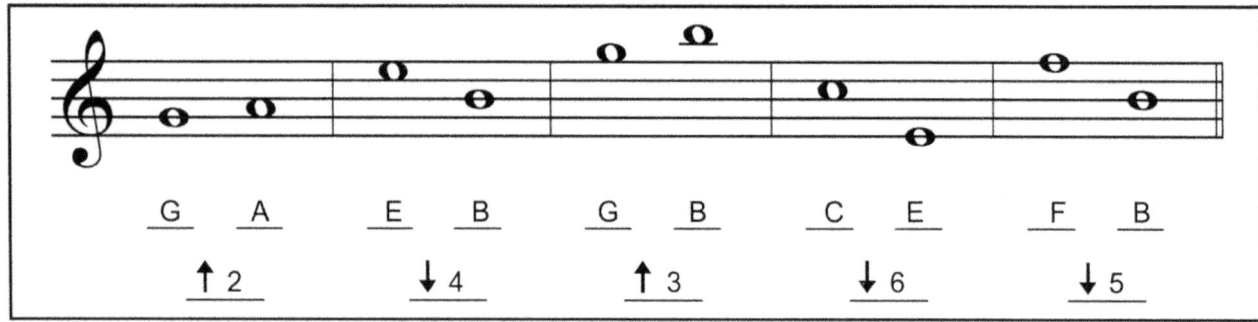

1. a) Name the following notes in the Treble Clef.
   b) Name the melodic interval (numerical size) between the notes in each measure. Use an "up" or a "down" arrow to indicate the direction of the interval.

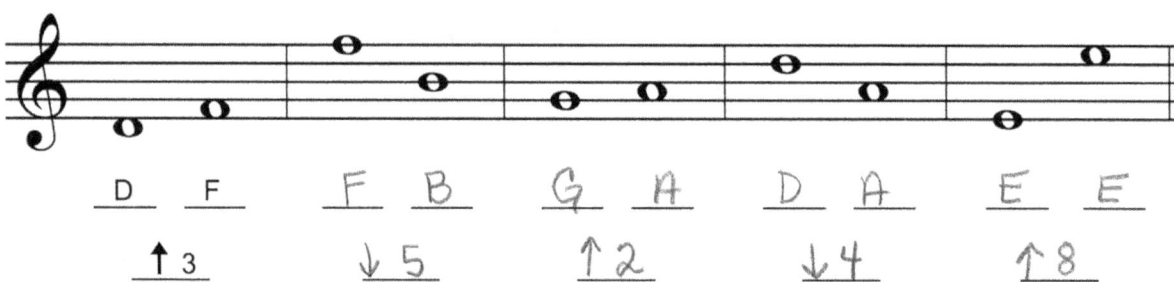

D F   F B   G A   D A   E E
↑ 3   ↓ 5   ↑ 2   ↓ 4   ↑ 8

♪ **Note:** An interval of a melodic 1st will use an "across" (horizontal) arrow (→).

2. a) In each measure, follow the interval pattern to locate the 2nd note of the melodic interval. Write the note in the Bass Clef. Use whole notes.
   b) Name the notes.

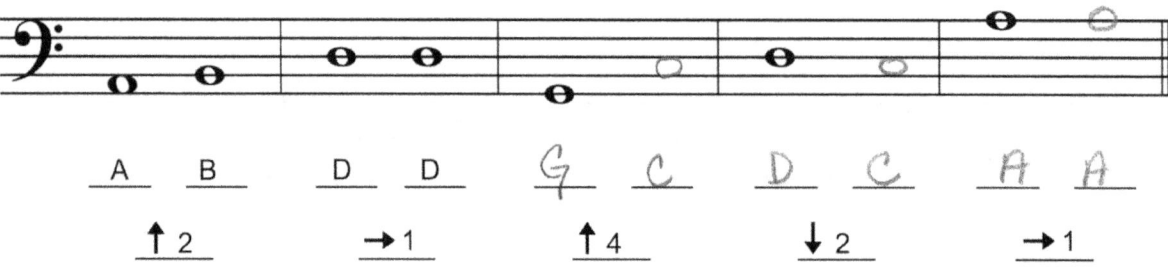

A B   D D   G C   D C   A A
↑ 2   → 1   ↑ 4   ↓ 2   → 1

NAMING MELODIC INTERVALS

When **NAMING MELODIC INTERVALS** the distance between the notes is called the numerical size.

♪ **Note:** An interval is the numerical size or distance between two notes.

1. a) Add stems to the following noteheads to create half notes.
   b) Name the melodic interval (numerical size) between the notes. Use an up, down or across arrow to indicate the direction of each interval.
   c) Name the notes.

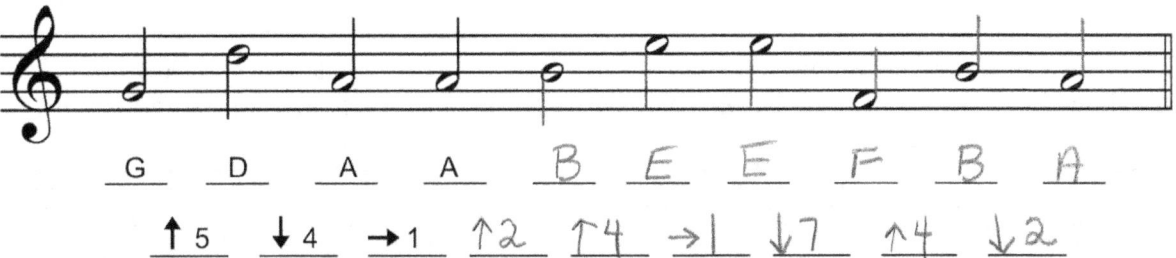

G D A A B E E F B A
↑5 ↓4 →1 ↑2 ↑4 →1 ↓7 ↑4 ↓2

2. a) Add stems to the following noteheads to create quarter notes.
   b) Name the melodic interval (numerical size) between the notes. Use an up, down or across arrow to indicate the direction of each interval.
   c) Name the notes.

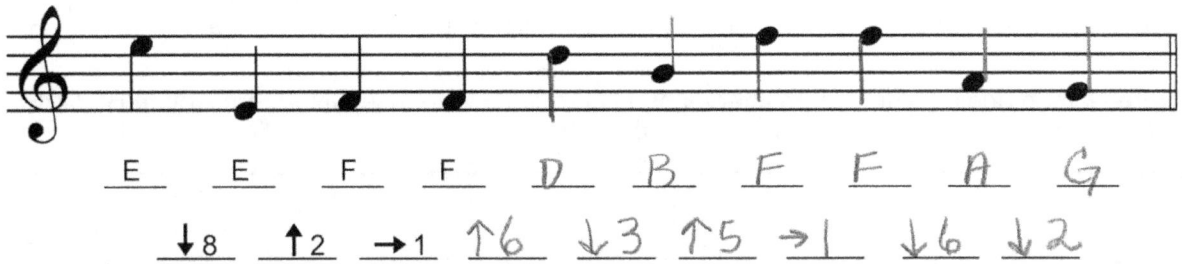

E E F F D B F F A G
↓8 ↑2 →1 ↑6 ↓3 ↑5 →1 ↓6 ↓2

♪ **Note:** When beaming eighth notes, the stems follow the "**Stem Rules**" of the note furthest away from the middle line. The beam joins at the end of the stems. When both notes are the same distance from the middle line, the stems can go either up or down.

3. a) Add stems and beams to the following noteheads to create pairs of beamed eight notes.
   b) Name the melodic interval (numerical size) between the notes. Use an up, down or across arrow to indicate the direction of each interval.
   c) Name the notes.

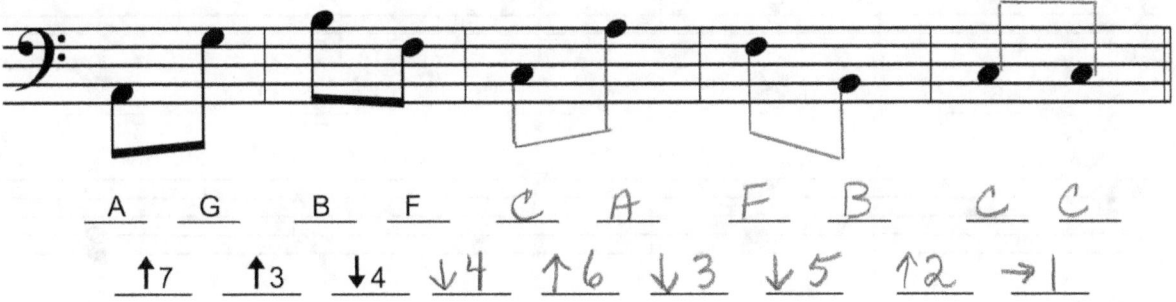

A G B F C A F B C C
↑7 ↑3 ↓4 ↓4 ↑6 ↓3 ↓5 ↑2 →1

HARMONIC INTERVALS

♪ **Note:** A **HARMONIC** interval is two notes written one note **ABOVE** the other. Harmonic intervals are played together, two notes at the same time.

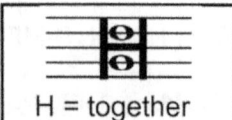

H = together

1. Name the following harmonic intervals (numerical size).

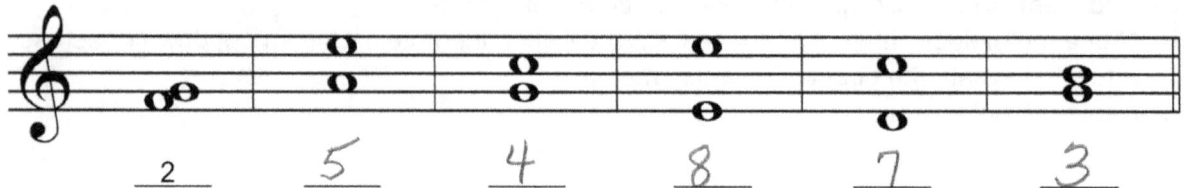

2. a) Write the following harmonic intervals above each of the given notes. Use whole notes.
   b) Name both notes. Name the lower (bottom) note first, then the higher (upper) note.

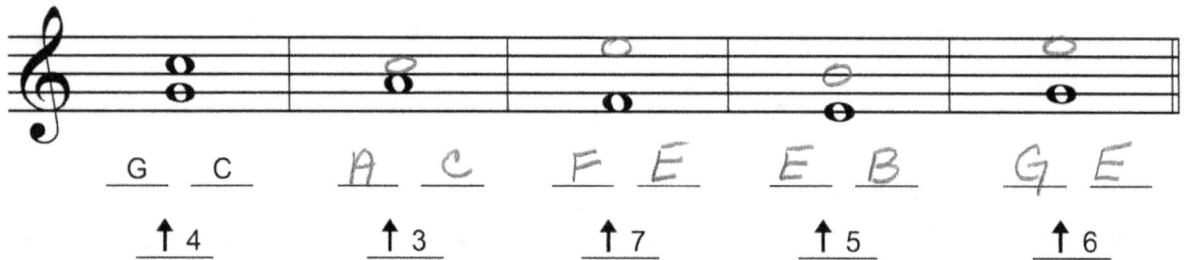

In a **HARMONIC** interval when one note is **ABOVE** the middle line and the other note is **BELOW** the middle line, the note **FURTHEST** away from the middle line determines the stem direction.
When both notes are the same distance from the middle line, the stem can go either up or down.

♪ **Note:** When adding stems to an interval of a first or a second, use ONE stem written BETWEEN the two notes and follow the Stem Rules.

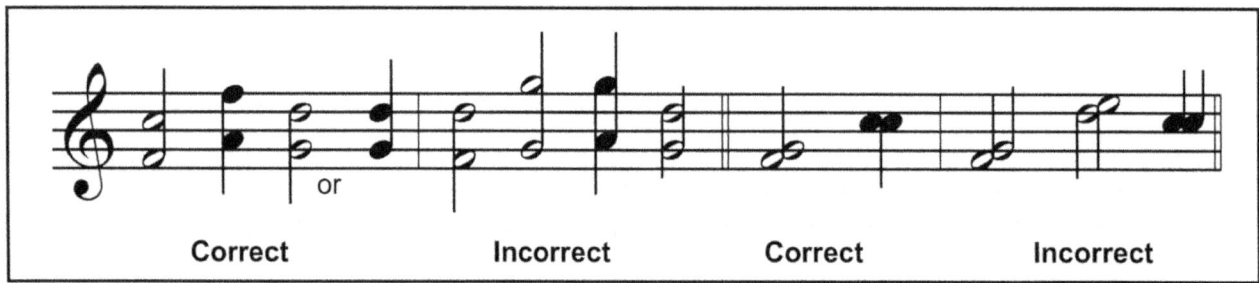

3. a) Add stems to the noteheads to create half notes (Treble Clef) and quarter notes (Bass Clef).
   b) Name each harmonic interval (numerical size).

DOTTED NOTES, STEMS and FLAGS on HARMONIC INTERVALS

A **HARMONIC** interval that is written as **EIGHTH NOTES** uses only **ONE** flag.
The flag ALWAYS goes to the RIGHT.

♪ **Note:** To identify the direction of the stem, follow the **Stem Rules**.

1. a) Add stems and flags to the following noteheads to create eighth notes.
   b) Name both notes. Name the lower (bottom) note first, then the higher (upper) note.
   c) Name each harmonic interval (numerical size).

F C   A B   C E   B F   E A
  5   2   3   5   4

A **HARMONIC** interval that is written as **DOTTED** notes will use one dot for each note. The dot is written to the right in the same space as a space note, and in the space above for a line note.

♪ **Note:** When using DOTTED notes, if the lower note of the harmonic 2nd is on a line, the interval will use TWO dots, one in the space below the line and one in the space above the line.

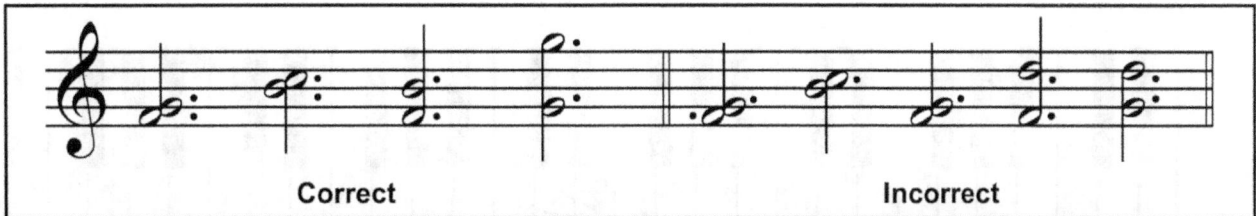

2. a) Add stems and dots to the following noteheads to create dotted half notes.
   b) Name both notes. Name the lower (bottom) note first, then the higher (upper) note.
   c) Name each harmonic interval (numerical size).

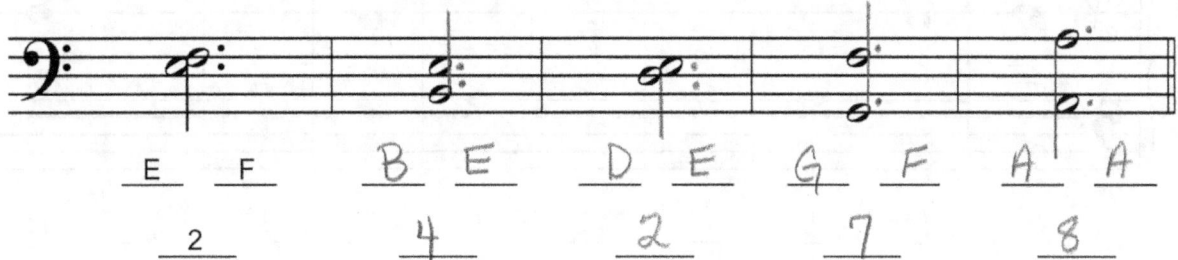

E F   B E   D E   G F   A A
  2   4   2   7   8

Lesson 2   Review Test

Total Score: ____
                100

1. a) Draw a **Treble Clef** ("G" Clef) on the staff below.
   b) Name the notes.

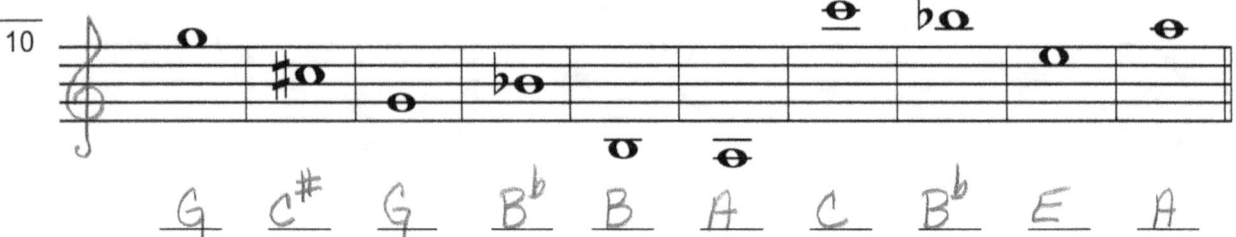

2. a) Add **STEMS** and a **BEAM** to create a pair of beamed eighth notes in each measure.
   b) Name the notes.

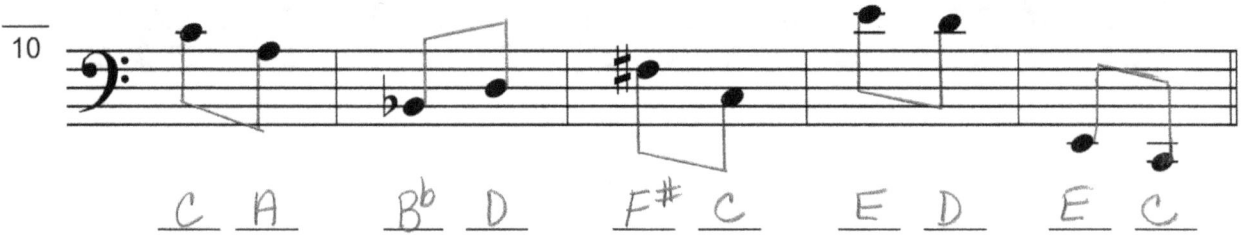

3. a) Rewrite the given notes at the **SAME PITCH** in the alternate clef (either ABOVE the Bass Clef or BELOW the Treble Clef). Use LEDGER lines. Use whole notes.
   b) Name the notes.
   c) Draw a line from each note to the corresponding key on the keyboard (at the correct pitch).

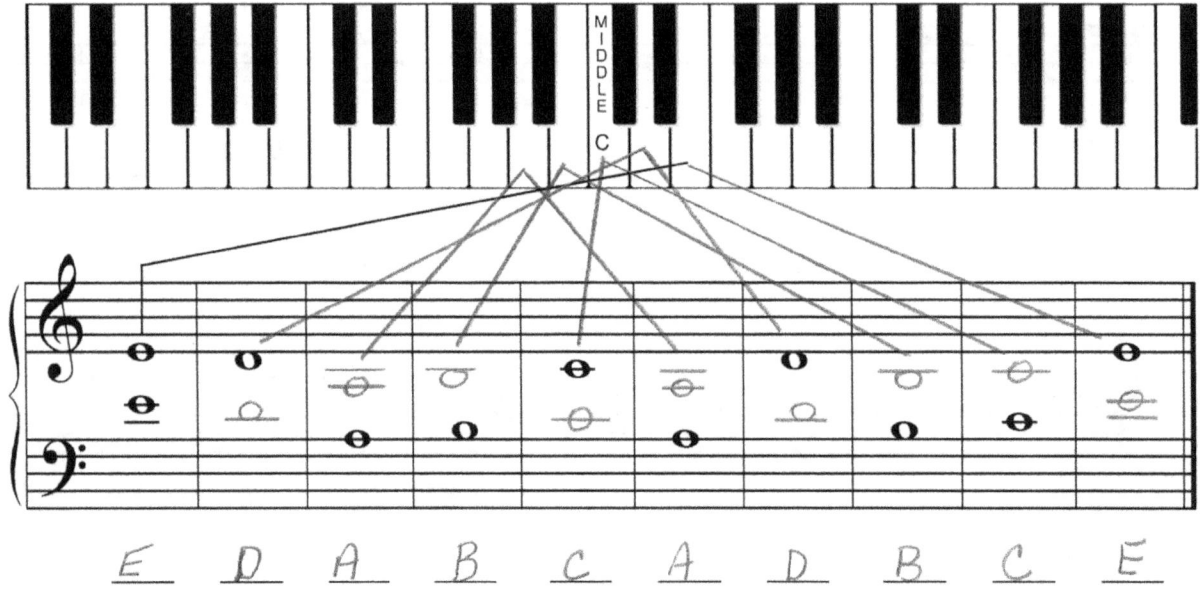

4. a) Add a **STEM** to the noteheads in each measure to create half notes.
    b) Name the following harmonic intervals (numerical size only).

    5   2   3   6   4   1   7   7   5   4

5. Write the following notes. Use ledger lines. Use whole notes.

    a) **ABOVE** the Treble Clef.   b) **BELOW** the Treble Clef.

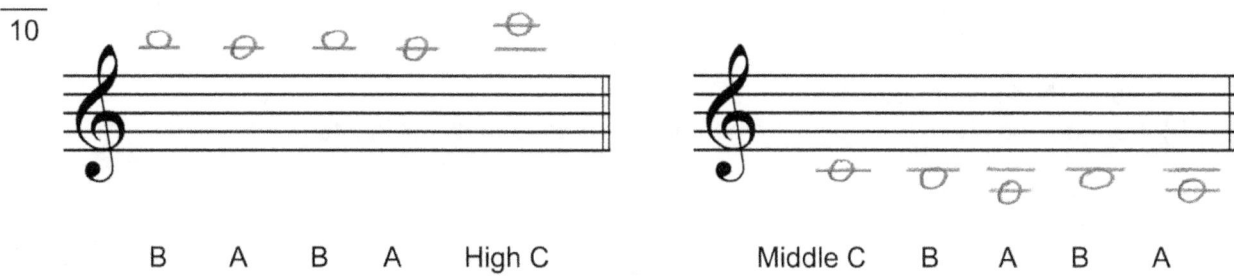

    B   A   B   A   High C   Middle C   B   A   B   A

6. a) Write the following harmonic intervals above each of the given notes. Use whole notes.
    b) Name both notes. Write the name of the LOWER note first, then the HIGHER note.

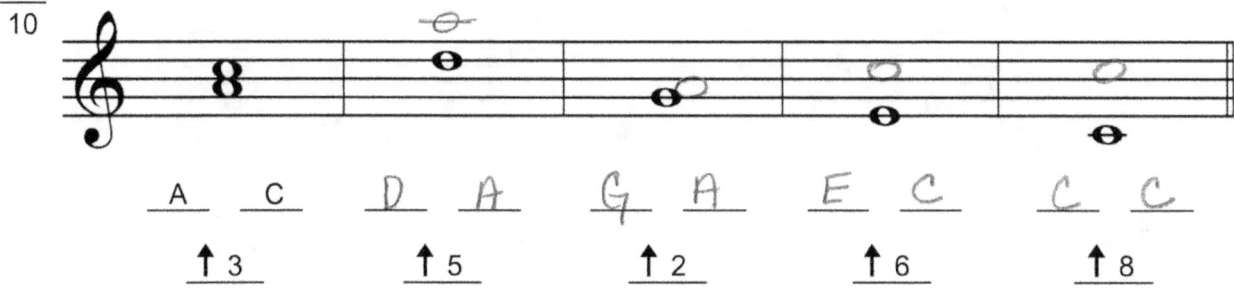

    A C   D A   G A   E C   C C
    ↑3   ↑5   ↑2   ↑6   ↑8

7. a) In each measure, follow the interval pattern to locate the 2nd note of the melodic interval.
       Write the note in the Bass Clef. Use whole notes.
    b) Name the notes.

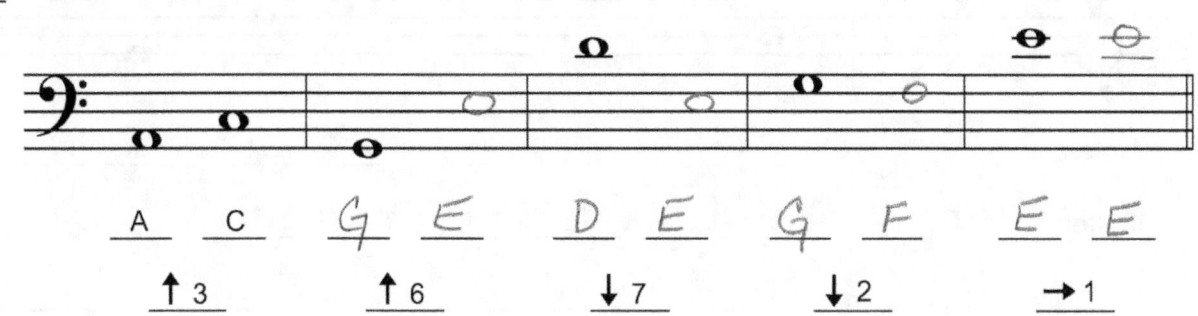

    A C   G E   D E   G F   E E
    ↑3   ↑6   ↓7   ↓2   →1

8. Copy the music below in the Bass Clef. Correct any stem direction as necessary.

9. a) Name the following notes.
   b) For each pair of notes, circle the note which sounds **LOWER** in pitch.

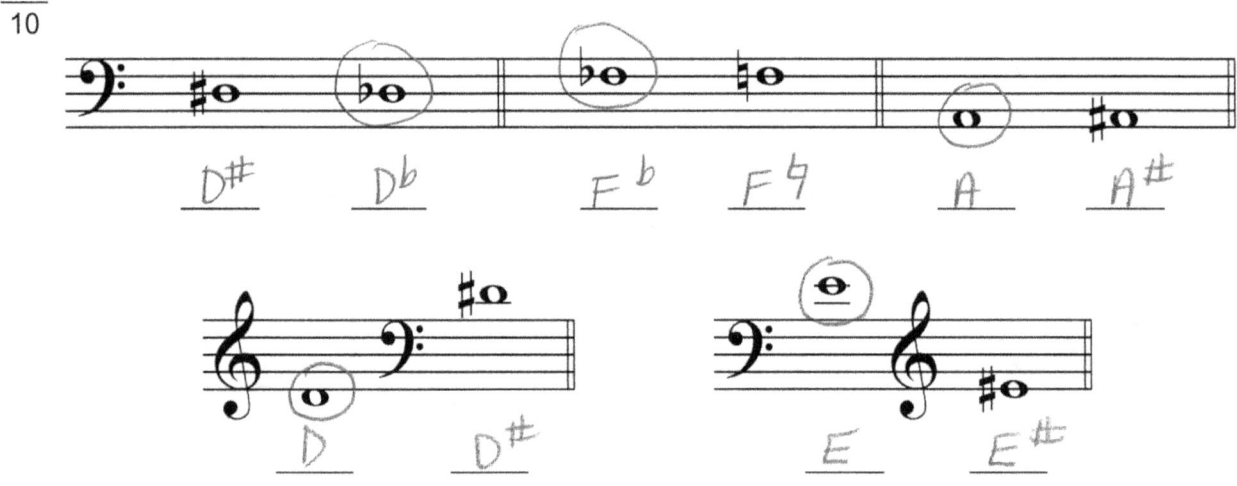

10. a) Name the following notes.
    b) Identify the melodic pattern in each measure as either:
       same line, same space, step up, step down, skip up or skip down.

Notes: F# G   Bb Bb   C A   Eb D   G B
Pattern: step   same   skip   step   skip
         up   line   down   down   up

Lesson 3 — Simple Time

A **TIME SIGNATURE** has two numbers and is written on the staff after the clef.

The **TOP** number **2**, **3** or **4** indicates the number of beats per measure.
Each beat has a **Pulse**: **S** = Strong, **w** = weak or **M** = Medium.

Pulse:	**2**	**S**trong weak
Pulse:	**3**	**S**trong weak weak
Pulse:	**4**	**S**trong weak **M**edium weak

The **BOTTOM** number **4** indicates **one quarter note** (♩) is equal to **ONE** Basic Beat.

One SCOOP is equal to one Basic Beat. Scoops are joined together to indicate note or rest values.

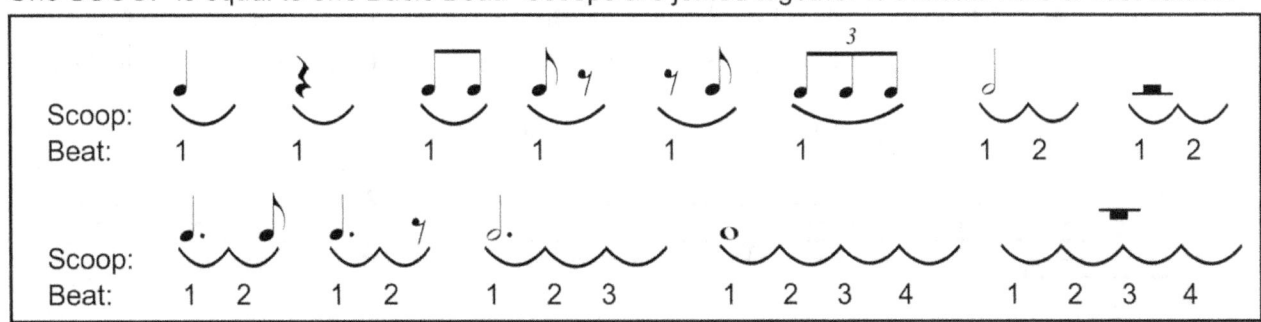

♪ **Note:** The **PULSE** is where the rhythmic emphasis falls in a measure.
UPPER case letter for **S** (Strong) and **M** (Medium); and lower case letter for **w** (weak).

1. a) Scoop each Basic Beat in each measure.
   b) Write the pulse below each Basic Beat.

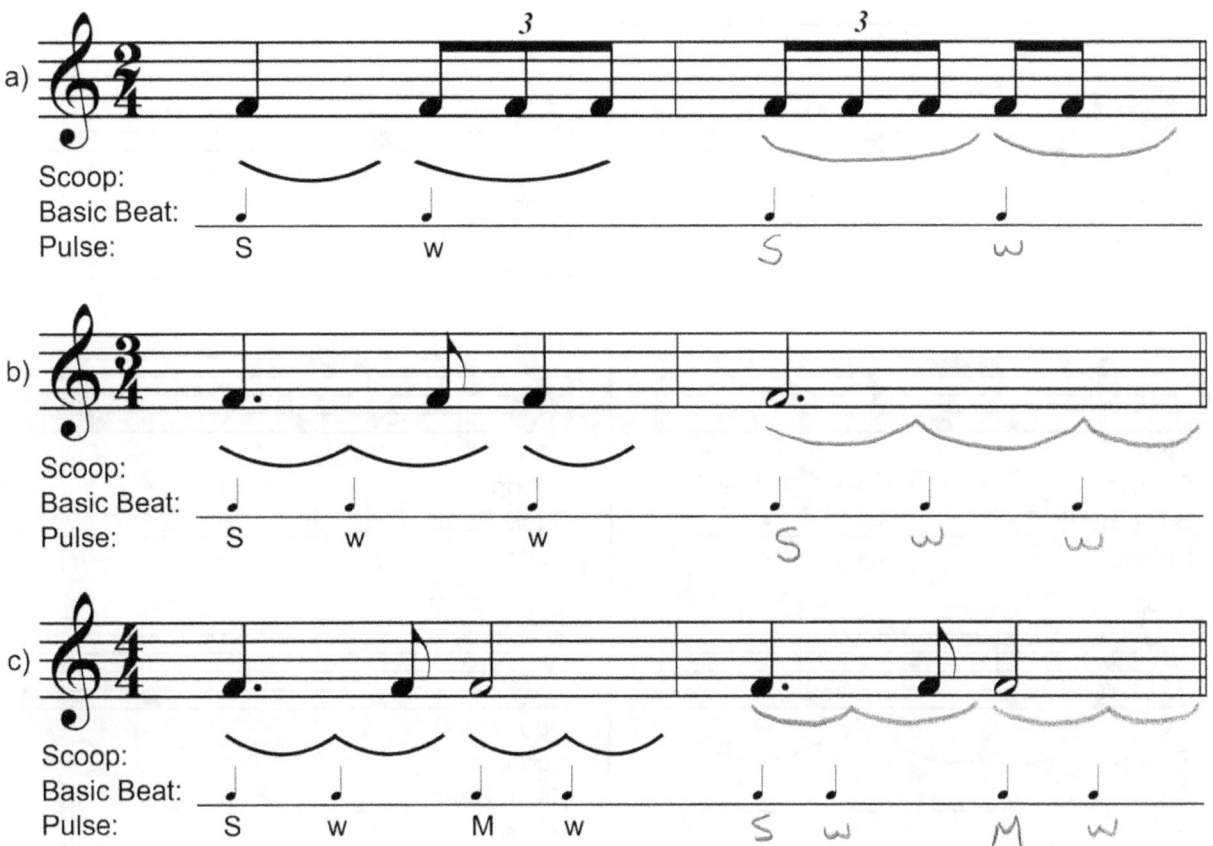

29

COMMON TIME

$\frac{4}{4}$ Time is also known as Common Time. The symbol for Common Time is **C**.

A Time Signature is written once at the beginning of the first measure, after the clef.

Bar lines are thin lines that separate music into equal measures of time.

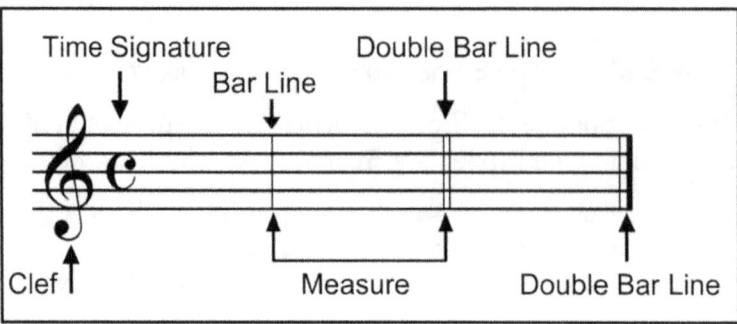

A double bar line (two thin bar lines together) indicates the end of a section of music.
A double bar line (a thin bar line and a thick bar line together) indicates the end of a piece of music.

♪ **Note:** A double bar line is also referred to as a final bar line when used at the end of a piece of music.

1. Write the symbol for Common Time ("**C**") below the bracket for each measure of Common Time.

2. Following the examples below:

    a) Scoop each Basic Beat in each measure.
    b) Write the Basic Beat and pulse below each scoop.
    c) Add the correct Time Signature below the bracket.

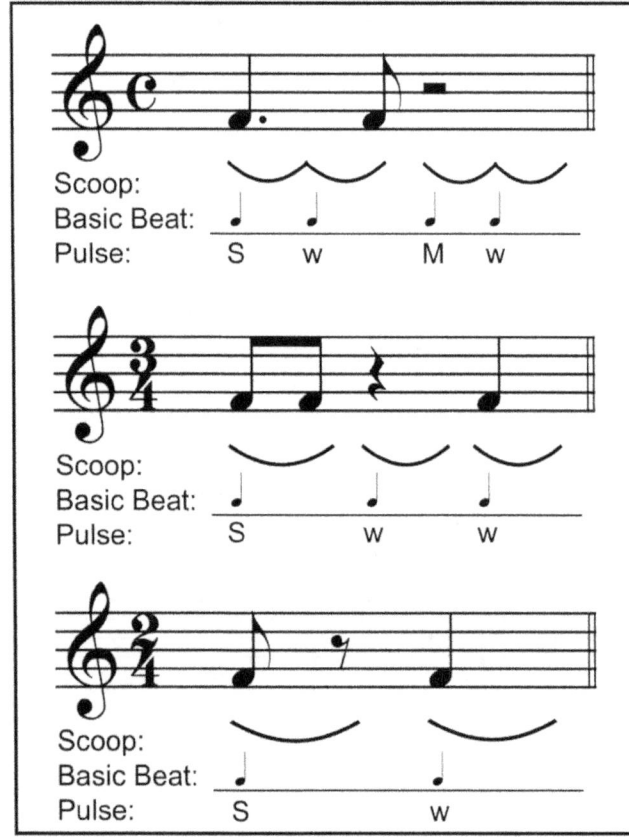
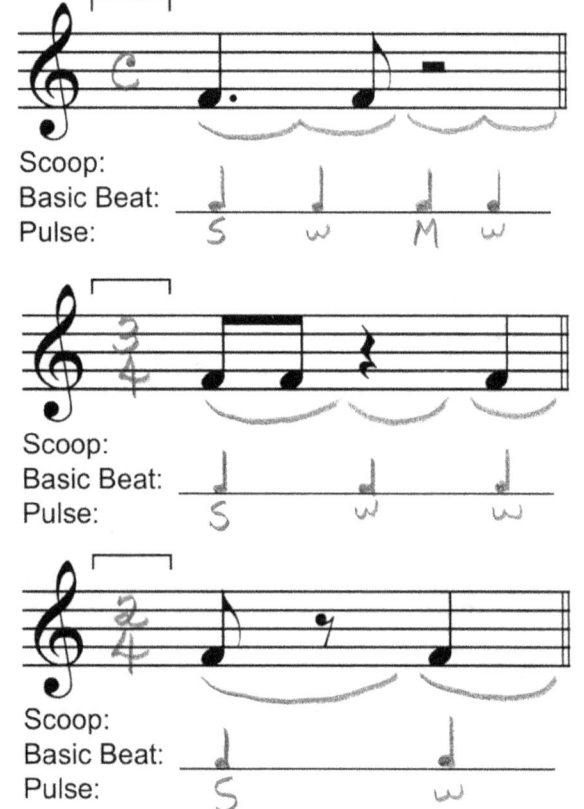

30

ADDING RESTS

1. Write the number of beats that each rest receives in 4/4 Time.

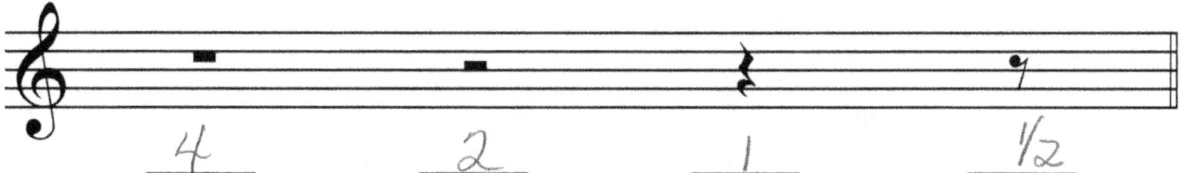

2. a) Write the pulse below each Basic Beat.
   b) Add one rest below each bracket to complete each measure.
   c) Cross off the Basic Beat as each beat is completed.

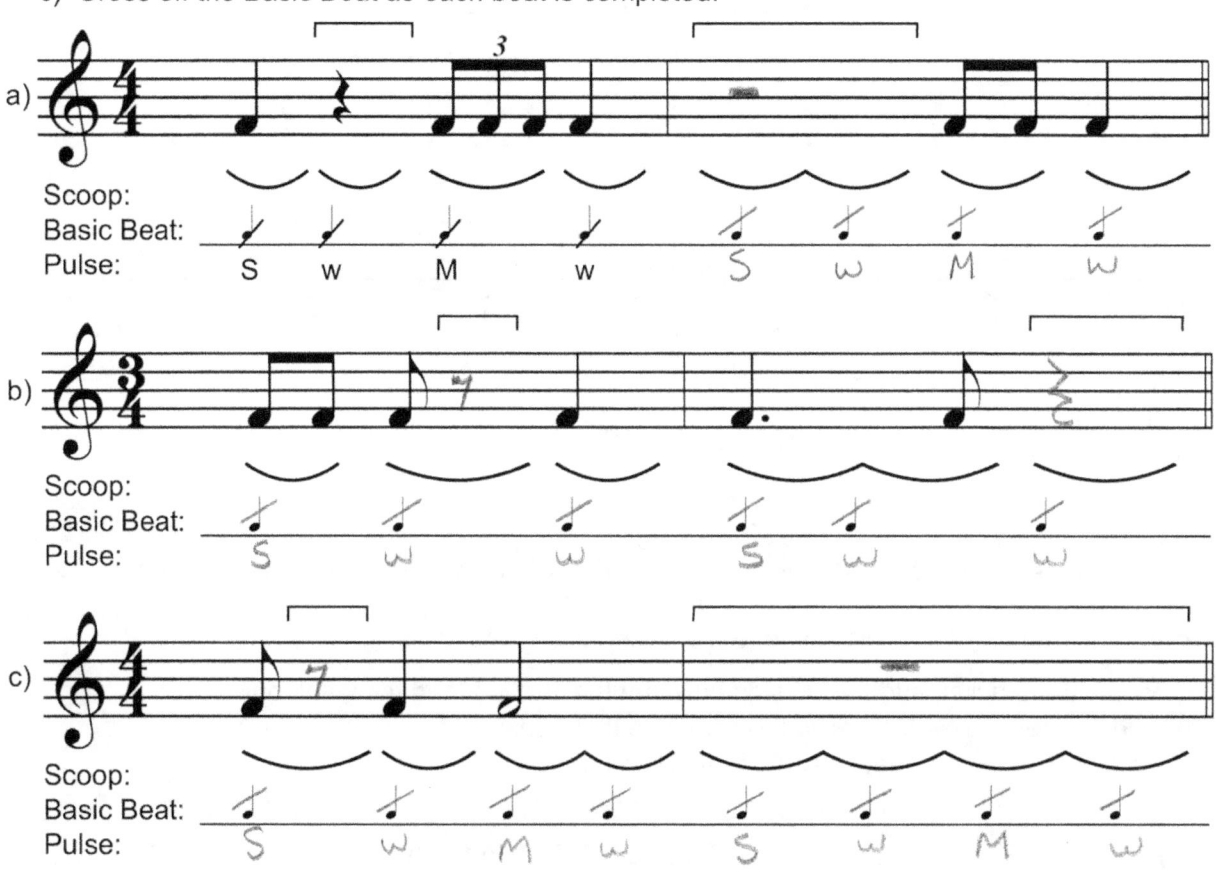

♪ **Note:** A whole rest is used to indicate silence for a whole measure in 2/4, 3/4 and 4/4 Time.

3. a) Scoop each Basic Beat. b) Add bar lines to complete each measure.

31

JOIN STRONG + WEAK and MEDIUM + WEAK BEATS into ONE REST

When adding rests, a **STRONG (S)** beat can join a **weak (w)** beat into **ONE** rest (**S + w**).

♪ **Note:** The **plus (+)** sign indicates to **join** the Strong + weak pulses.

1. a) Below the bracket, add the "+" sign between the Strong and the weak pulses.
   b) Add one rest below the bracket to complete the measure.
   c) Cross off the Basic Beat as each beat is completed.

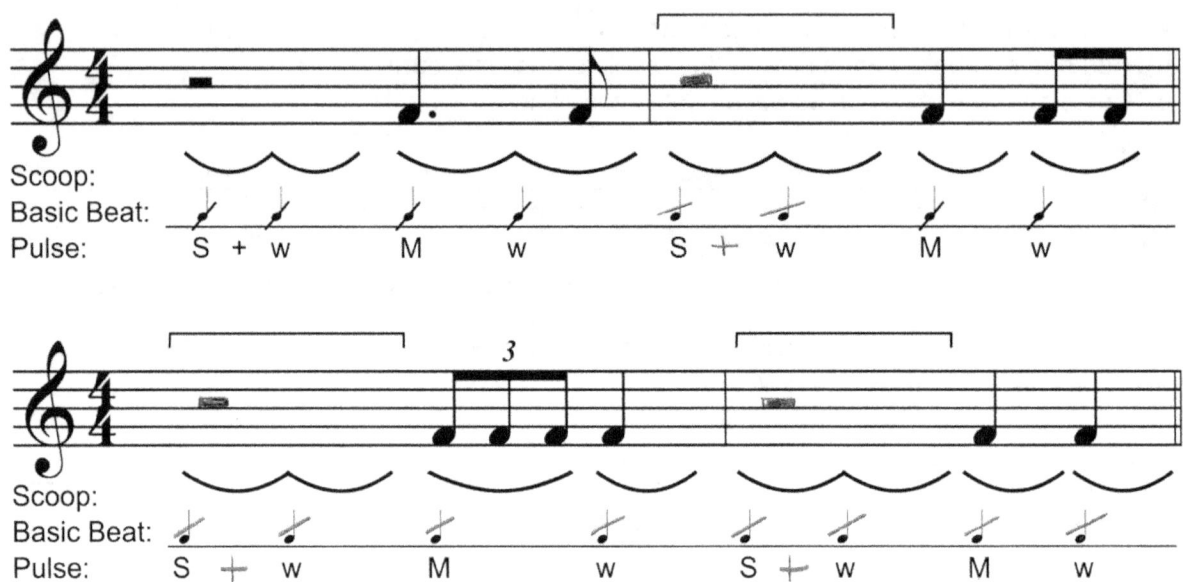

When adding rests, a **MEDIUM (M)** beat can join a **WEAK (w)** beat into **ONE** rest (**M + w**).

♪ **Note:** The **plus (+)** sign indicates to **join** the Medium + weak pulses.

2. a) Below the bracket, add the "+" sign between the Medium and the weak pulses.
   b) Add one rest below the bracket to complete the measure.
   c) Cross off the Basic Beat as each beat is completed.

ADDING a SCOOP, PULSE and REST

SCOOP: One scoop equals one Basic Beat. Join scoops together when notes or rests equal more than one Basic Beat.

PULSE: A **Strong** beat can join a **weak** beat or a **Medium** beat can join a **weak** beat into **ONE** rest.

♪ **Note:** When adding **RESTS**, combined pulses: **S + w** or **M + w**.

1. a) Scoop each Basic Beat in each measure.
   b) Below the bracket, add the "+" sign between the **S + w** or **M + w** pulses.
   c) Add one rest below each bracket to complete each measure.
   d) Cross off the Basic Beat as each beat is completed.

WEAK BEATS

A **WEAK** beat can **NOT** hold on to another beat. A weak beat always stands alone.

The **tilde** (~) sign (pronounced TILL-day) indicates to **NOT** join the **weak** and **Medium** pulses (**w ~ M**) or the **weak** and **weak** pulses (**w ~ w**). Use two separate rests.

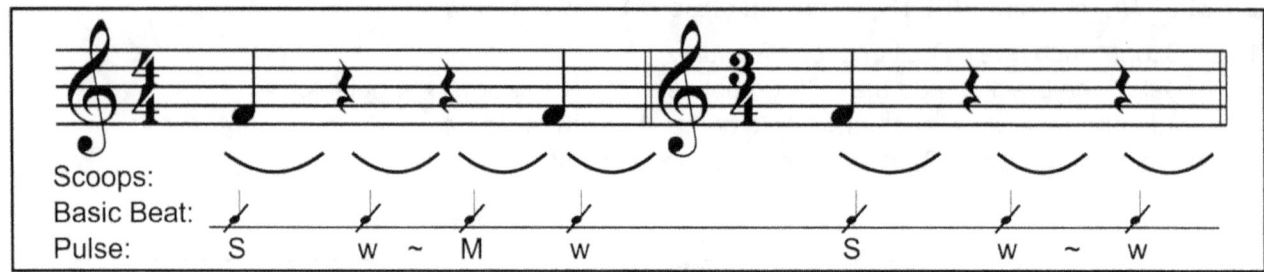

♪ **Note:** A weak beat can **NOT** be combined with another beat.   w ~ M   or   w ~ w

1. a) Below the bracket, add the "+" or "~" sign between the pulses (S + w; M + w; w ~ M; w ~ w).
   b) Add rests below the bracket to complete each measure.
   c) Cross off the Basic Beat as each beat is completed.

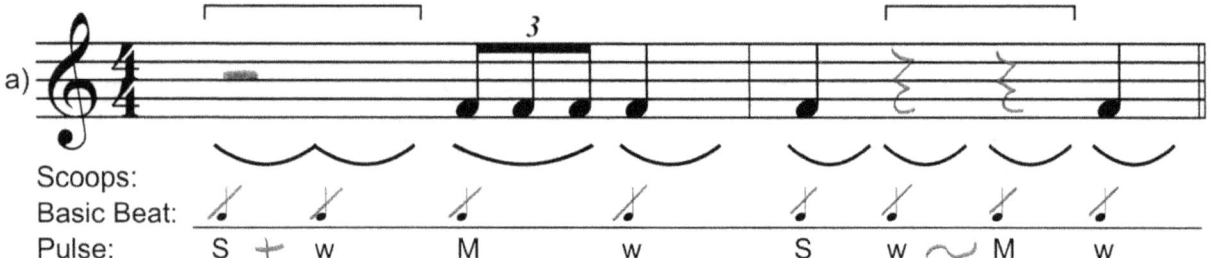

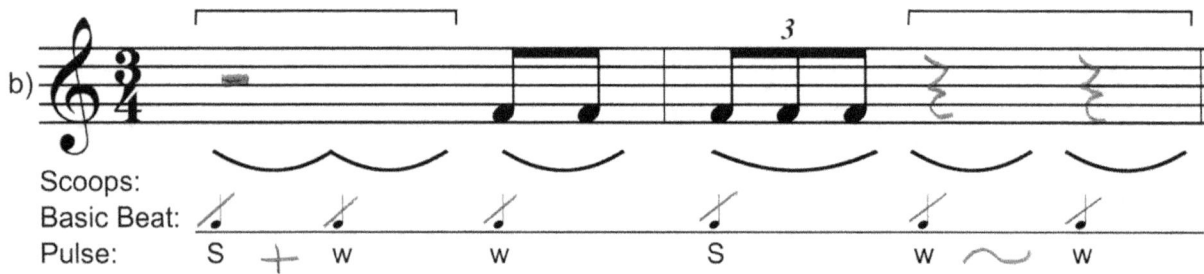

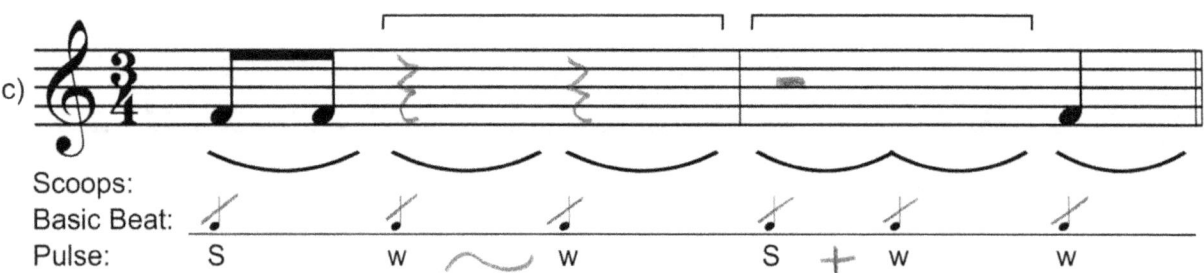

ADDING RESTS to COMPLETE a MEASURE

When **ADDING RESTS to COMPLETE a MEASURE**, complete **ONE** Basic Beat at a time. Cross off the Basic Beat as each beat is completed.

♪ **Note:** Join S + w and M + w. Do NOT join w ~ w and w ~ M.

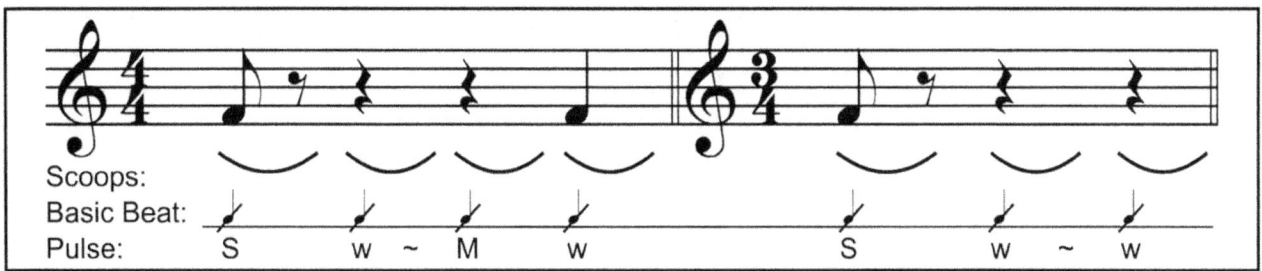

♪ **Note:** When completing one Basic Beat that only has an eighth note, use an eighth rest.

1. a) Scoop each Basic Beat in each measure.
   b) Below the bracket, add the "+" or "~" sign between the pulses (S + w; M + w; w ~ M; w ~ w).
   c) Add one or more rests below each bracket to complete each measure.
   d) Cross off the Basic Beat as each beat is completed.

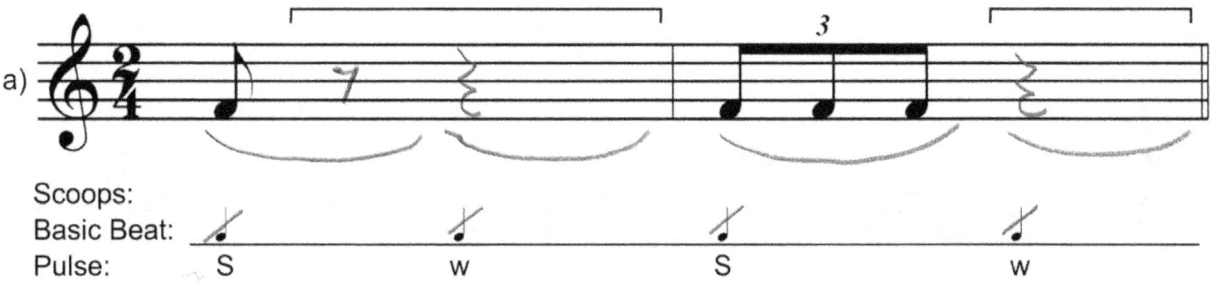

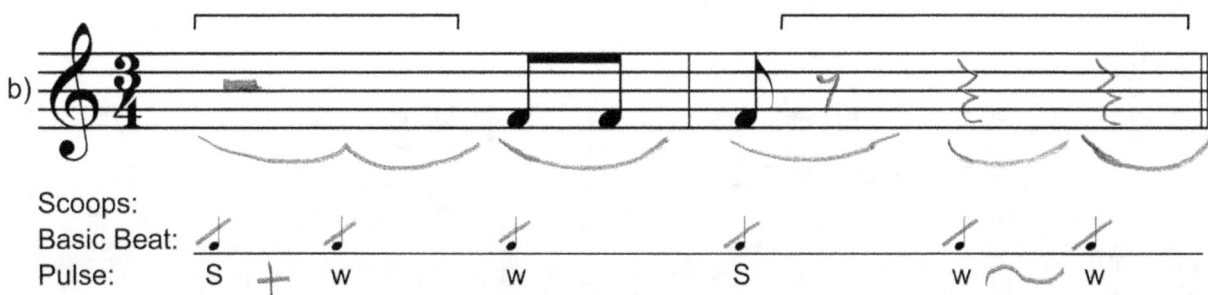

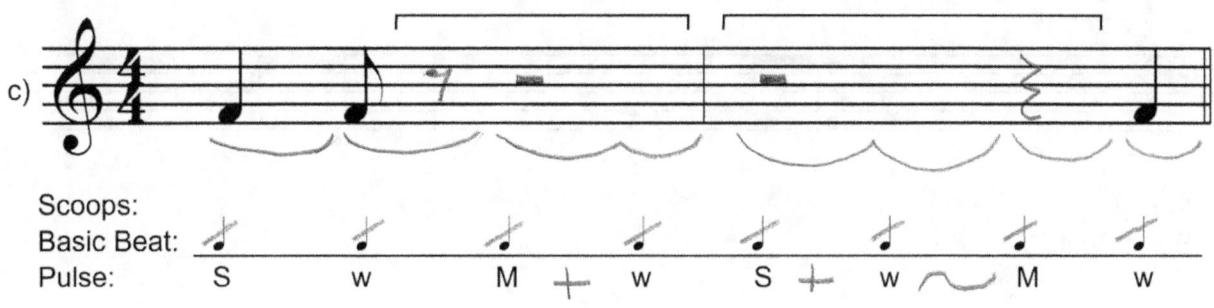

ADDING TIME SIGNATURES

1. a) Scoop each Basic Beat in each measure.
   b) Write the Basic Beat and pulse below each scoop.
   c) Add the correct Time Signature below the bracket.

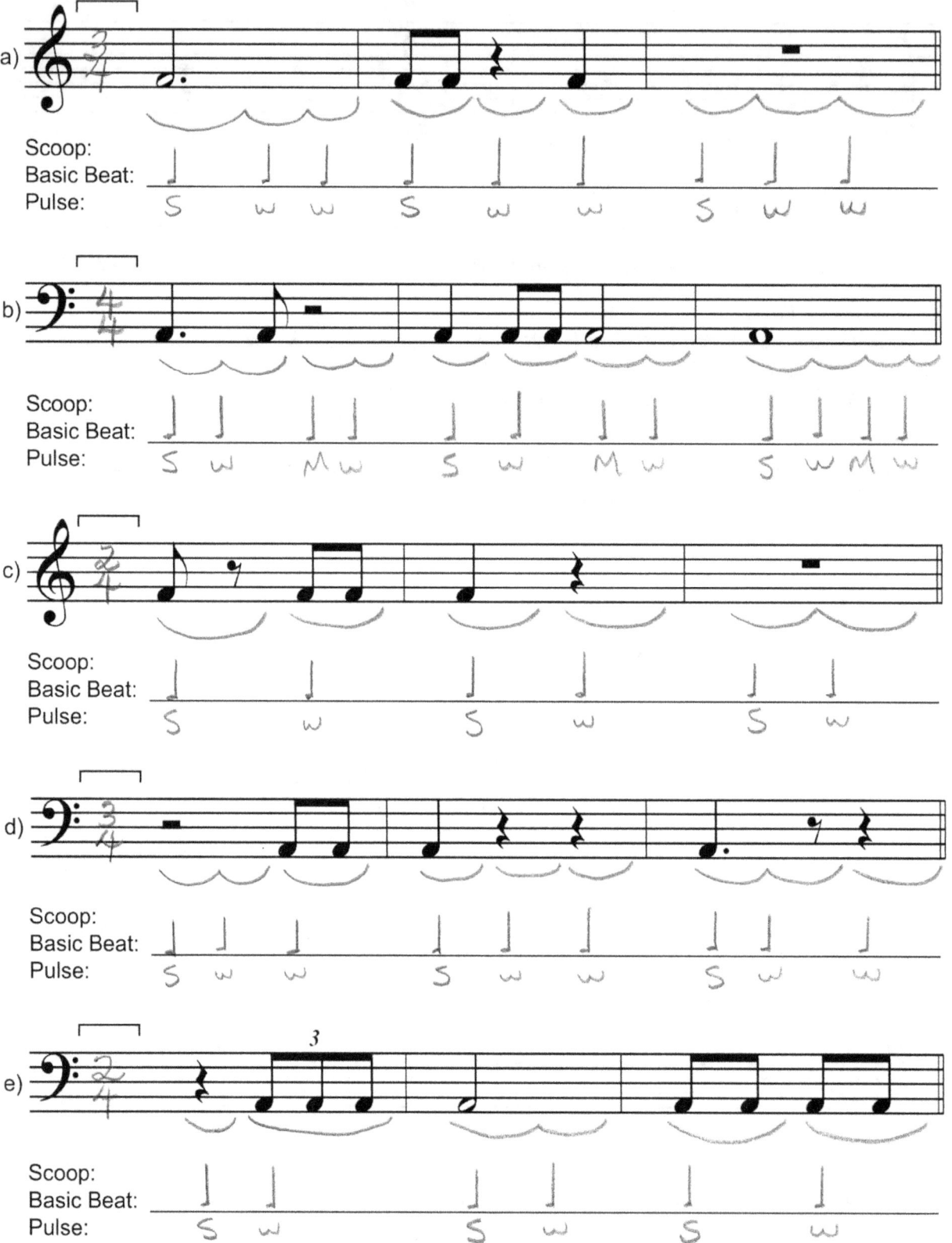

ADDING BAR LINES

♪ **Note:** Check the Time Signature to determine the number of beats per measure.

1. a) Scoop each Basic Beat in each measure.
   b) Write the Basic Beat and pulse below each scoop.
   c) Add bar lines.

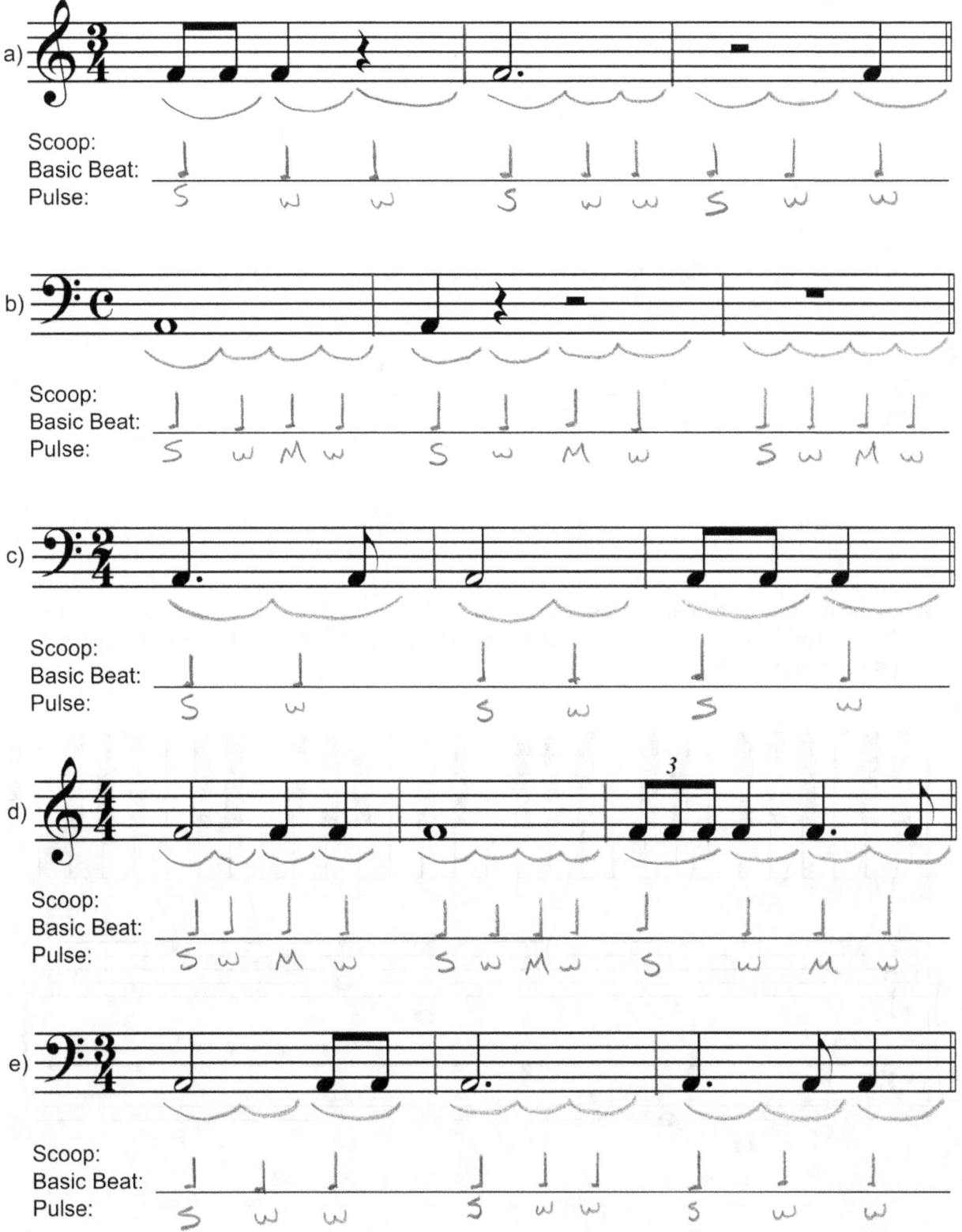

Lesson 3 **Review Test**

Total Score: ____ / 100

1. a) Draw a **Bass Clef** ("F" Clef) on the staff below.
   b) Name the notes.

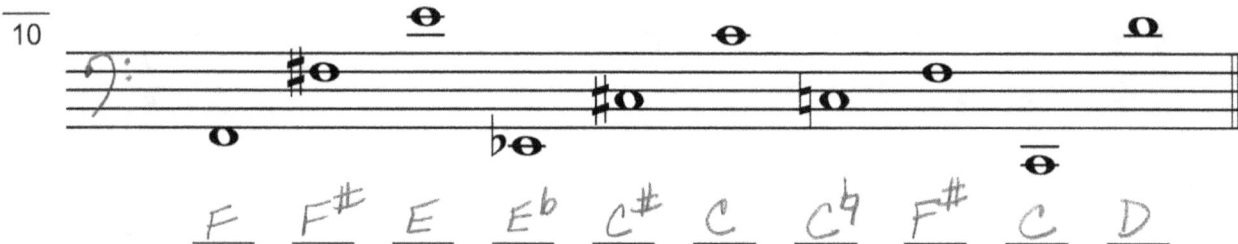

F F# E E♭ C# C C♮ F# C D

2. a) Add a **STEM** and a **FLAG** to each notehead to create an eighth note in each measure.
   b) Name the notes.

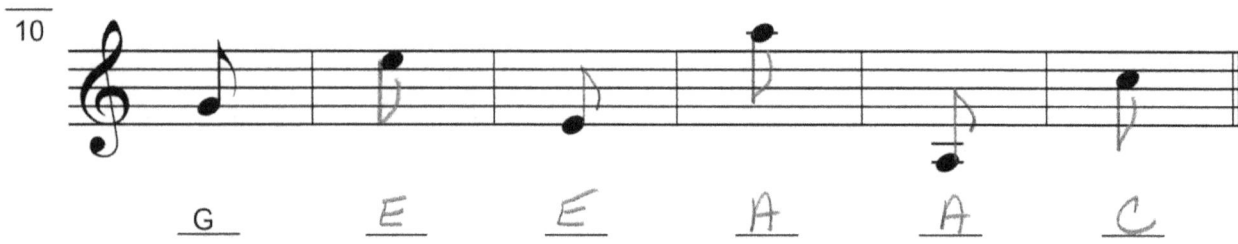

G E E A A C

3. a) Name the following notes on the Grand Staff.
   b) Draw a line from each note on the Grand Staff to the corresponding key on the keyboard (at the correct pitch).

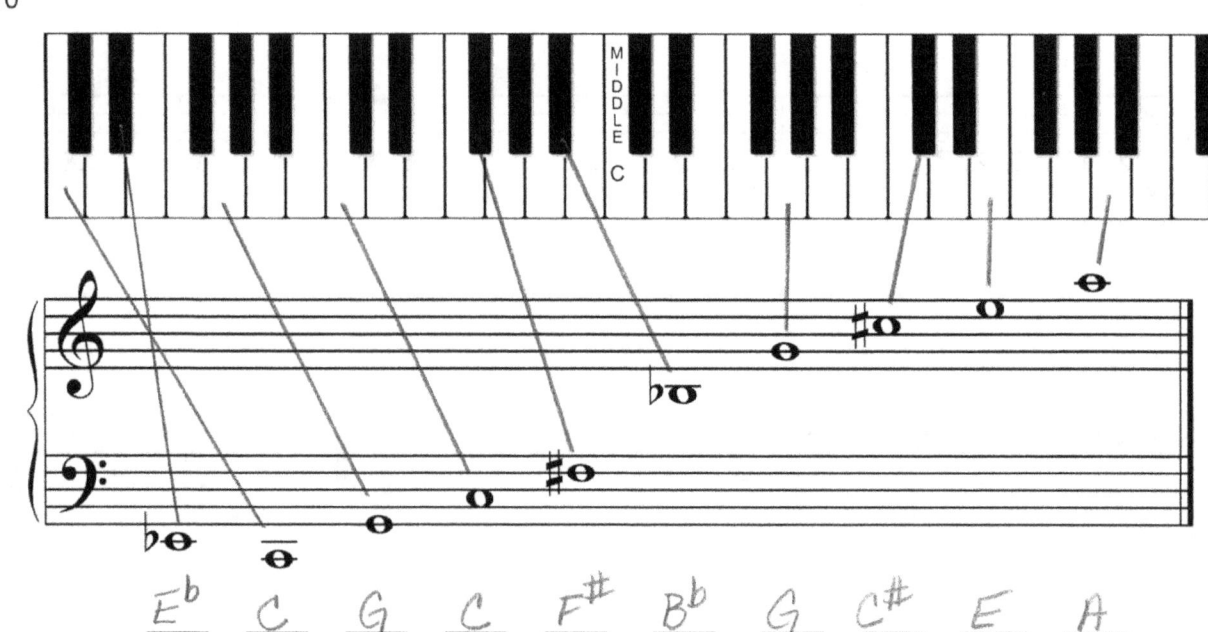

E♭ C G C F# B♭ G C# E A

38

4. a) Add **DOTS** to the following quarter notes to create dotted quarter notes.
b) Name the following harmonic intervals (numerical size only).

___
10

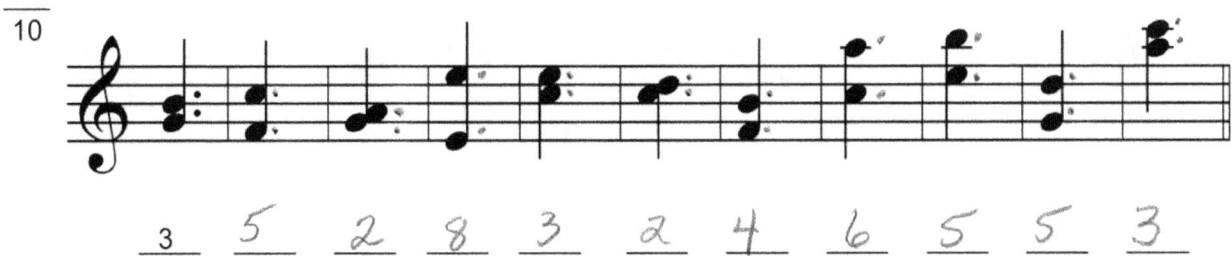

3 5 2 8 3 2 4 6 5 5 3

5. a) **SCOOP** each Basic Beat in each measure.
b) Write the **PULSE** below each Basic Beat.
c) Add **RESTS** below each bracket to complete each measure.
d) Cross off the Basic Beat as each beat is completed.

___
10

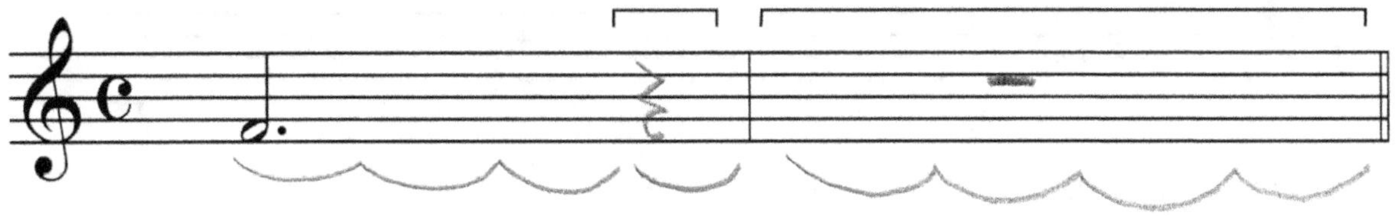

Scoop:
Basic Beat:
Pulse: S W M W S + W + M + W

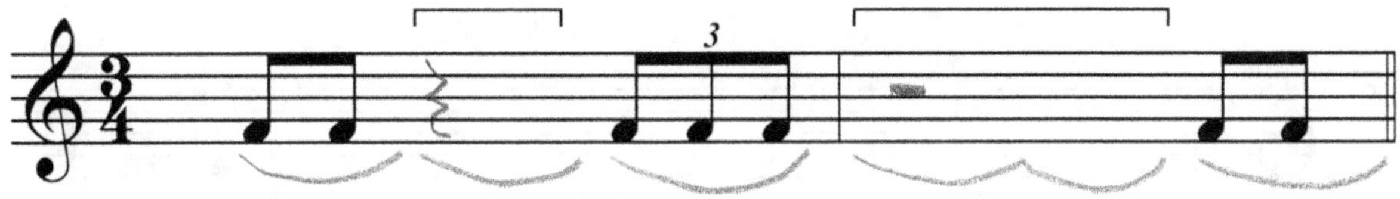

Scoop:
Basic Beat:
Pulse: S W W S + W W

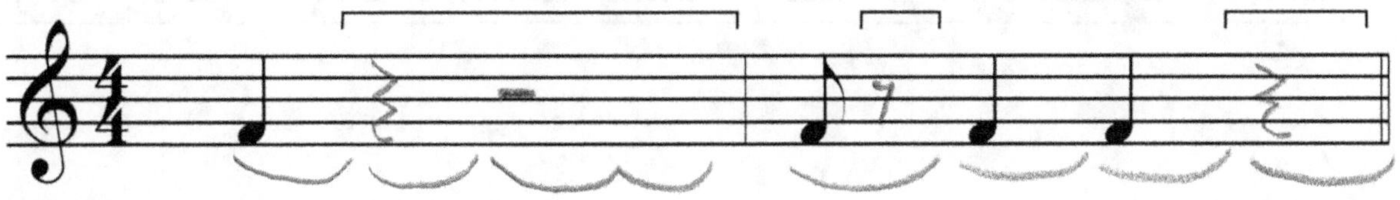

Scoop:
Basic Beat:
Pulse: S W ~ M + W S W M W

6. a) Write the following harmonic intervals above each of the given notes. Use whole notes.
   b) Name the notes. Write the name of the LOWER note first, then the HIGHER note.

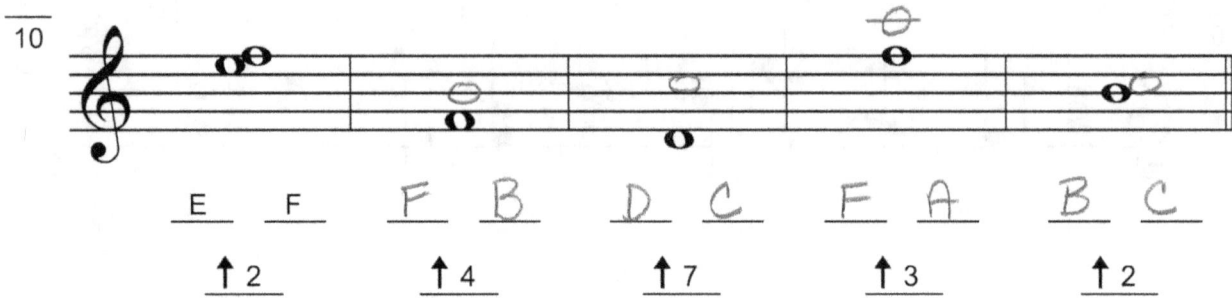

7. a) In each measure, follow the interval pattern to locate the 2nd note of the melodic interval. Write the note in the Bass Clef. Use whole notes.
   b) Name the notes.

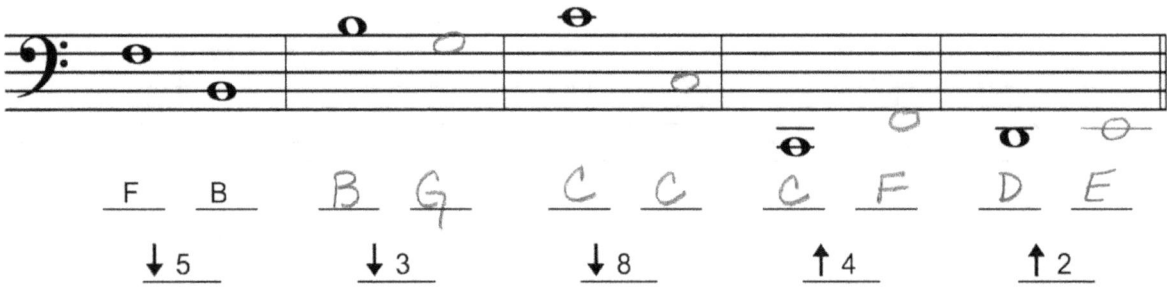

8. Add bar lines to complete the following rhythms.

9. Match each musical term with the English definition. (Not all definitions will be used.)

Term		Definition
bar lines	e	a) indicates how many beats in a measure
half note	j	b) receives one beat
double bar line	h	c) hold for the combined value of the tied notes
quarter note	b	d) curved line indicating to play the notes legato
Time Signature	a	e) lines that separate music into equal measures of time
pulse	i	f) 2 notes played separately, one after the other
tie	c	g) 2 notes played together, both at the same time
slur	d	h) indicates the end of a piece of music
melodic interval	f	i) where the rhythmic emphasis falls in a measure
whole note	k	j) receives two beats
		k) receives four beats

10. Draw **ONE NOTE** that is equal in value to the combined value of the given notes.

a) 𝅗𝅥 ♩ ♩ = 𝅝

b) 𝅗𝅥 ♩ = 𝅗𝅥.

c) ♫ ♫ = 𝅗𝅥

d) ♩ ♩ ♩ ♩ = 𝅝

e) ♩ ♫ = 𝅗𝅥

f) ♫ 𝅗𝅥. = 𝅝

g) ♩ ♫ ♫ = 𝅗𝅥.

h) ♩ ♩ = 𝅗𝅥

i) ♫ = ♩

j) 𝅗𝅥 ♩ ♫ = 𝅝

Lesson 4 Semitones, Whole Tones and Accidentals

A **SEMITONE** is the shortest distance between two neighbouring (next door) keys on the keyboard, black or white, no key in between.

A **SEMITONE SLUR** is used to identify a semitone.

♪ **Note:** A **semitone** is also known as a "**half step**".

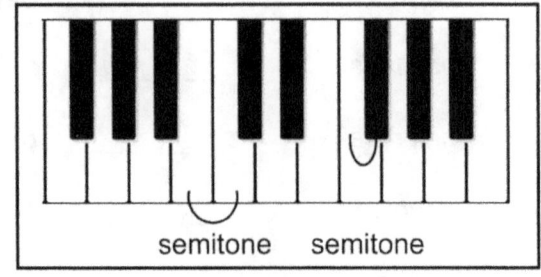

A **WHOLE TONE** is equal to TWO semitones. A whole tone is the distance from one key to another (black or white), with one key in between.

A **SQUARE** bracket is used to identify a whole tone.

♪ **Note:** A **whole tone** is also known as a "**whole step**".

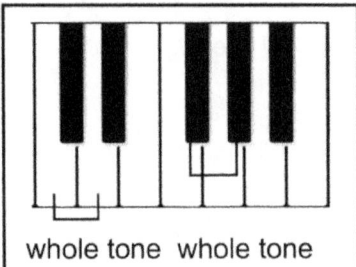

1. a) Identify the following pairs of keys labelled with a ☺ on the keyboard as semitone (ST) or whole tone (WT).
   b) Label the semitones with a slur and the whole tones with a square bracket.

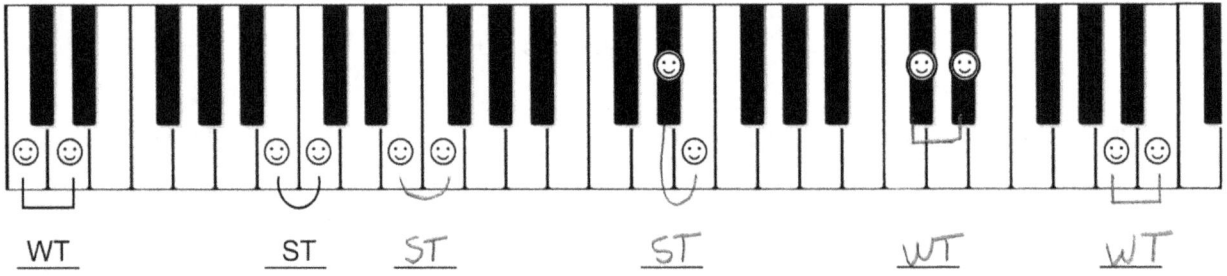

WT ST ST ST WT WT

An **ACCIDENTAL** is a sign placed IN FRONT of a note that raises or lowers the pitch.
A **SHARP** (♯) raises a note one semitone. A **FLAT** (♭) lowers a note one semitone.

2. a) Name the notes.
   b) Draw a line from each note on the staff to the corresponding key on the keyboard (at the correct pitch).

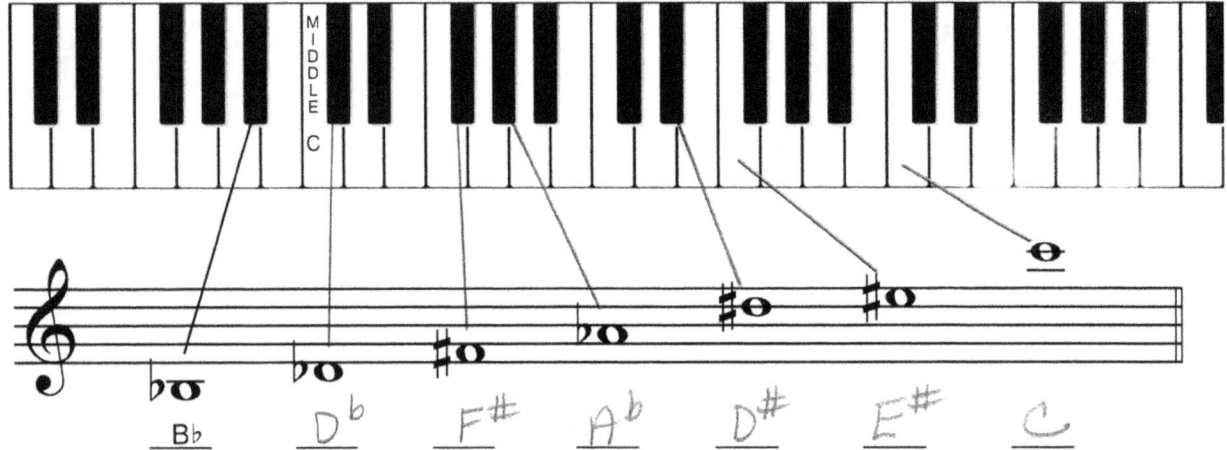

Bb Db F# Ab D# E# C

42

ACCIDENTALS - FLAT, NATURAL and SHARP

♪ **Note:** To RAISE a FLAT note one semitone, use a NATURAL sign.
To RAISE a NATURAL note one semitone, use a SHARP sign.

1. a) Raise the following notes one semitone. Use accidentals. Use the same letter name. Use whole notes.
   b) Name the notes.
   c) Draw a line from each note on the staff to the corresponding key on the keyboard.

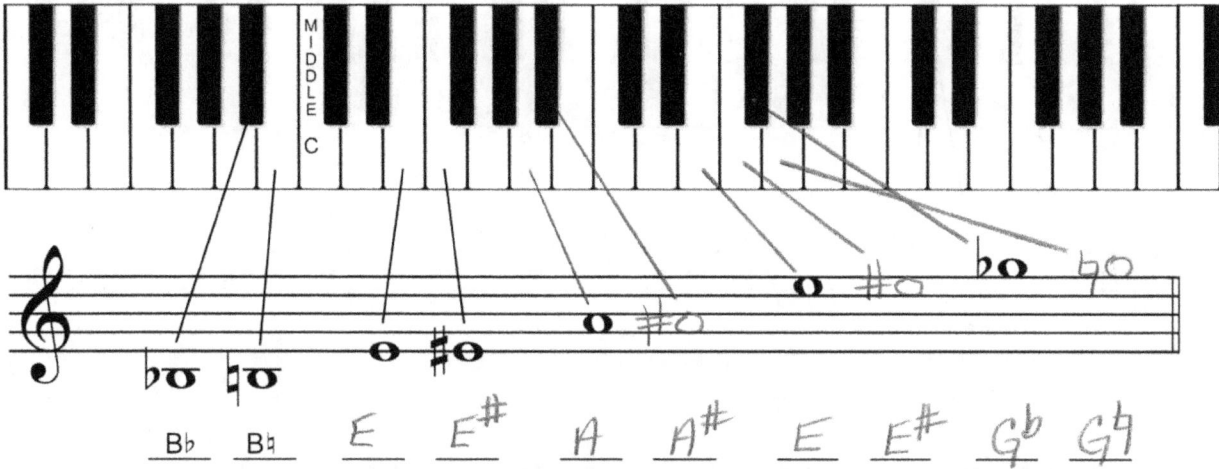

B♭ B♮ E E# A A# E E# G♭ G♮

♪ **Note:** To LOWER a SHARP note one semitone, use a NATURAL sign.
To LOWER a NATURAL note one semitone, use a FLAT sign.

2. a) Lower the following notes one semitone. Use accidentals. Use the same letter name. Use whole notes.
   b) Name the notes.
   c) Draw a line from each note on the staff to the corresponding key on the keyboard.

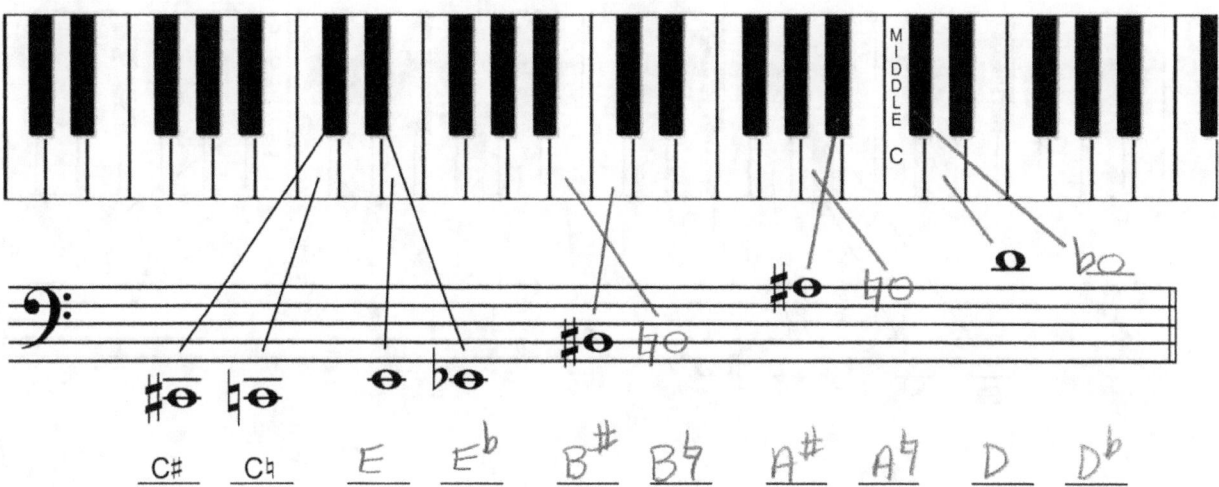

C# C♮ E E♭ B# B♮ A# A♮ D D♭

ENHARMONIC EQUIVALENTS

An **ENHARMONIC EQUIVALENT** is the SAME pitch (tone) using a DIFFERENT letter name.

♪ **Note:** Enharmonic equivalent tones have the SAME pitch and use the SAME key on the keyboard, but they use different letter names and are written differently on the staff.

An enharmonic equivalent is written as an interval of a 2nd (a step).

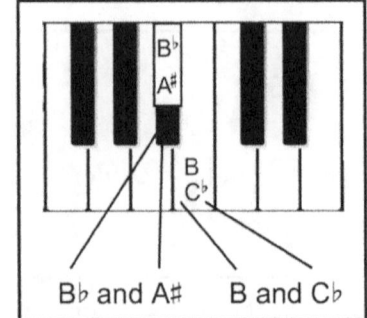

B♭ and A♯   B and C♭

1. a) Write the enharmonic equivalent for each of the following notes. Use whole notes.
   b) Name the notes.
   c) Draw a line from each note on the staff to the corresponding key on the keyboard.

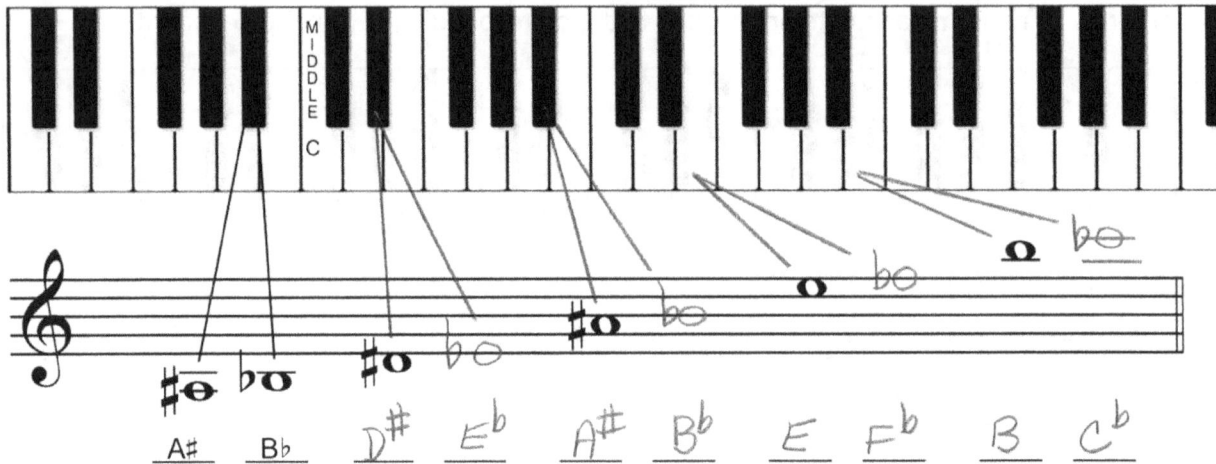

A♯   B♭   D♯   E♭   A♯   B♭   E   F♭   B   C♭

A **WHOLE TONE** (whole step) is equal to TWO semitones (half steps).

♪ **Note:** When raising or lowering a note one whole tone, the notes will be moving by step (an interval of a 2nd).

2. a) Raise the following notes one whole tone. Use whole notes.
   b) Name the notes.
   c) Draw a line from each note on the staff to the corresponding key on the keyboard.

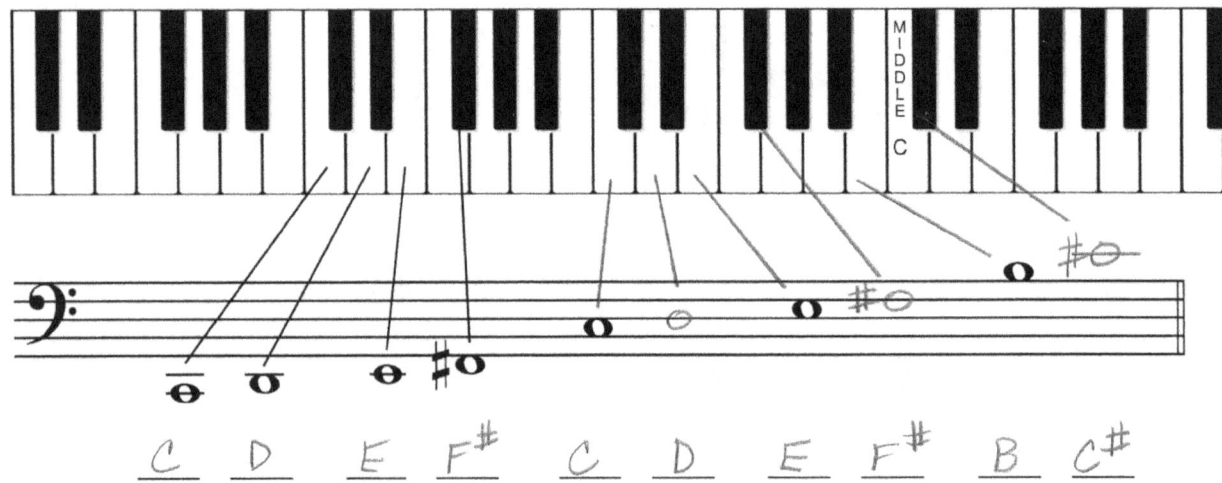

C   D   E   F♯   C   D   E   F♯   B   C♯

KEYS on the KEYBOARD and NOTES on the STAFF

1. a) Write the following notes on the Grand Staff for the keys labelled with a ☺ on the keyboard.
      Use **SHARPS** for the ☺ marked on the black keys. Use whole notes.
   b) Name the notes.
   c) Draw a line from each note on the staff to the corresponding key on the keyboard.

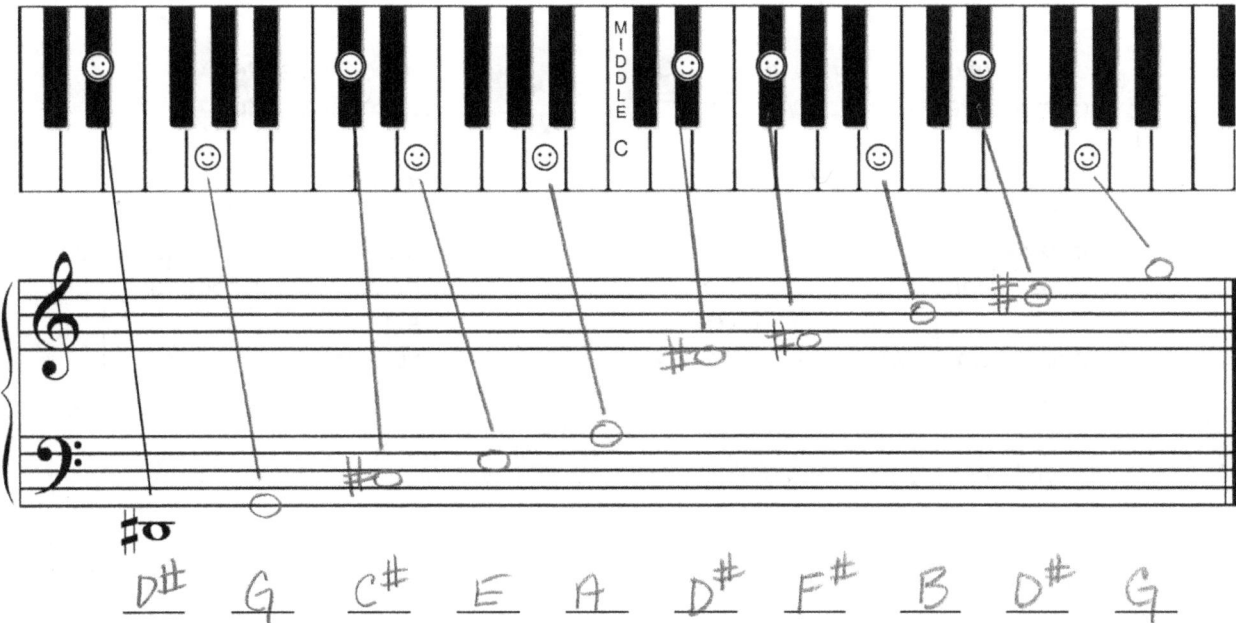

D# G C# E A D# F# B D# G

2. a) Write the following notes on the Grand Staff for the keys labelled with a ☺ on the keyboard.
      Use **FLATS** for the ☺ marked on the black keys. Use whole notes.
   b) Name the notes.
   c) Draw a line from each note on the staff to the corresponding key on the keyboard.

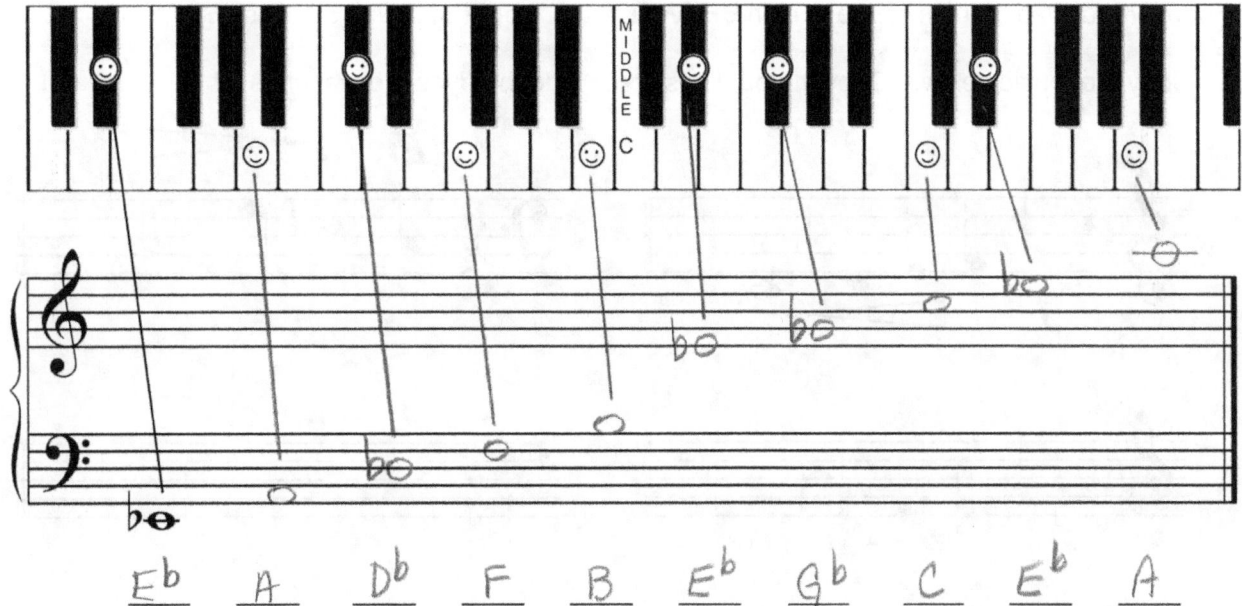

Eb A Db F B Eb Gb C Eb A

DYNAMICS

"**Dynamics**" refer to the varying degrees of loudness or softness.
Dynamic Markings are symbols or signs written in music to indicate different volumes of sound.

Term	Symbol or Sign	Definition
crescendo	cresc. or <	becoming louder
diminuendo	dim. or >	becoming softer
decrescendo	decresc. or >	becoming softer
fortissimo	*ff*	very loud
forte	*f*	loud
mezzo forte	*mf*	medium loud (moderately loud)
mezzo piano	*mp*	medium soft (moderately soft)
piano	*p*	soft
pianissimo	*pp*	very soft

1. Write the symbol or sign for each definition. (Use each symbol or sign only once.)

pp	*p*	*mp*	*mf*	*f*	*ff*
very soft	soft	medium soft	medium loud	loud	very loud

cresc.		&lt;	
becoming louder		becoming louder	

dim.	*decresc.*	&gt;
becoming softer	becoming softer	becoming softer

On a single staff, dynamics are written **BELOW** the Treble Staff or **ABOVE** the Bass Staff.
For a Grand Staff, dynamics are written **BETWEEN** the Treble Staff and the Bass Staff.

2. Copy the music below. (Copy the bar lines first.) Add the dynamic markings.

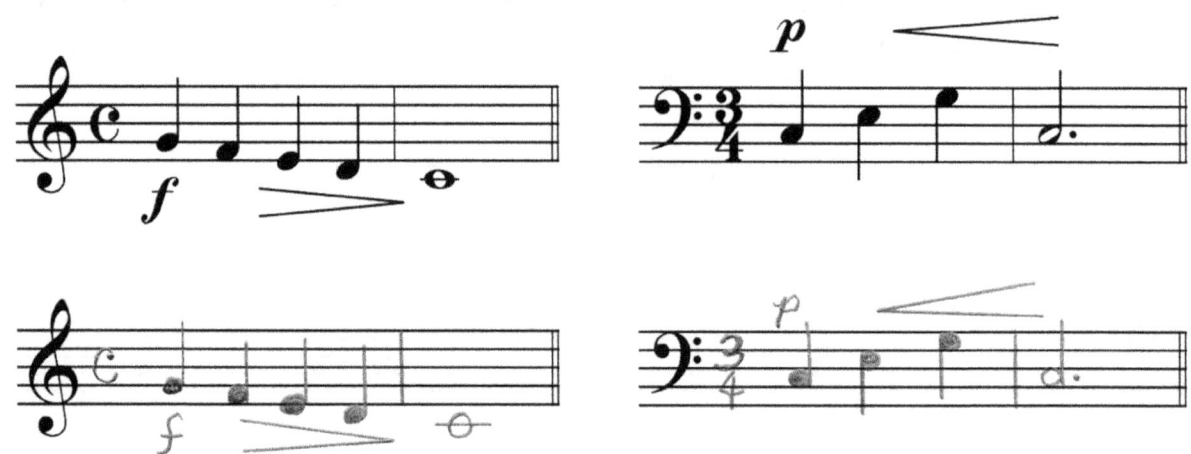

Lesson 4 — Review Test

Total Score: ____ / 100

1. a) Write a **Treble Clef** ("G" Clef) on the staff below.
   b) Name the notes.

___10___

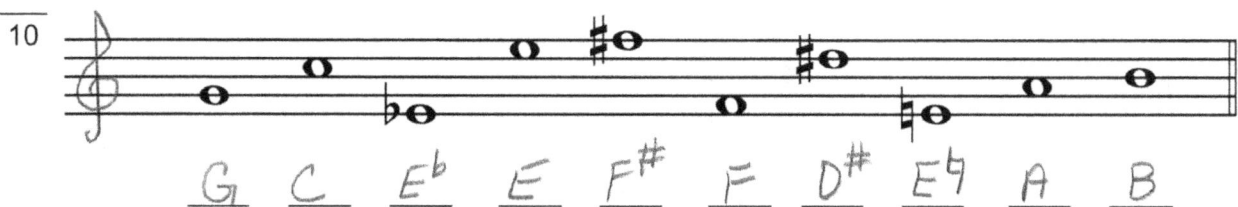

G   C   E♭   E   F♯   F   D♯   E♮   A   B

2. a) Name the notes in the **Bass Clef**.
   b) Identify the distance between the notes in each measure as **WT** (whole tone or whole step) or as **ST** (semitone or half step).

___10___

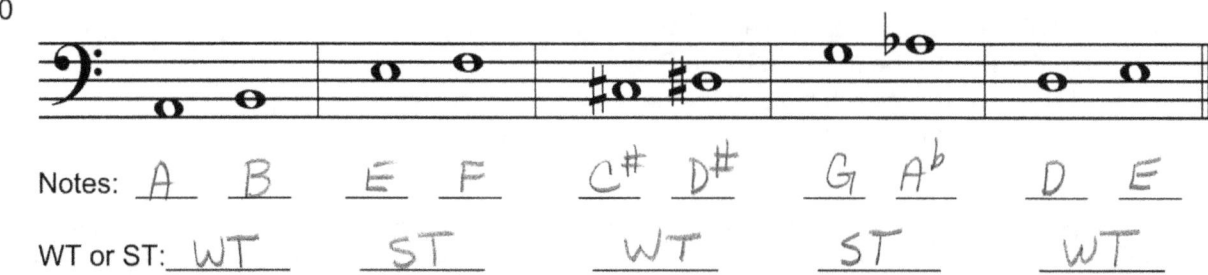

Notes: A B   E F   C♯ D♯   G A♭   D E
WT or ST: WT   ST   WT   ST   WT

3. a) Add a **Treble** ("G") Clef, **Bass** ("F") Clef and **Brace** to create the Grand Staff.
   b) Name the notes.
   c) Draw a line from each note on the staff to the corresponding key on the keyboard.

___10___

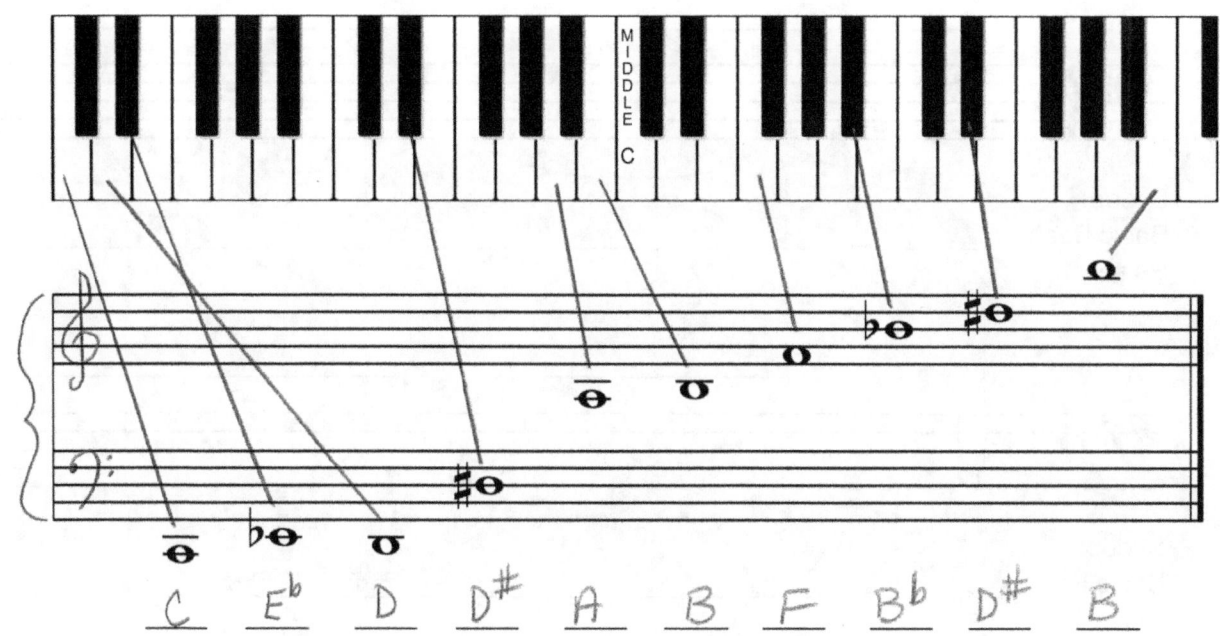

C   E♭   D   D♯   A   B   F   B♭   D♯   B

47

4. a) Write the names of the enharmonic equivalent notes in each measure.
b) Draw a line from each note on the staff to the corresponding key on the keyboard.

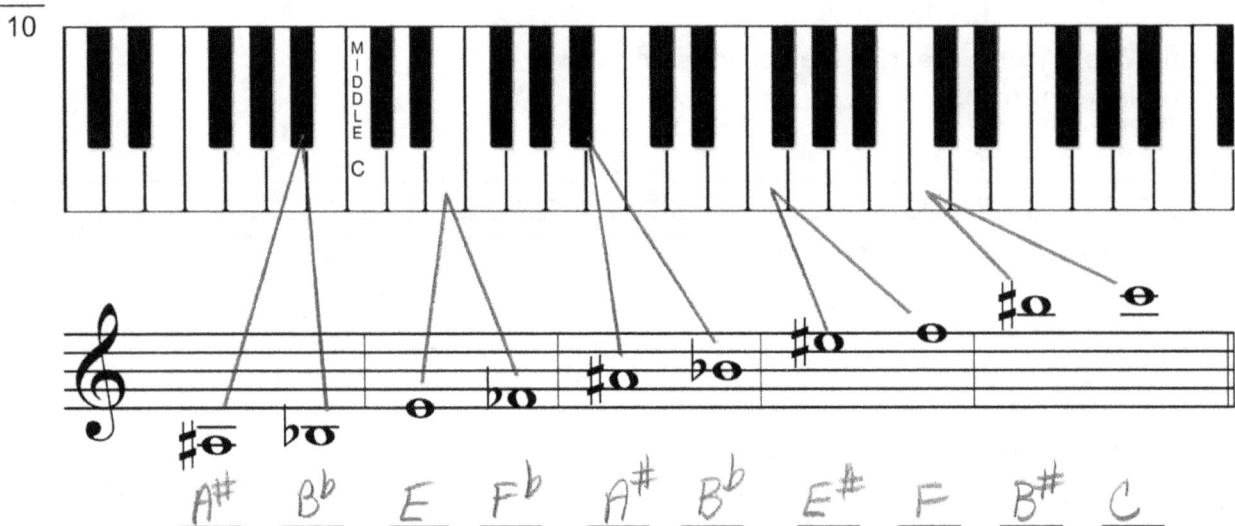

Measure 1: A# B♭
Measure 2: E F♭
Measure 3: A# B♭
Measure 4: E# F
Measure 5: B# C

5. a) **SCOOP** each Basic Beat in each measure.
b) Write the **PULSE** below each Basic Beat.
c) Add **RESTS** below each bracket to complete each measure.
d) Cross off the Basic Beat as each beat is completed.

Measure 1 (3/4):
Basic Beat: ♩ ♩ ♩ ♩ ♩ ♩
Pulse: S W W S W W

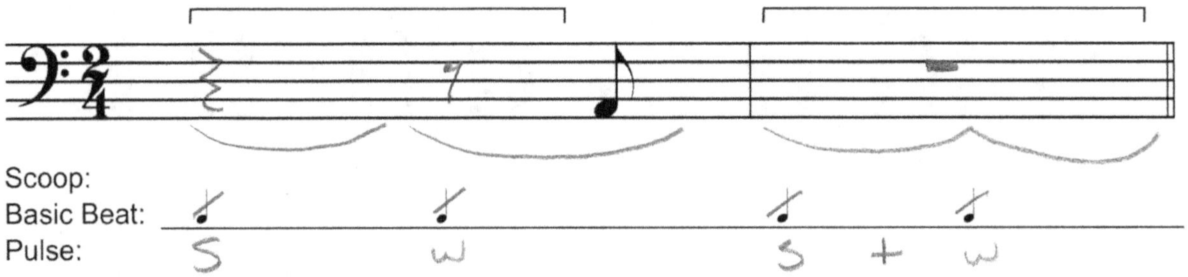

Measure 2 (2/4):
Basic Beat: ♩ ♩ ♩ ♩
Pulse: S W S + W

Measure 3 (C):
Basic Beat: ♩ ♩ ♩ ♩ ♩ ♩ ♩ ♩
Pulse: S W M+W S W M M+W

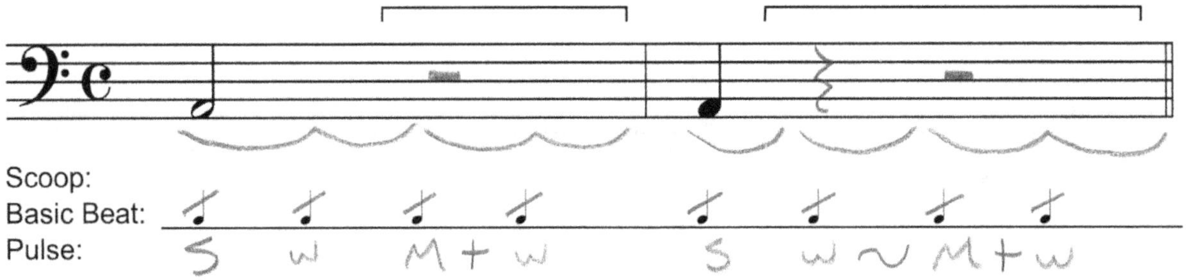

6. a) Name the notes.
   b) Name the melodic interval (numerical size only) in each measure. Use an up or a down arrow to indicate direction.

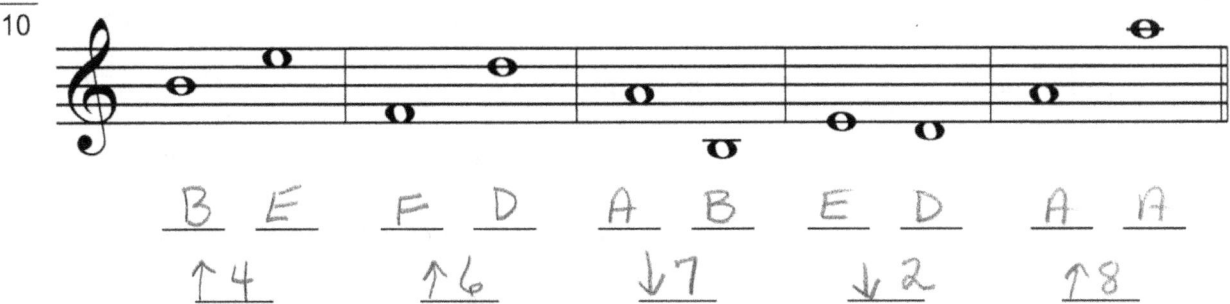

B E   F D   A B   E D   A A
↑4   ↑6   ↓7   ↓2   ↑8

7. Add bar lines to complete the following rhythms.

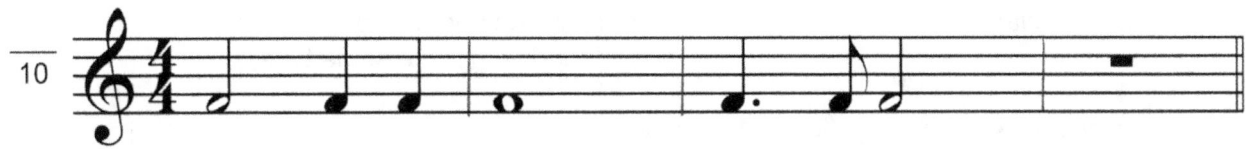

8. Write the following notes. Use ledger lines. Use whole notes.

a) **ABOVE** the Treble Clef   b) **BELOW** the Treble Clef

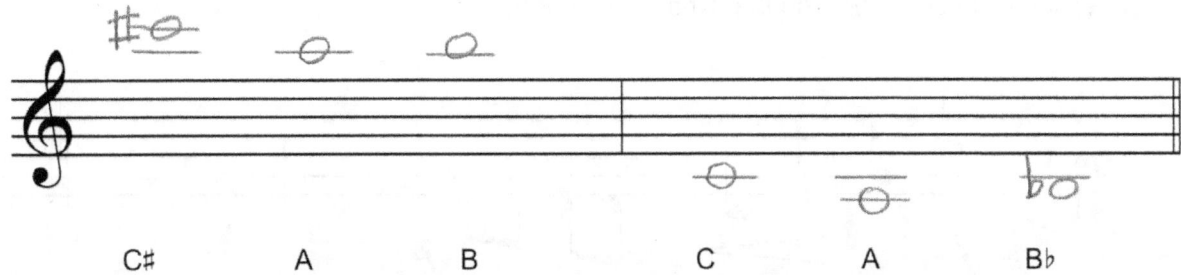

C#   A   B   C   A   B♭

c) **ABOVE** the Bass Clef   d) **BELOW** the Bass Clef

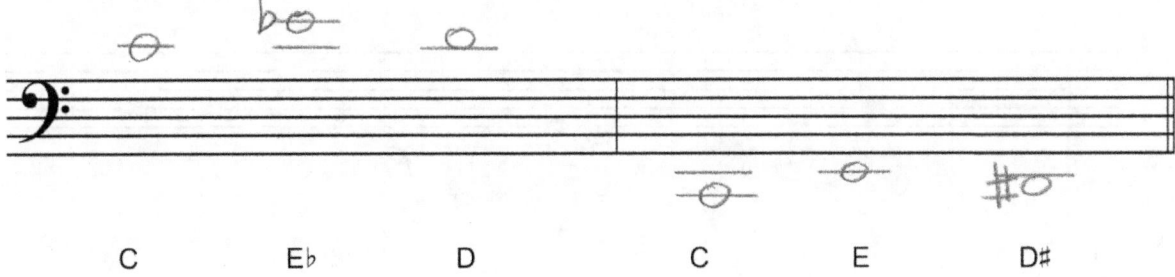

C   E♭   D   C   E   D#

9. Match each musical term with the English definition. (Not all definitions will be used.)

Term		Definition
crescendo	d	a) loud
piano	g	b) indicates a quarter note equals one beat
fortissimo	j	c) sharp, flat or natural sign in front of a note
diminuendo	i	d) becoming louder
forte	a	e) medium soft (moderately soft)
mezzo piano	e	f) 2 notes written one above the other, played together (at the same time)
accidentals	c	g) soft
whole tone	k	h) medium loud (moderately loud)
harmonic interval	f	i) becoming softer
mezzo forte	h	j) very loud
		k) two semitones

10. Copy the music below in the Treble Clef. (Copy the bar lines first.) Correct any stem direction as necessary. Add the dynamic markings.

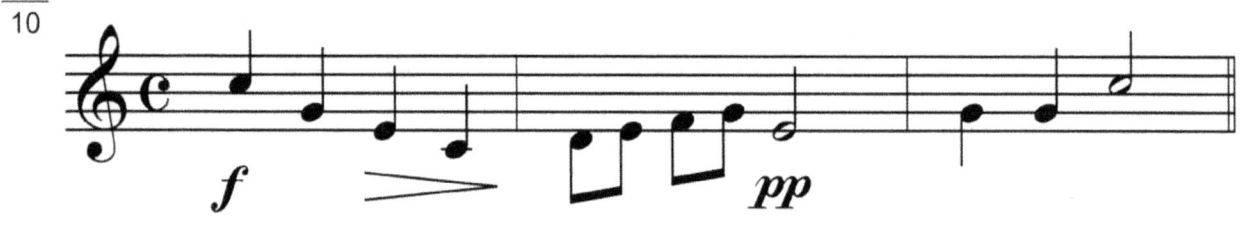

Lesson 5
Major Pentascales - Major Scales Outside the Circle of Fifths

A **Major Pentascale** is a series of 5 notes (degrees) in alphabetical order.

A **caret** sign " ^ " (or hat) above a number ($\hat{3}$) indicates the degree number of the scale.

A Major Pentascale uses the following pattern:

$\hat{1}$ |whole tone| $\hat{2}$ |whole tone| $\hat{3}$ semitone $\hat{4}$ |whole tone| $\hat{5}$
     WT   WT   ST   WT

The outside of the **CIRCLE OF FIFTHS** is a **MAP of the Major keys**. It is called the Circle of Fifths because when moving around the Circle of Fifths, the distance between each key is 5 letter names (a 5th). Major Pentascales create the **OUTSIDE** of the Circle of Fifths.

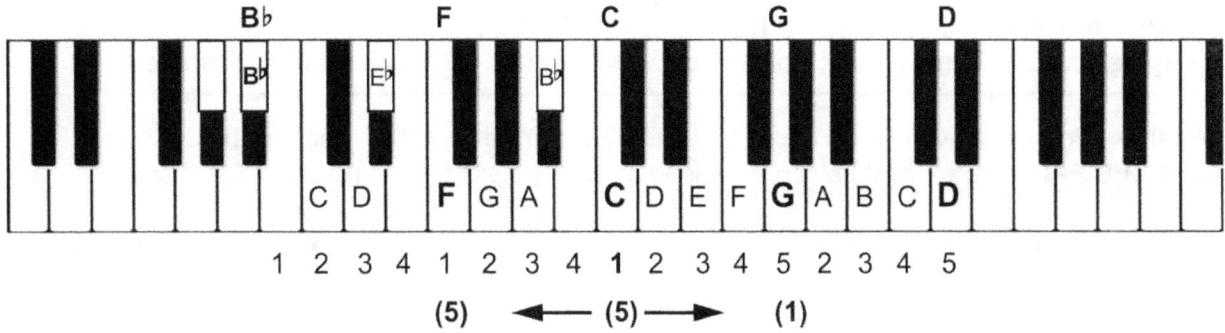

To identify the Keys of the Circle of Fifths: begin with C. Moving **CLOCKWISE** (to the right) around the Circle of Fifths, count UP 5 letter names. When moving **COUNTERCLOCKWISE** (to the left) around the Circle of Fifths, count DOWN 5 letter names.

♫ **Note:** When moving UP from C the 5th note is counted again as **(1)**: **1** 2 3 4 **5 (1)** 2 3 4 **5**.
           When moving DOWN from C the 1st note is counted again as **(5)**: **5** 4 3 2 **1 (5)** 4 3 2 **1**.

1. Trace the letter names (UPPER case) outside the Circle of Fifths.

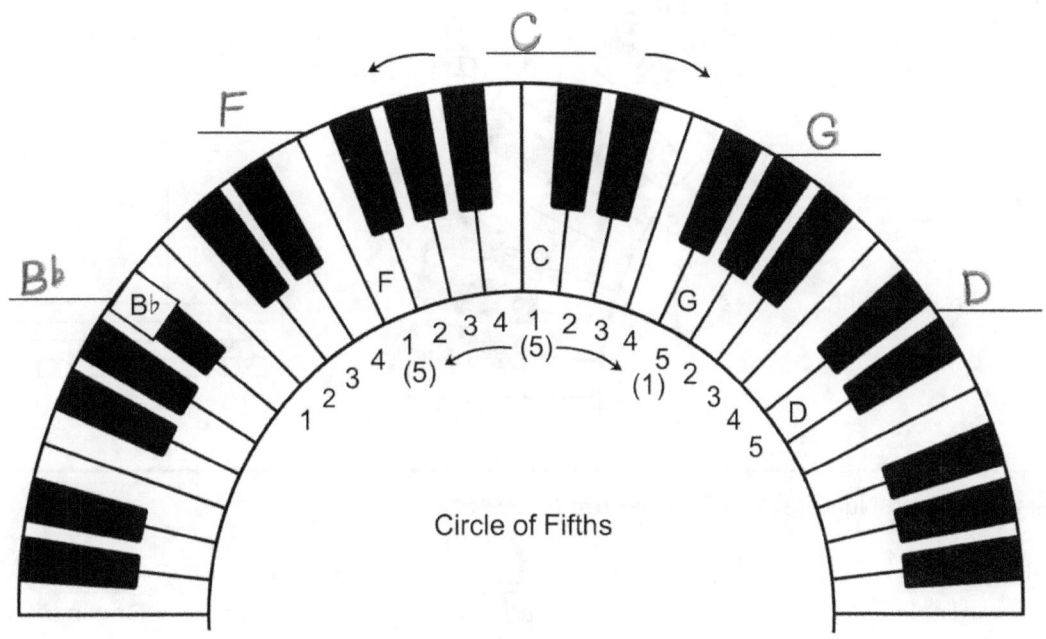

Circle of Fifths

MAJOR PENTASCALES with SHARPS

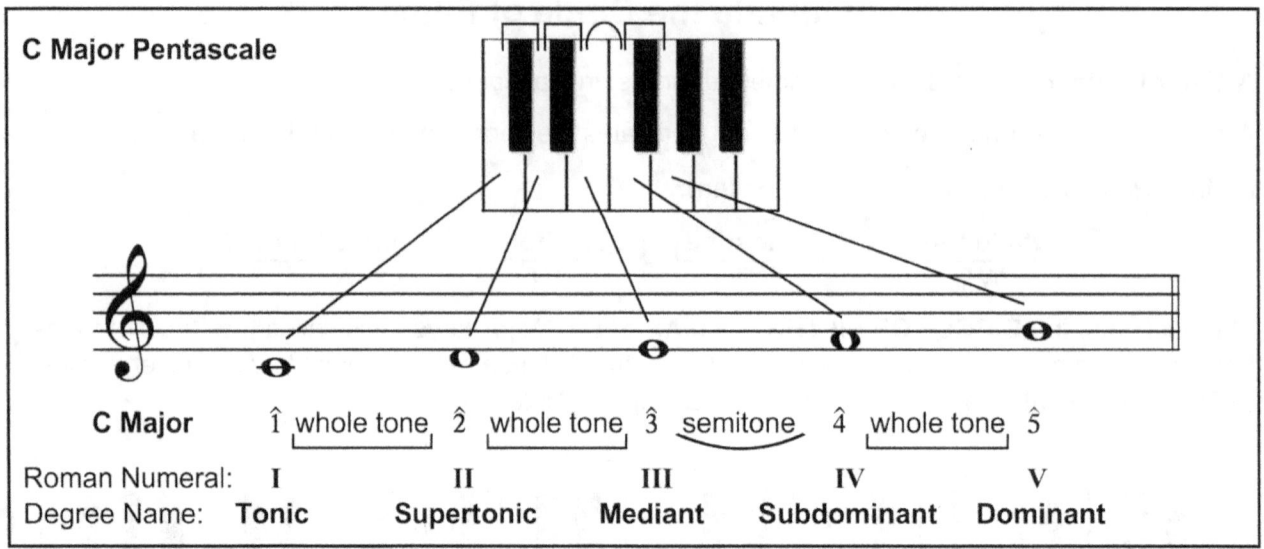

When moving **CLOCKWISE** (to the right) around the **Circle of Fifths**, begin with C. Count UP 5 from C: **C D E F G**. G is the next key on the Circle of Fifths. (G is the Dominant of C Major.)

To find the next key on the Circle of Fifths, count UP 5 from G: **G A B C D**. D is the next key on the Circle of Fifths. (D is the Dominant of G Major.)

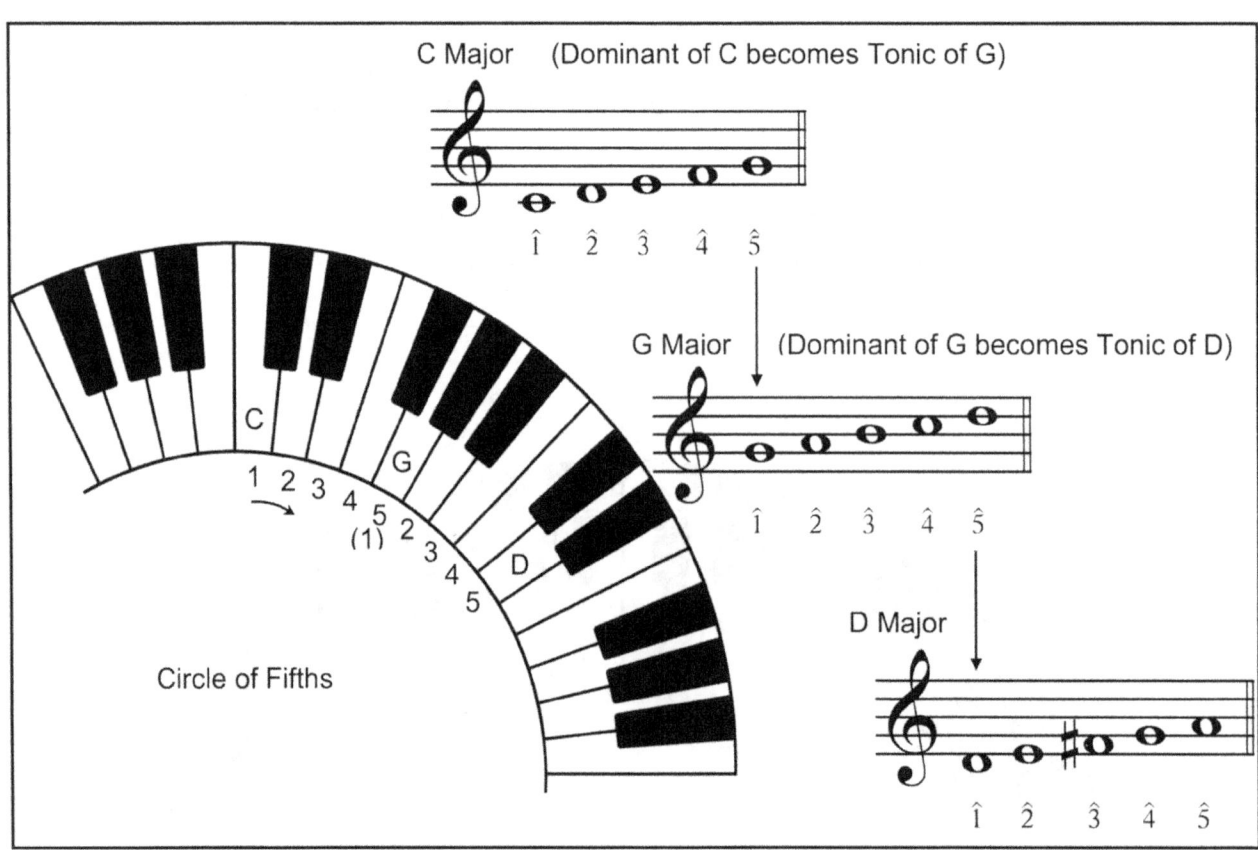

1. Write the Roman Numeral for each Degree Name.

I	II	III	IV	V
Tonic	Supertonic	Mediant	Subdominant	Dominant

MAJOR KEYS WRITTEN OUTSIDE the CIRCLE of FIFTHS with SHARPS

Beginning with the Key of C Major, when moving clockwise (to the RIGHT) around the Circle of Fifths, the **Major keys** will have **SHARPS**. Count UP 5 from the key of C to find the next key on the Circle of Fifths. The 5th note (Dominant) of C Major becomes the 1st note (Tonic) of G Major.

♫ **Note:** Use the keyboard to identify the Major Pentascale pattern of: whole tone, whole tone, semitone, whole tone. The semitone is ALWAYS between degrees $\hat{3}$ and $\hat{4}$.

1. a) Write each Major Pentascale on the Treble Clef below. Use accidentals (sharps) when necessary. Use whole notes.
   b) Write the name of the Tonic note of each Major Pentascale directly on the keyboard of the Circle of Fifths. Use an UPPER case letter.

Key of C Major   (Dominant of C Major becomes Tonic of G Major)

Key of G Major   (Dominant of G Major becomes Tonic of D Major)

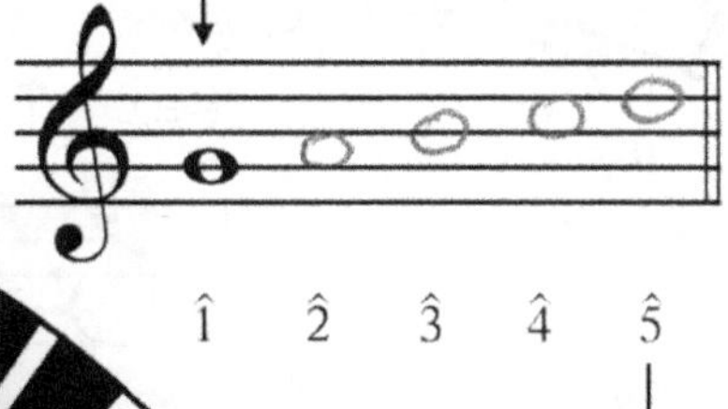

Key of D Major

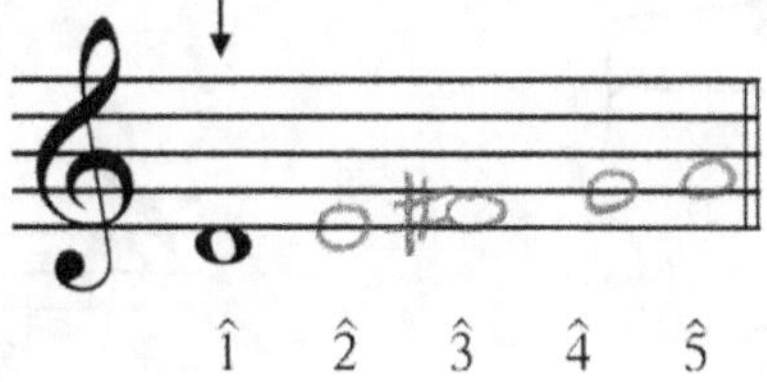

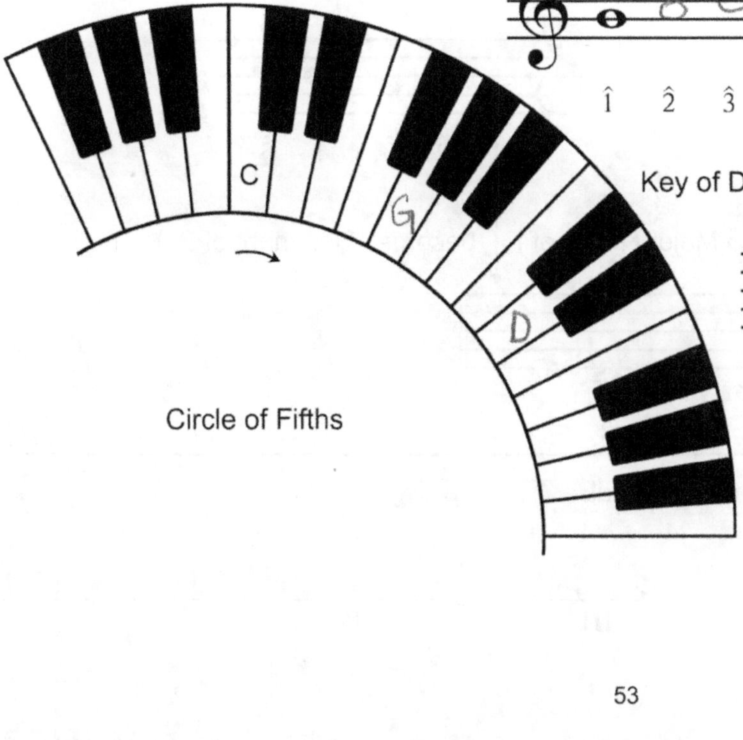

Circle of Fifths

MAJOR PENTASCALES with FLATS

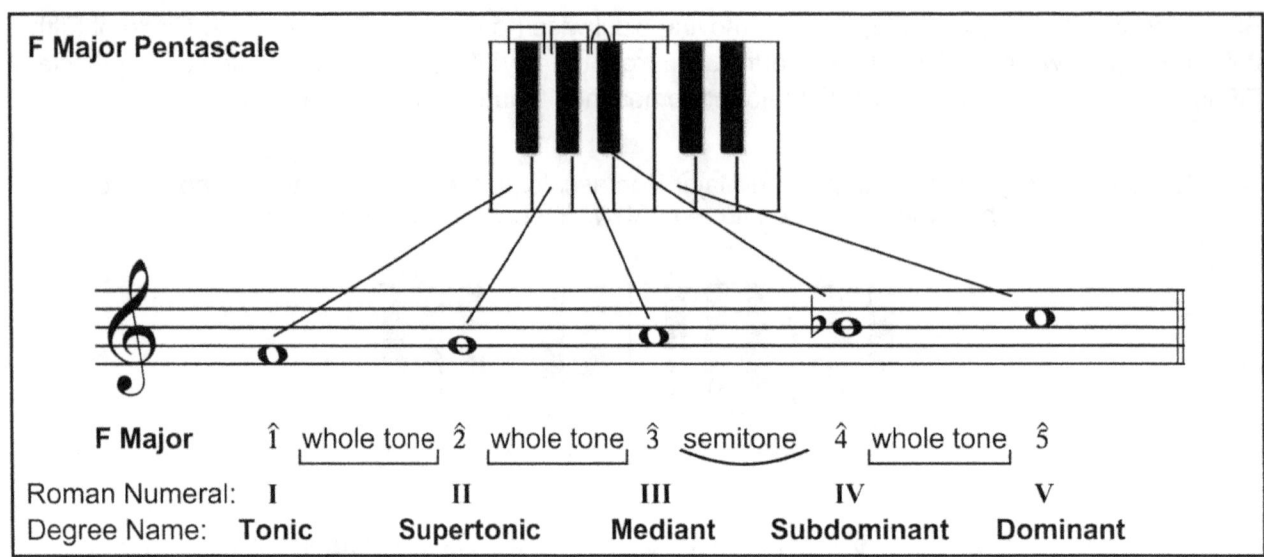

When moving **COUNTERCLOCKWISE** (to the left) around the **Circle of Fifths**, begin with C. Count DOWN 5 from C: **C B♭ A G F**. F is the next key on the Circle of Fifths. (C is the Dominant of F Major.)

To find the next key on the Circle of Fifths, count DOWN 5 from F: **F E♭ D C B♭**. B♭ is the next key on the Circle of Fifths. (F is the Dominant of B♭ Major.)

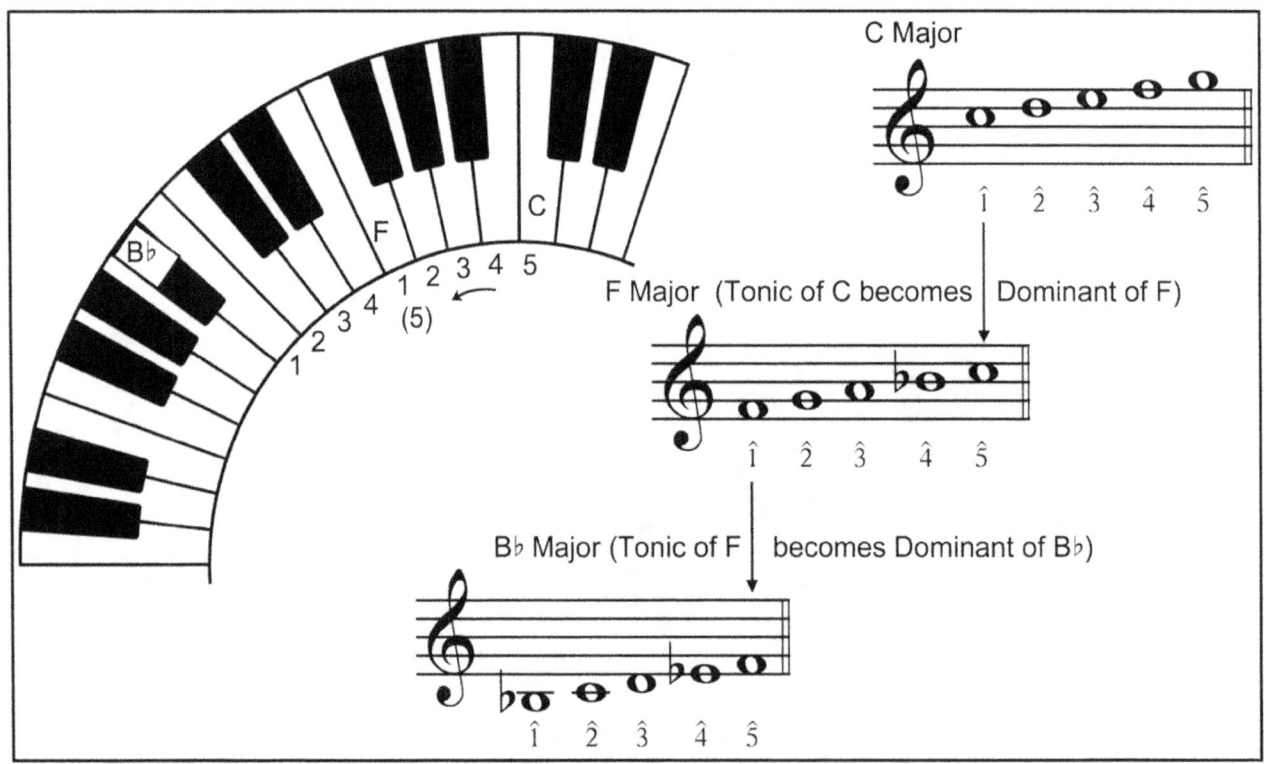

1. Write the Degree Name for each Roman Numeral.

Tonic	Supertonic	Mediant	Subdominant	Dominant
I	II	III	IV	V

MAJOR KEYS WRITTEN OUTSIDE the CIRCLE of FIFTHS with FLATS

Beginning with the Key of C Major, when moving counterclockwise (to the LEFT) around the Circle of Fifths, the **Major keys** will have **FLATS**. Count DOWN 5 from the key of C to find the next key on the Circle of Fifths. The 1st note (Tonic) of C Major becomes the 5th note (Dominant) of F Major.

♫ **Note:** Use the keyboard to identify the Major Pentascale pattern of: whole tone, whole tone, semitone, whole tone. The semitone is ALWAYS between degrees $\hat{3}$ and $\hat{4}$.

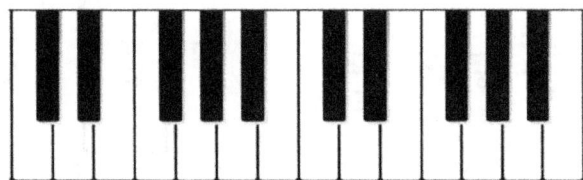

1. a) Write each Major Pentascale on the Treble Clef below. Use accidentals (flats) when necessary. Use whole notes.
   b) Write the name of the Tonic note of each Major Pentascale directly on the keyboard of the Circle of Fifths. Use an UPPER case letter.

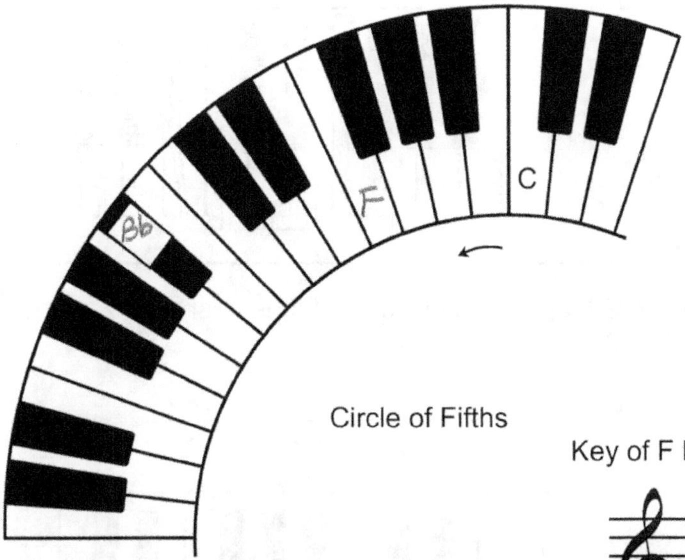

Circle of Fifths

Key of C Major

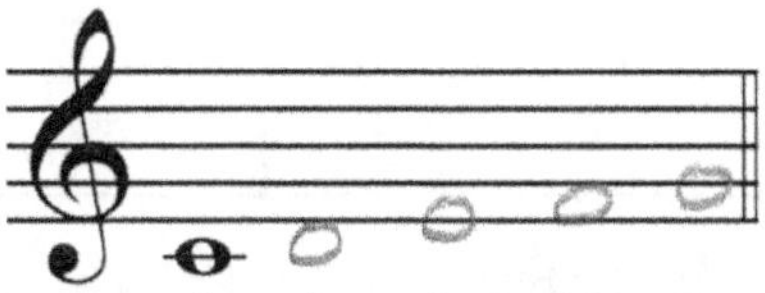

$\hat{1}$ $\hat{2}$ $\hat{3}$ $\hat{4}$ $\hat{5}$

Key of F Major

becomes (Tonic of C Major Dominant of F Major)

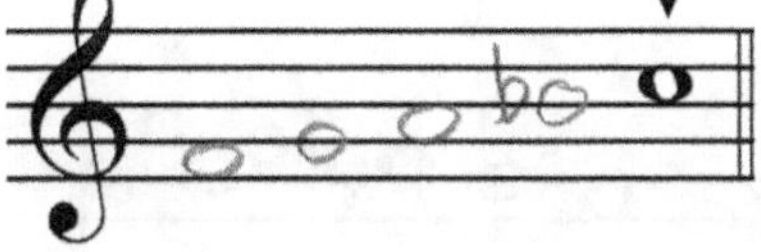

$\hat{1}$ $\hat{2}$ $\hat{3}$ $\hat{4}$ $\hat{5}$

Key of B♭ Major

(Tonic of F Major becomes Dominant of B♭ Major)

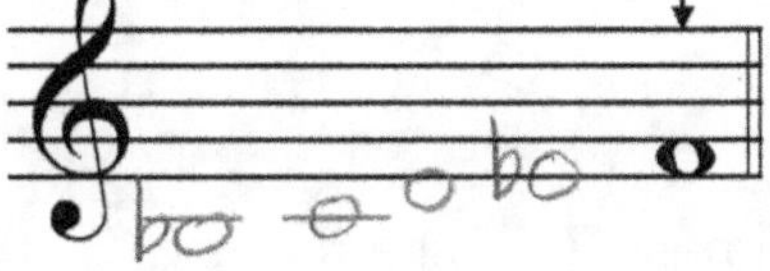

$\hat{1}$ $\hat{2}$ $\hat{3}$ $\hat{4}$ $\hat{5}$

MAJOR SCALES with SHARPS

A **Major scale** is a series of 8 notes in a specific pattern:
$\hat{1}$ whole tone $\hat{2}$ whole tone $\hat{3}$ semitone $\hat{4}$ whole tone $\hat{5}$ whole tone $\hat{6}$ whole tone $\hat{7}$ semitone $\hat{8}$ ($\hat{1}$).

The semitones are between degrees $\hat{3}$ and $\hat{4}$, and between degrees $\hat{7}$ and $\hat{8}$ of the Major scale. Semitones are indicated by a semitone slur.

♪ **Note:** This pattern will create a MAJOR SCALE beginning on any note.

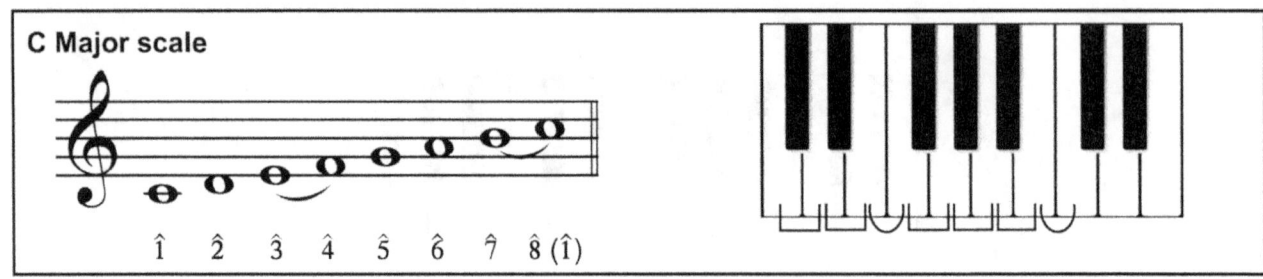

C Major has **0** (zero) sharps or flats. The 0 is written below C Major on the Circle of Fifths. Moving clockwise around the Circle of Fifths, the Dominant of C Major is G.

1. Write the letter names above the numbers: C D E F G
   $\hat{1}$ $\hat{2}$ $\hat{3}$ $\hat{4}$ $\hat{5}$

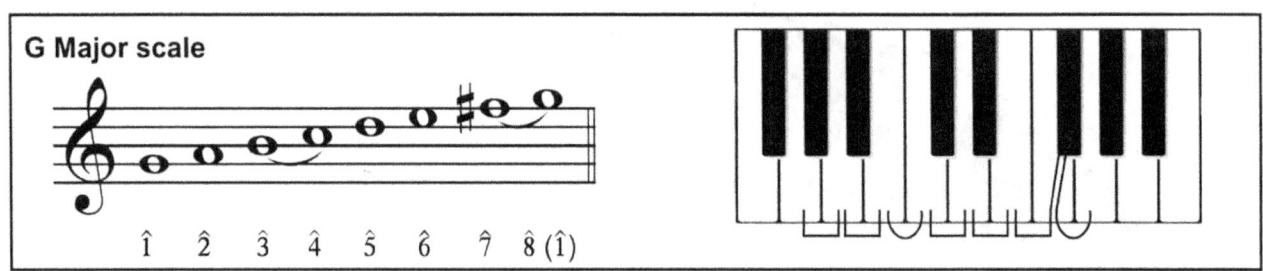

G Major has 1 sharp, **F♯**. The 1 is written beside G Major on the Circle of Fifths (1 sharp). Moving clockwise around the Circle of Fifths, the Dominant of G Major is D.

2. Write the letter names above the numbers: G A B C D
   $\hat{1}$ $\hat{2}$ $\hat{3}$ $\hat{4}$ $\hat{5}$

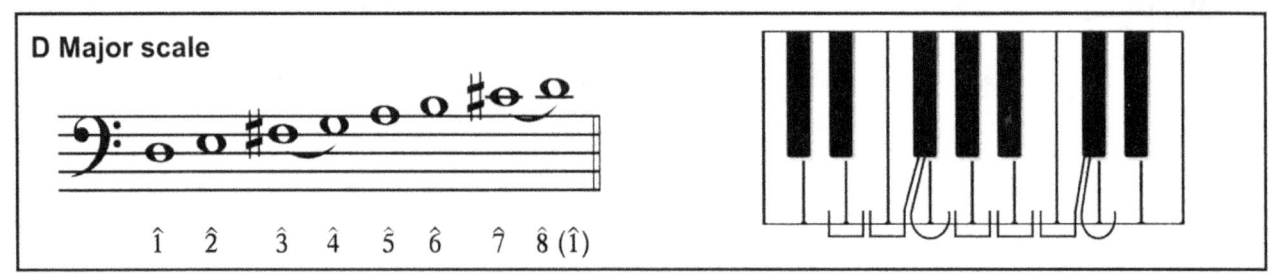

D Major has 2 sharps, **F♯** and **C♯**. The 2 is written beside D Major on the Circle of Fifths (2 sharps).

3. Complete the following.

   C Major has __0__ sharps. G Major has __1__ sharp. It is __F__ sharp.
   D Major has __2__ sharps. They are __F__ sharp and __C__ sharp.

CIRCLE of FIFTHS - MAJOR SCALES with SHARPS

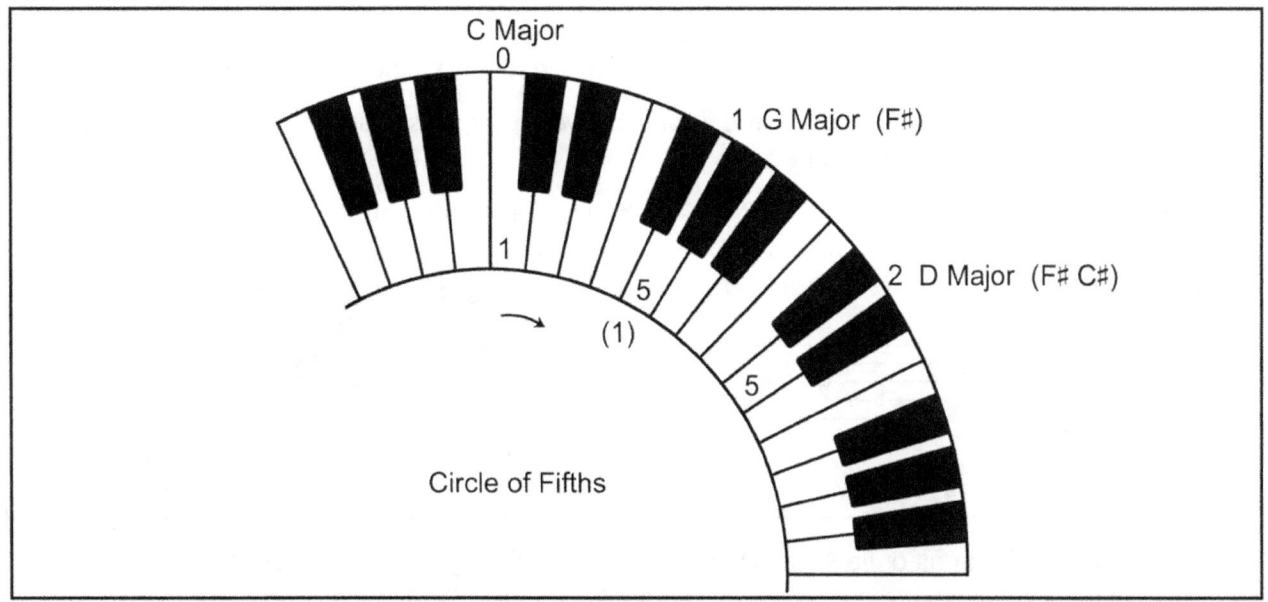

A Major scale can be written **WITH** or **WITHOUT** a center bar line after the highest note.

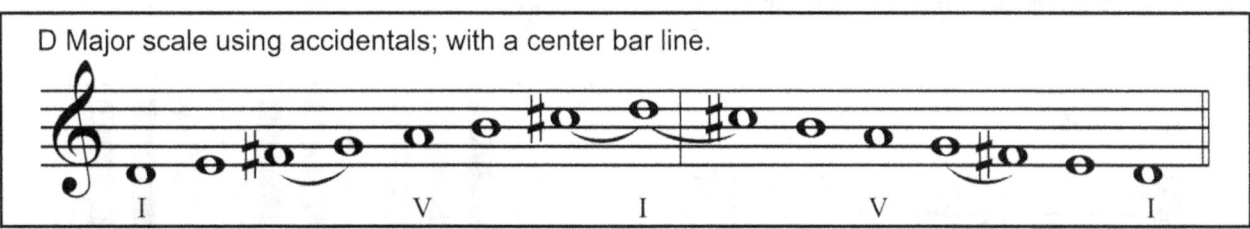

D Major scale using accidentals; with a center bar line.

♪ **Note:** Always write scales in the **SAME WAY**, either **WITH** or **WITHOUT** a center bar line.

1. a) Write the following scales, ascending and descending, in the given clef. Use whole notes. Use accidentals (sharps) when necessary.
   b) Label the Tonic (I) and Dominant (V) notes.

a) C Major scale

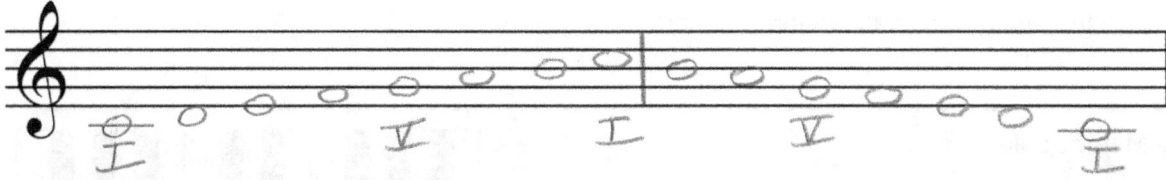

b) G Major scale

c) D Major scale

MAJOR SCALES with FLATS

A **Major scale** is a series of 8 notes in a specific pattern:
$\hat{1}$ whole tone $\hat{2}$ whole tone $\hat{3}$ semitone $\hat{4}$ whole tone $\hat{5}$ whole tone $\hat{6}$ whole tone $\hat{7}$ semitone $\hat{8}$ ($\hat{1}$).

The semitones are between degrees $\hat{3}$ and $\hat{4}$, and between degrees $\hat{7}$ and $\hat{8}$ of the Major Scale. Semitones are indicated by a semitone slur.

♪ **Note:** This pattern will create a MAJOR SCALE beginning on any note.

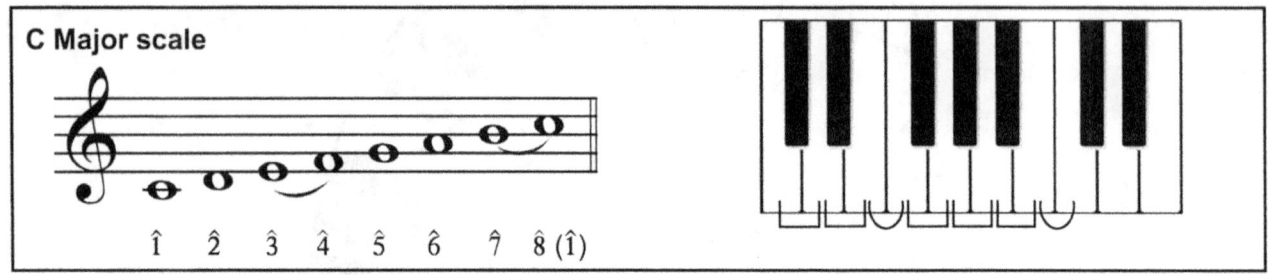

C Major has **0** (zero) sharps or flats. The 0 is written below C Major on the Circle of Fifths. Moving counterclockwise around the Circle of Fifths, C becomes the Dominant of F Major.

1. Write the letter names above the numbers: _F_ _G_ _A_ _B♭_ _C_
   $\hat{1}$ $\hat{2}$ $\hat{3}$ $\hat{4}$ $\hat{5}$

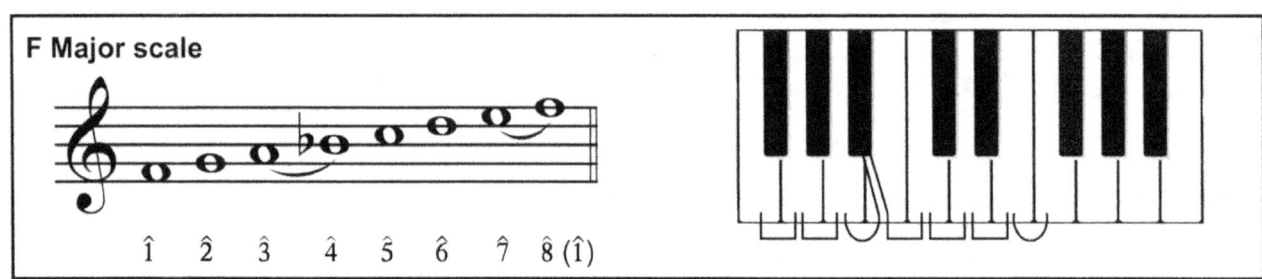

F Major has 1 flat, **B♭**. The 1 is written beside F Major on the Circle of Fifths (1 flat). Moving counterclockwise around the Circle of Fifths, F becomes the Dominant of B♭ Major.

2. Write the letter names above the numbers: _B♭_ _C_ _D_ _E♭_ _F_
   $\hat{1}$ $\hat{2}$ $\hat{3}$ $\hat{4}$ $\hat{5}$

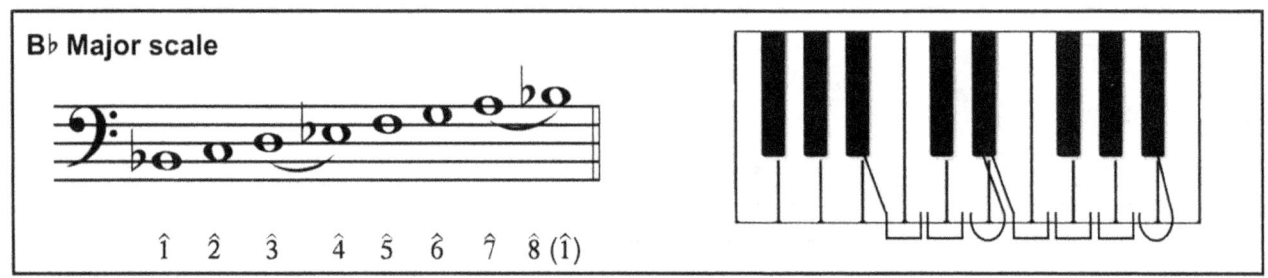

B♭ Major has 2 flats, **B♭** and **E♭**. The 2 is written beside B♭ Major on the Circle of Fifths (2 flats).

3. Complete the following.

   C Major has __0__ flats. F Major has __1__ flat. It is __B__ flat.
   B♭ Major has __2__ flats. They are __B__ flat and __E__ flat.

CIRCLE of FIFTHS - MAJOR KEYS with FLATS

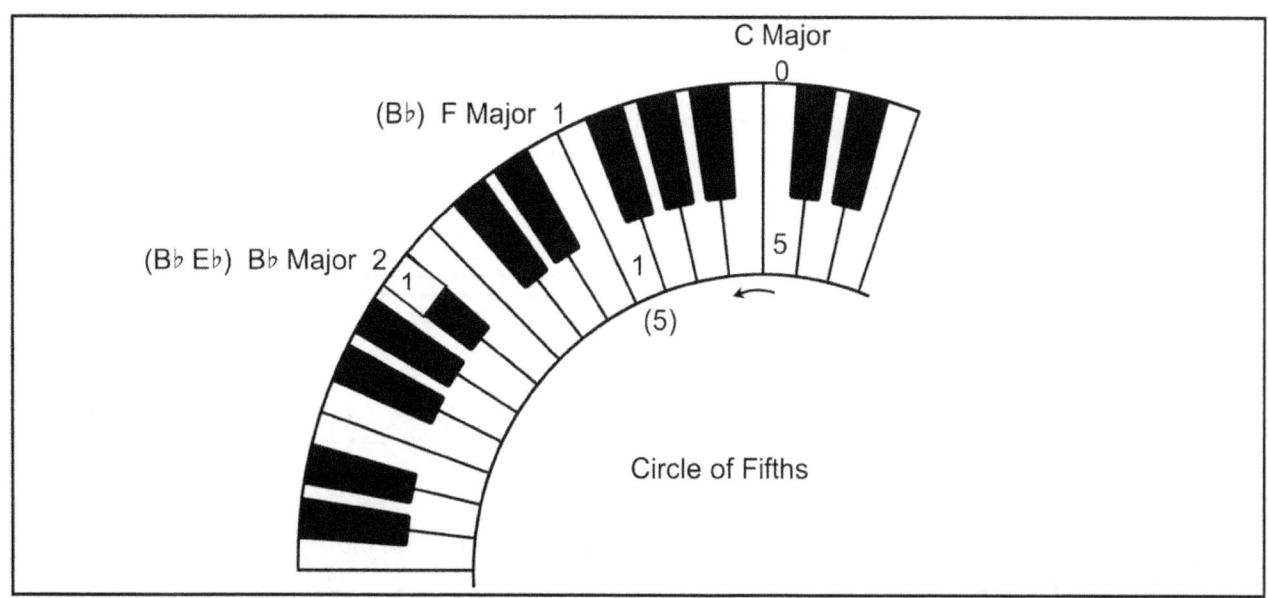

When writing a scale using accidentals **WITH** a center bar line, the accidentals must be repeated in the descending scale. When writing a scale using accidentals **WITHOUT** a center bar line, accidentals are **ONLY** written in the ascending scale.

1. a) Write the following scales, ascending and descending, in the given clef. Use whole notes. Use accidentals (flats) when necessary.
   b) Label the Tonic (I) and Dominant (V) notes.

a) C Major scale

b) F Major scale

c) B♭ Major scale

Lesson 5 — Review Test

Total Score: ____ / 100

1. Write the following notes. Use **ledger lines**. Use whole notes.

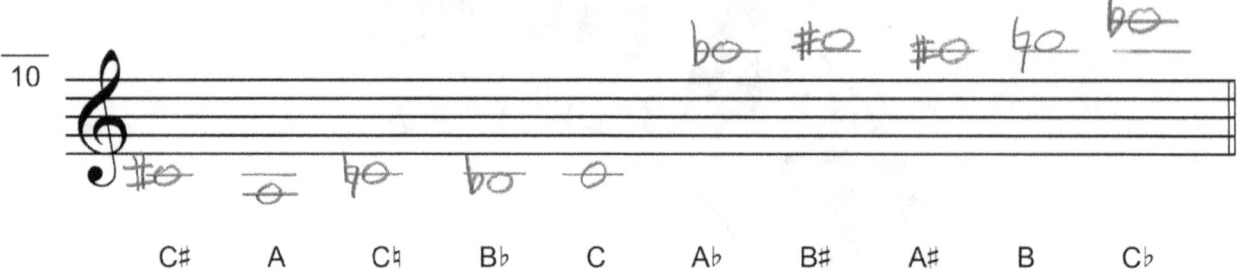

C#   A   C♮   B♭   C   A♭   B#   A#   B   C♭

2. a) Add a **STEM** to each notehead to create a quarter note in each measure.
   b) Name the notes.

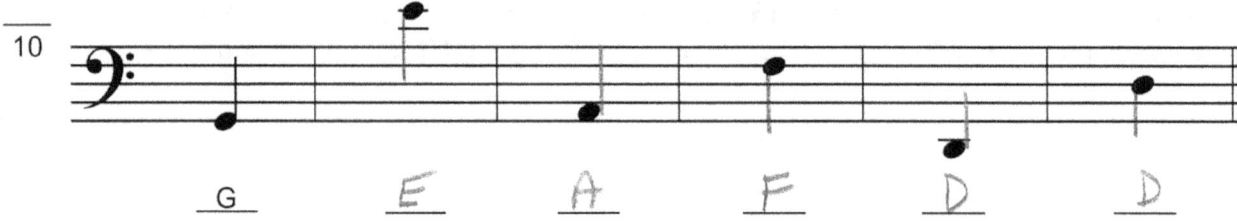

G   E   A   F   D   D

3. Name the following notes on the Grand Staff.

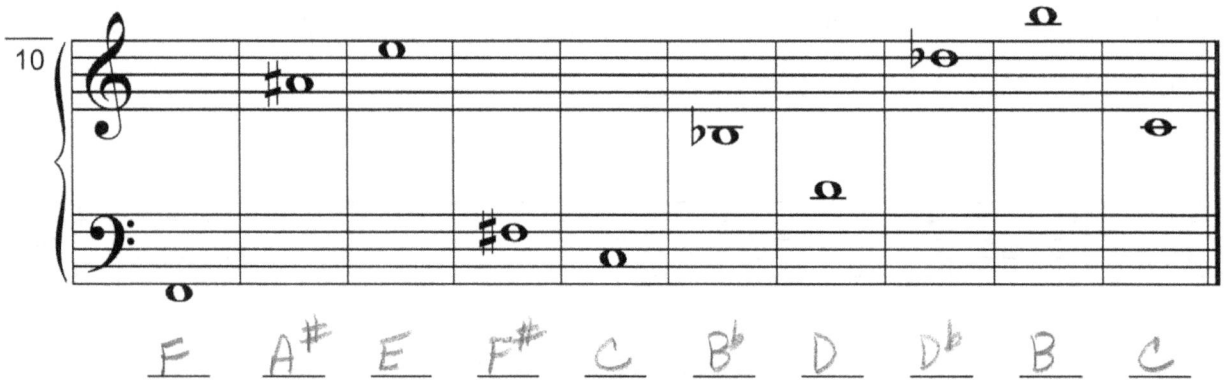

F   A#   E   F#   C   B♭   D   D♭   B   C

4. a) Add a **DOT** to each note to create dotted half notes in each measure.
   b) Name the following harmonic intervals (numerical size only).

3   5   2   7   4   6   2   2   6   3   8

5. a) **SCOOP** each Basic Beat in each measure.
   b) Write the **PULSE** below each Basic Beat.
   c) Add **RESTS** below each bracket to complete each measure.
   d) Cross off the Basic Beat as each beat is completed.

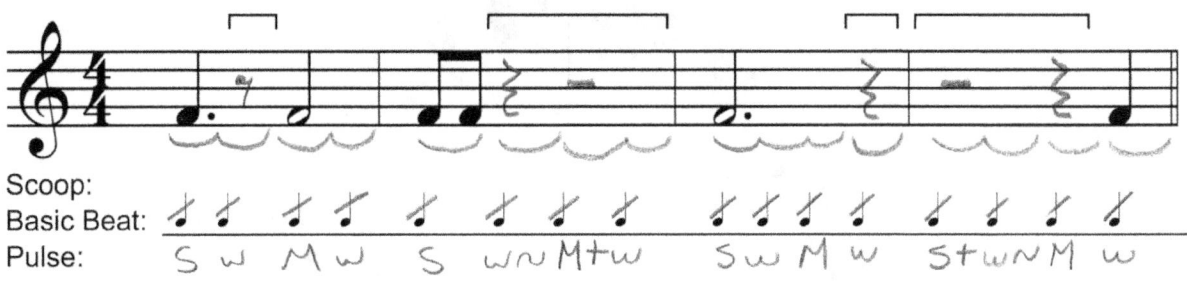

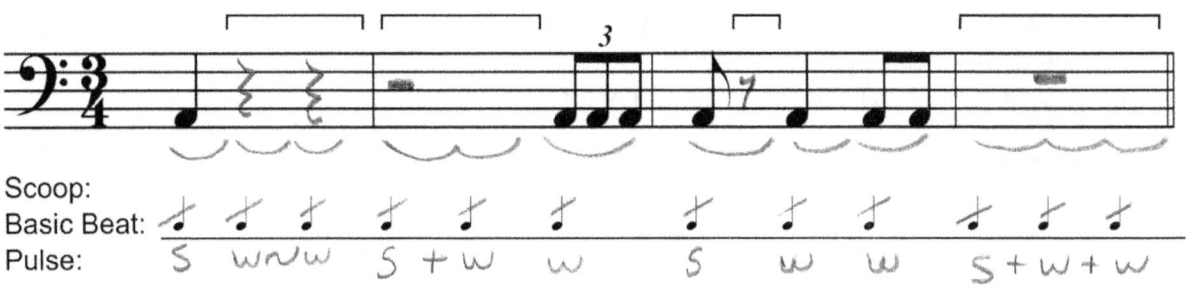

6. a) Write the following harmonic intervals above each of the given notes. Use whole notes.
   b) Name the notes. Write the name of the LOWER note first, then the HIGHER note.

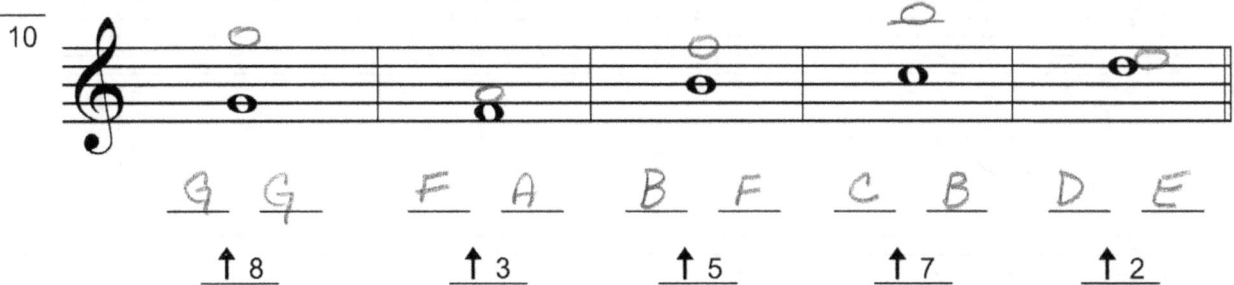

7. a) Name the notes.
   b) Name the melodic interval between the notes. Use an up or a down arrow to indicate direction.

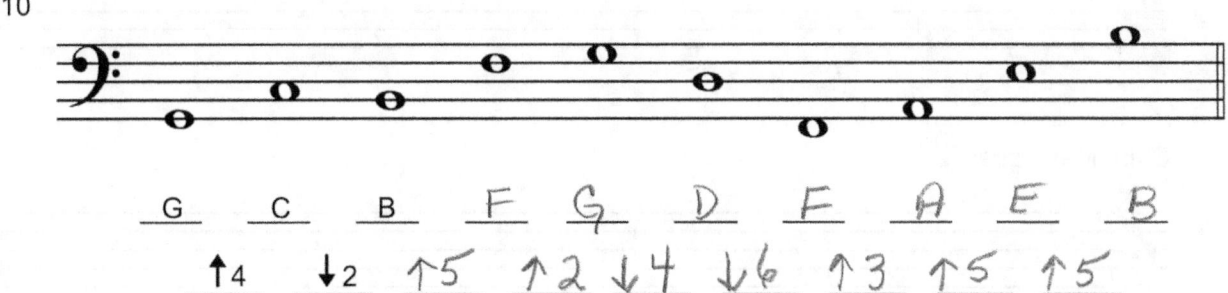

8. a) Complete the Circle of Fifths by adding the Major keys.
   b) Write the flats or sharps for each key.

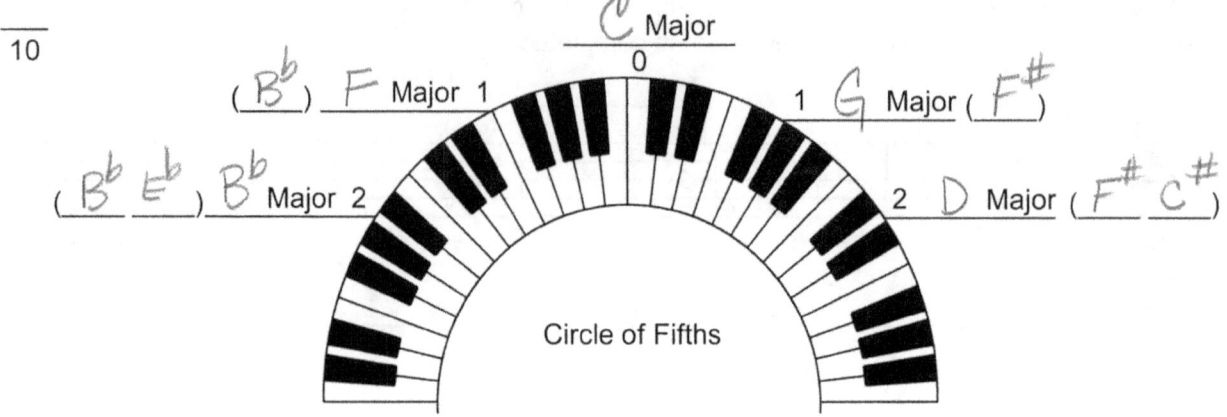

c) Write the following scales ascending and descending, in the given clef. Use whole notes. Use accidentals when necessary.
d) Label the Tonic (**I**) and Dominant (**V**) notes.

C Major scale

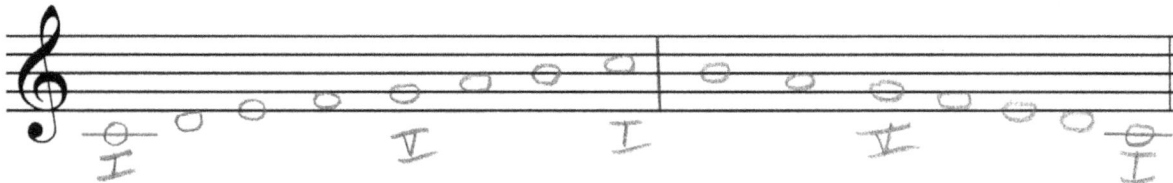

G Major scale

D Major scale

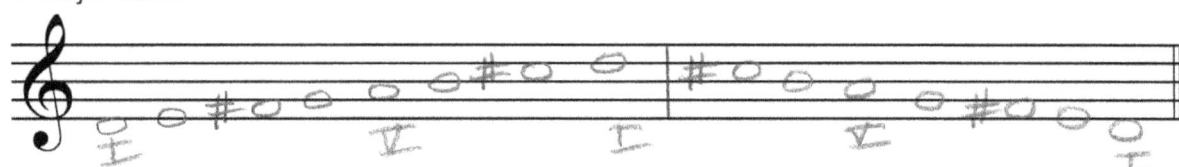

F Major scale

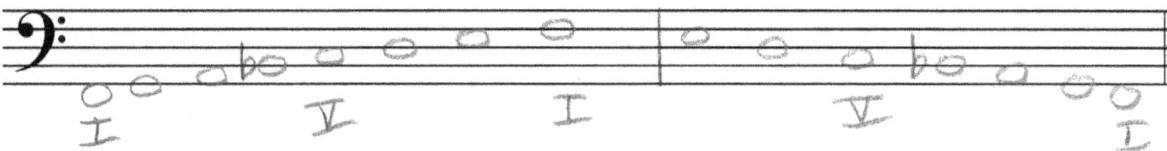

B flat Major scale

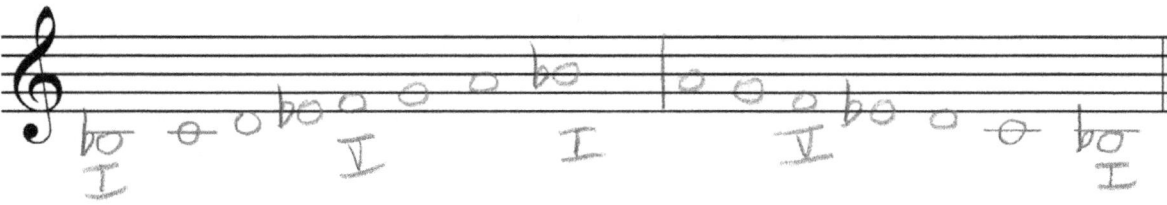

9. Copy the music below in the Bass Staff. (Copy the bar lines first.) Correct any stem direction as necessary.

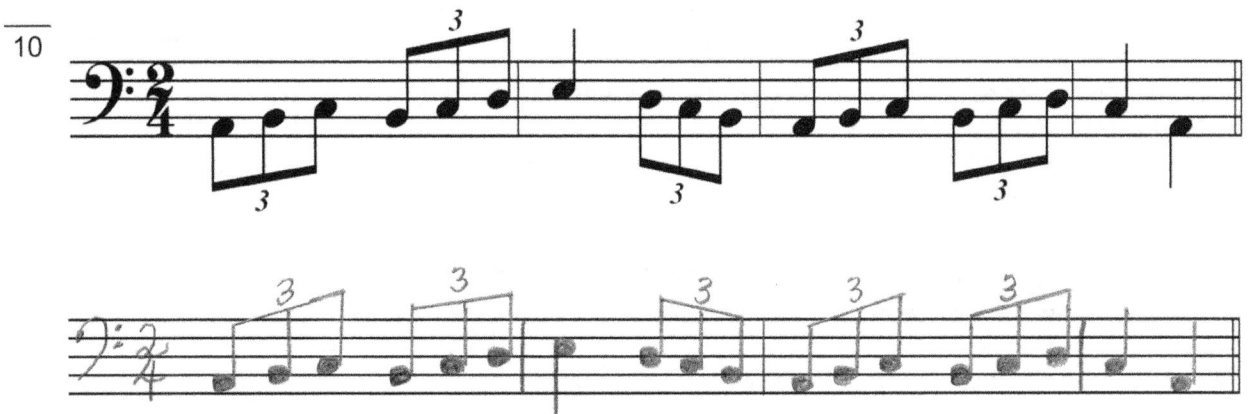

10. Match each musical term with the English definition. (Not all definitions will be used.)

Term		Definition
Grand Staff	j	a) raises a note one semitone (half step)
ledger line	g	b) first note (degree) of a scale
brace	d	c) 2 notes played separately, one after the other
sharp	a	d) bracket that joins the Treble Staff and Bass Staff
flat	h	e) fifth note (degree) of a scale
melodic interval	c	f) series of 5 notes in alphabetical order with a pattern of WT - WT - ST - WT
whole tone (whole step)	i	g) short line used to extend notation above and below the staff
Major Pentascale	f	h) lowers a note one semitone (half step)
Tonic	b	i) two semitones, two notes with one key (black or white) in between them
Dominant	e	j) Treble Staff and Bass Staff joined together
		k) 2 notes written one above the other, played together (at the same time)

Lesson 6   Minor Pentascales - Natural Minor Scales
Inside the Circle of Fifths

Every **MAJOR KEY** has a **RELATIVE MINOR** key.
Major keys and their relative minor keys share the same sharps or flats.

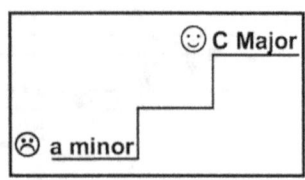

When moving from a Major key to its relative minor key, descend (go down) **THREE** semitones and **THREE** letter names.

When moving from a minor key to its relative Major key, ascend (go up) **THREE** semitones and **THREE** letter names.

♪ **No**te: Use UPPER case letters for Major keys and lower case letters for minor keys.

1. Name the following Major keys and their relative minor keys below.

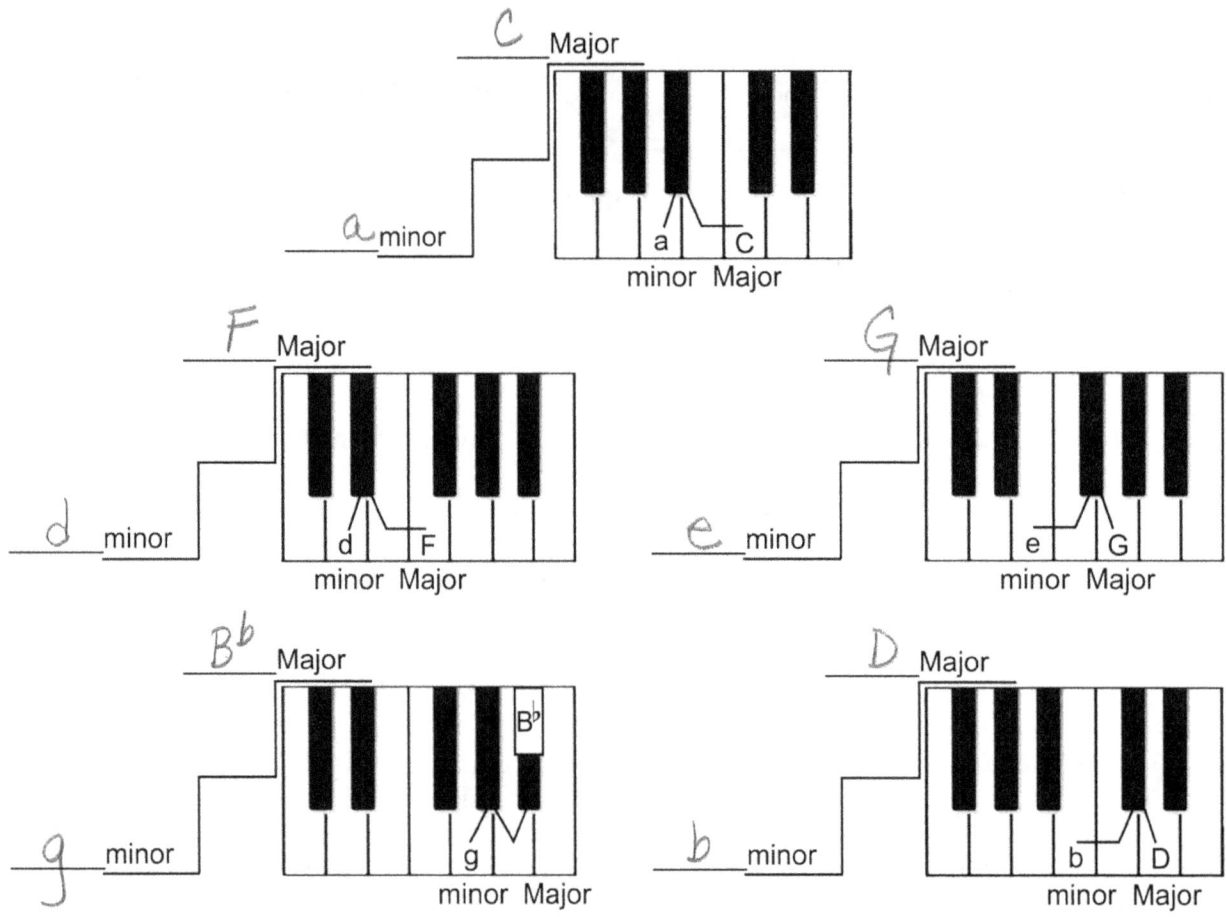

2. Name the relative minor key for each of the following Major keys.

           C Major's relative minor key is __a__ minor.

F Major's relative minor key is __d__ minor.   G Major's relative minor key is __e__ minor.

B♭ Major's relative minor key is __g__ minor.   D Major's relative minor key is __b__ minor.

64

CIRCLE of FIFTHS - MAJOR and RELATIVE MINOR KEYS

Major keys are written on the **OUTSIDE** of the Circle of Fifths and **minor keys** are written on the **INSIDE** of the **Circle of Fifths**. UPPER case letters are used for Major keys and lower case letters are used for minor keys.

♪ **Note:** When writing sharps, flats or note names, ALWAYS use UPPER case letters.

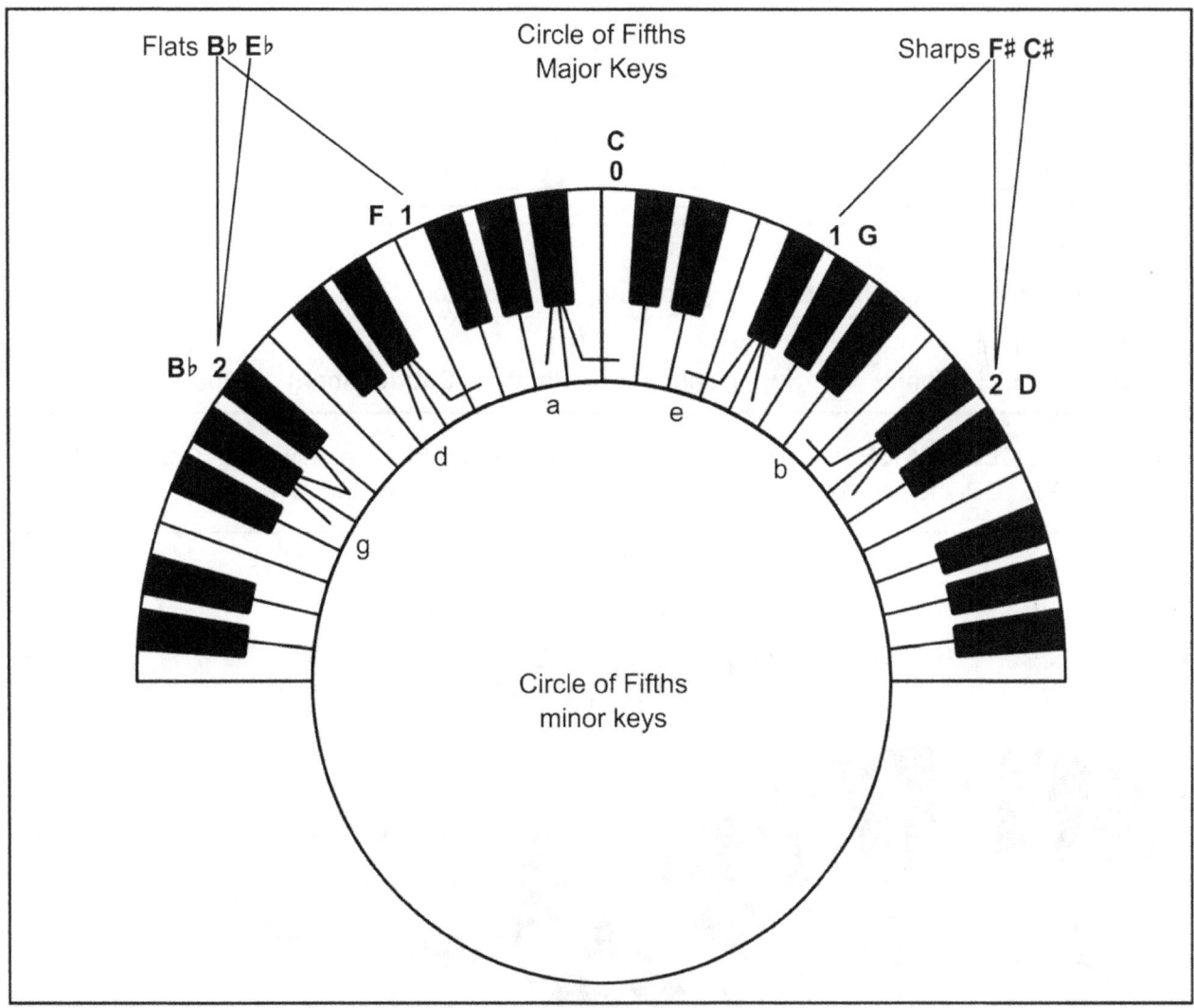

Major keys and their relative minor keys share the same sharps or flats.

1. a) Name the relative minor key for each Major key below.
   b) Write the sharps or flats for each Major and relative minor key.

Major keys	relative minor keys	Sharps	Flats
C Major	_a_ minor		
G Major	_e_ minor	F#	
D Major	_b_ minor	F# C#	
F Major	_d_ minor		B♭
B♭ Major	_g_ minor		B♭ E♭

MINOR PENTASCALES with SHARPS

A **MINOR Pentascale** is a series of 5 notes (degrees) in alphabetical order, using the following pattern: $\hat{1}$ whole tone $\hat{2}$ semitone $\hat{3}$ whole tone $\hat{4}$ whole tone $\hat{5}$.

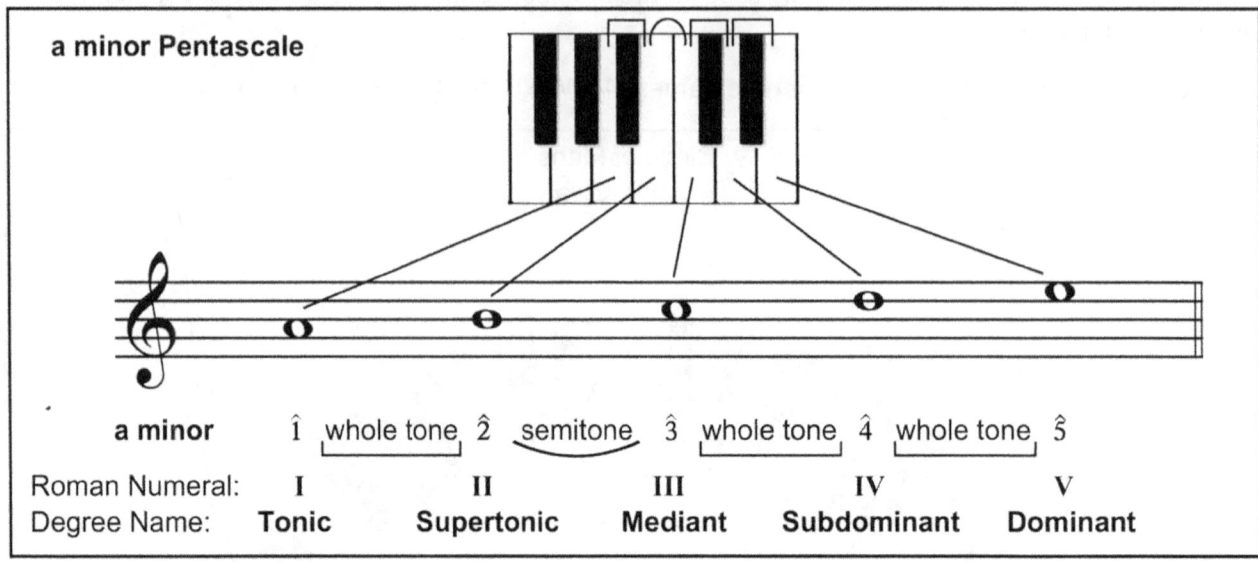

When moving **CLOCKWISE** (to the right) around the **Circle of Fifths**, begin with A. Count UP 5 from A: **A B C D E**. E is the next key on the Circle of Fifths. (E is the Dominant of a minor.)

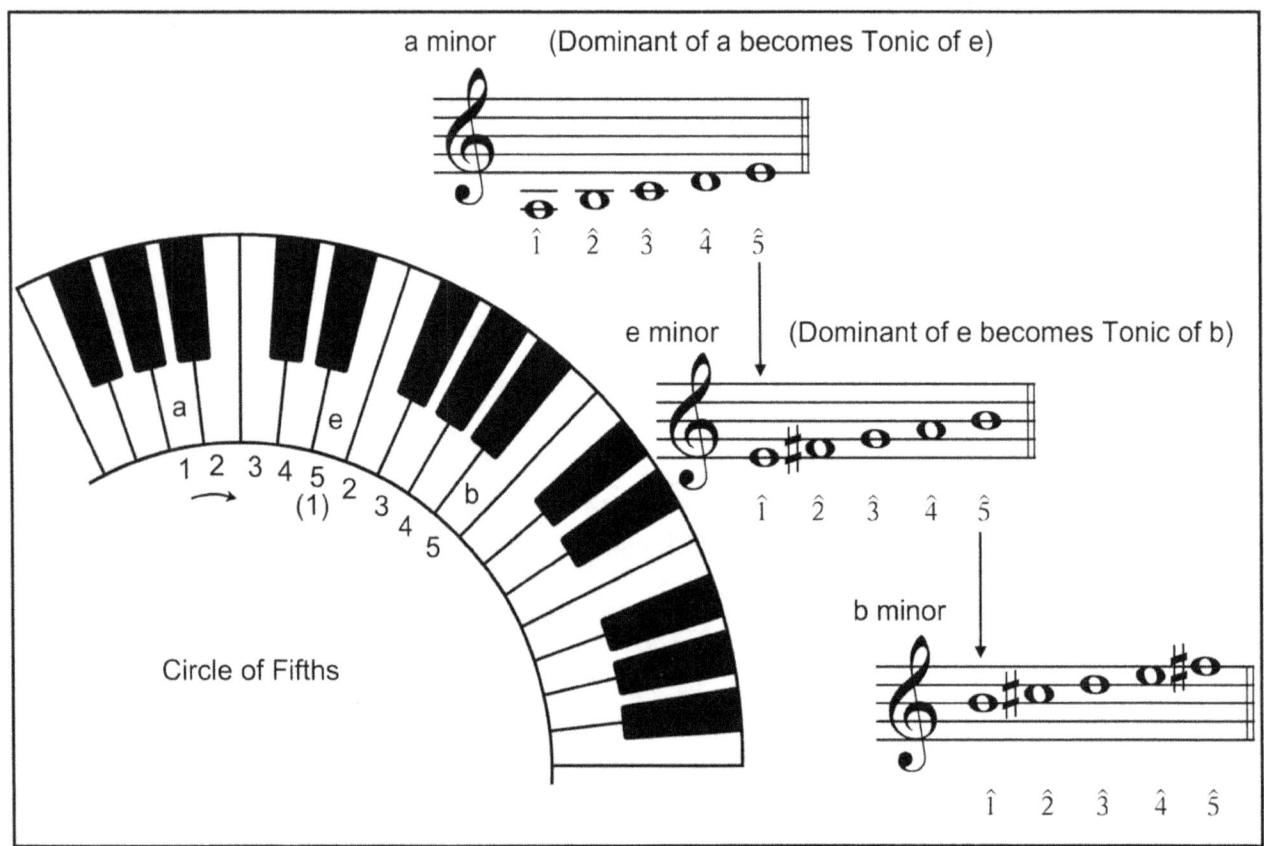

1. Write the Roman Numeral for each Degree Name.

I	II	III	IV	V
Tonic	Supertonic	Mediant	Subdominant	Dominant

MINOR KEYS WRITTEN INSIDE the CIRCLE OF FIFTHS with SHARPS

Beginning with the key of "**a**" minor, when moving clockwise (to the RIGHT) around the Circle of Fifths, the **minor keys** will have **SHARPS**. Count UP 5 from the key of "**a**" to find the next key on the Circle of Fifths. The 5th note (Dominant) of "**a**" minor becomes the 1st note (Tonic) of **e** minor.

♫ **Note:** Use the keyboard to identify the minor Pentascale pattern of: whole tone, semitone, whole tone, whole tone. The semitone is ALWAYS between degrees $\hat{2}$ and $\hat{3}$.

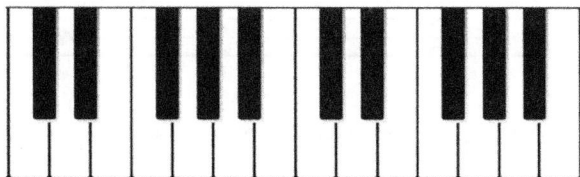

1. a) Write each minor Pentascale on the Treble Clef below. Use accidentals (sharps) when necessary. Use whole notes.
   b) Write the name of the TONIC note of each minor Pentascale DIRECTLY on the keyboard of the Circle of Fifths. Use a lower case letter.

Key of a minor (Dominant of a minor becomes Tonic of e minor)

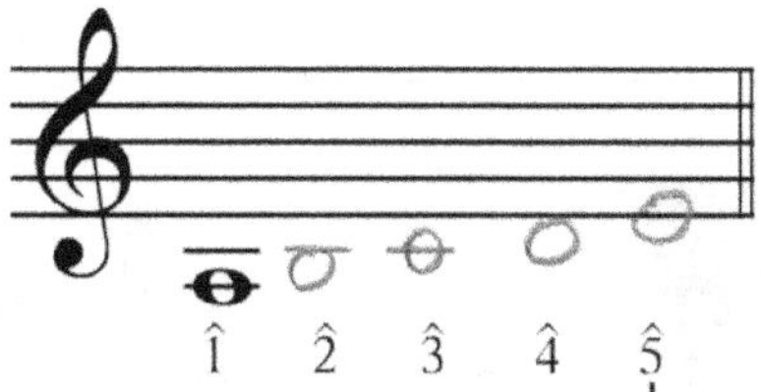

Key of e minor (Dominant of e minor becomes Tonic of b minor)

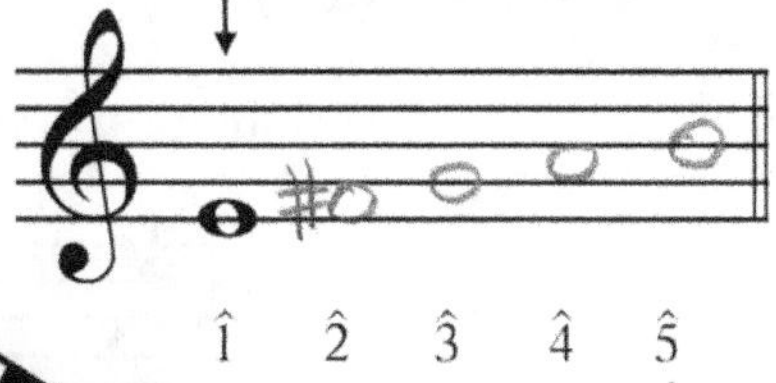

Key of b minor

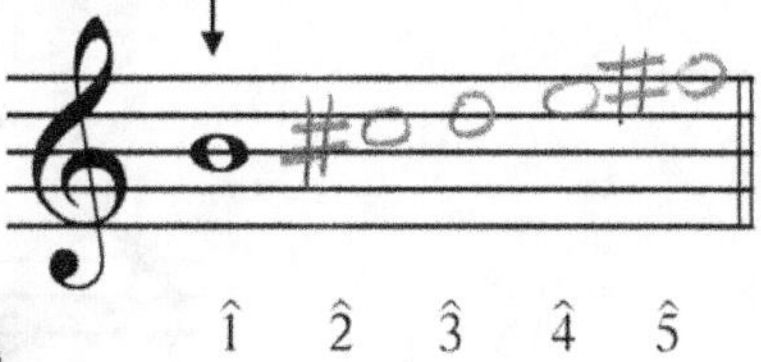

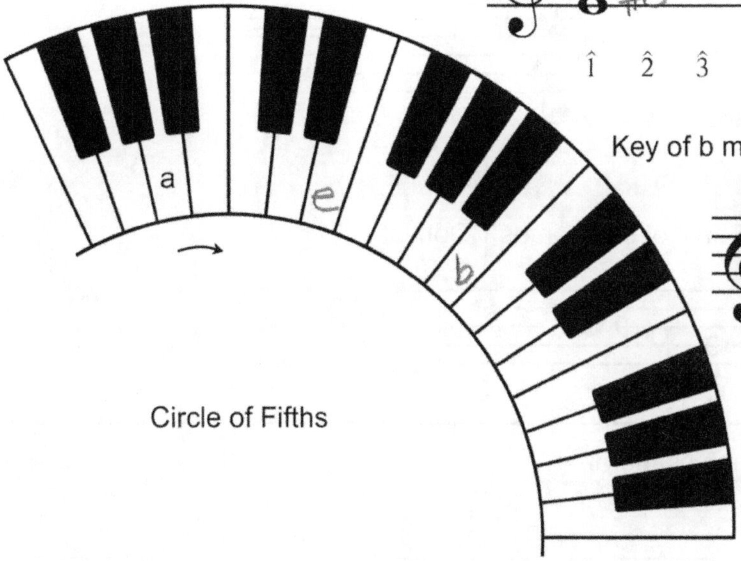

Circle of Fifths

MINOR PENTASCALES with FLATS

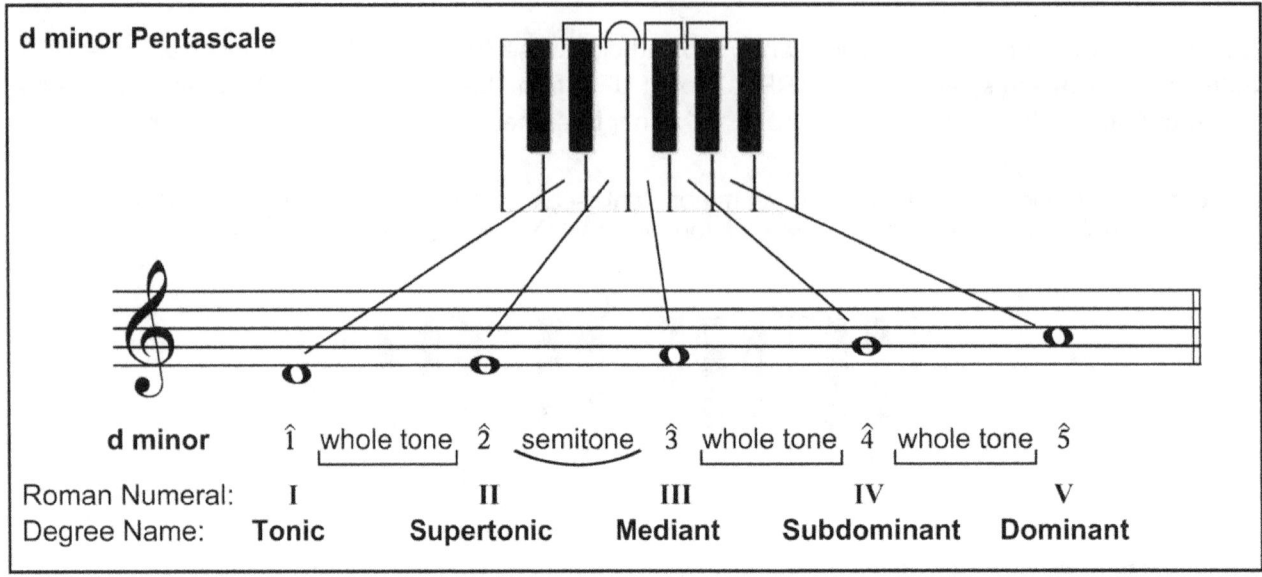

When moving **COUNTERCLOCKWISE** (to the left) around the **Circle of Fifths**, begin with a. Count DOWN 5 from A: **A G F E D**. D is the next key on the Circle of Fifths. (A is the Dominant of d minor.)

To find the next key on the Circle of Fifths, count DOWN 5 from D: **D C B♭ A G**. G is the next key on the Circle of Fifths. (D is the Dominant of g minor.)

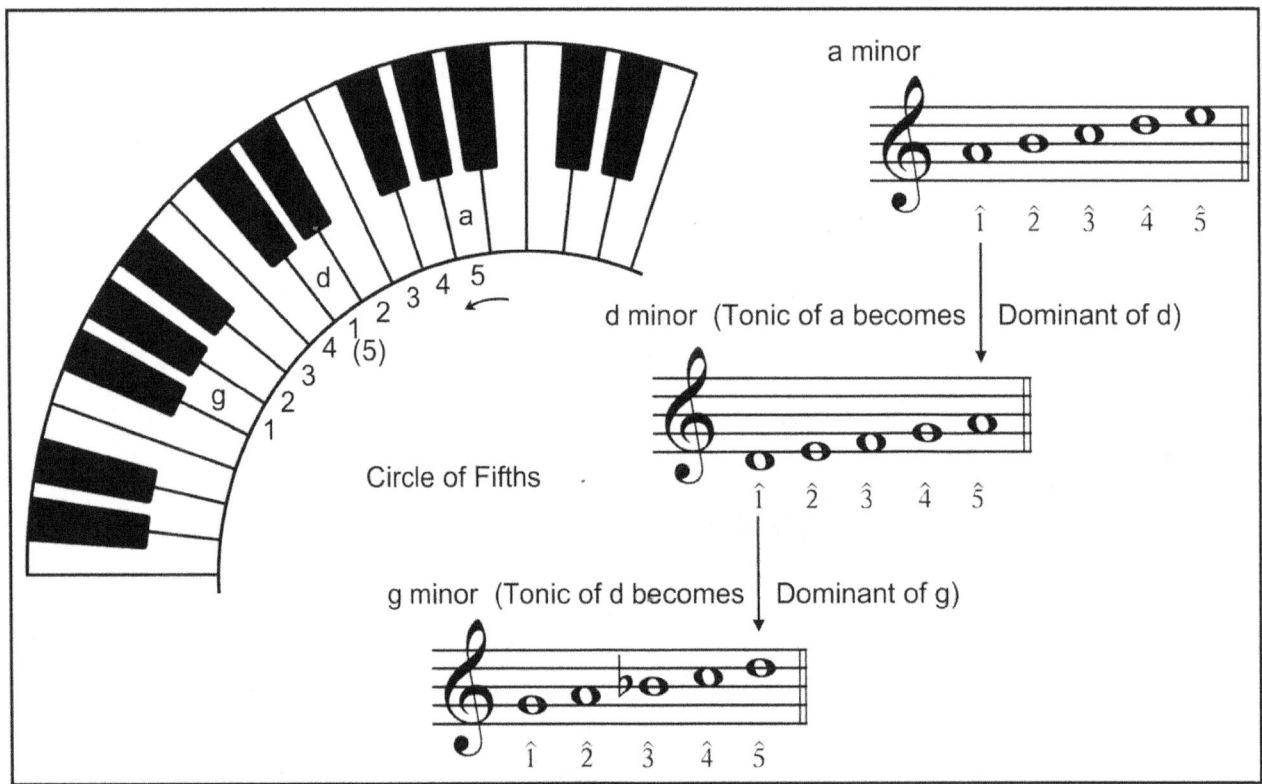

1. Write the Degree Name for each Roman Numeral.

Tonic	Supertonic	Mediant	Subdominant	Dominant
I	II	III	IV	V

MINOR KEYS WRITTEN INSIDE the CIRCLE of FIFTHS with FLATS

Beginning with the key of "**a**" minor, when moving counterclockwise (to the LEFT) around the Circle of Fifths, the **minor keys** will have **FLATS**. Count DOWN 5 from the key of "a" to find the next key on the Circle of Fifths. The 1st note (Tonic) of "a" minor becomes the 5th note (Dominant) of d minor.

♫ **Note:** Use the keyboard to identify the minor Pentascale pattern of: whole tone, semitone, whole tone, whole tone. The semitone is ALWAYS between degrees $\hat{2}$ and $\hat{3}$.

1. a) Write each minor Pentascale on the Treble Staff below. Use accidentals (flats) when necessary. Use whole notes.
   b) Write the name of the Tonic note of each minor Pentascale directly on the keyboard of the Circle of Fifths. Use a lower case letter.

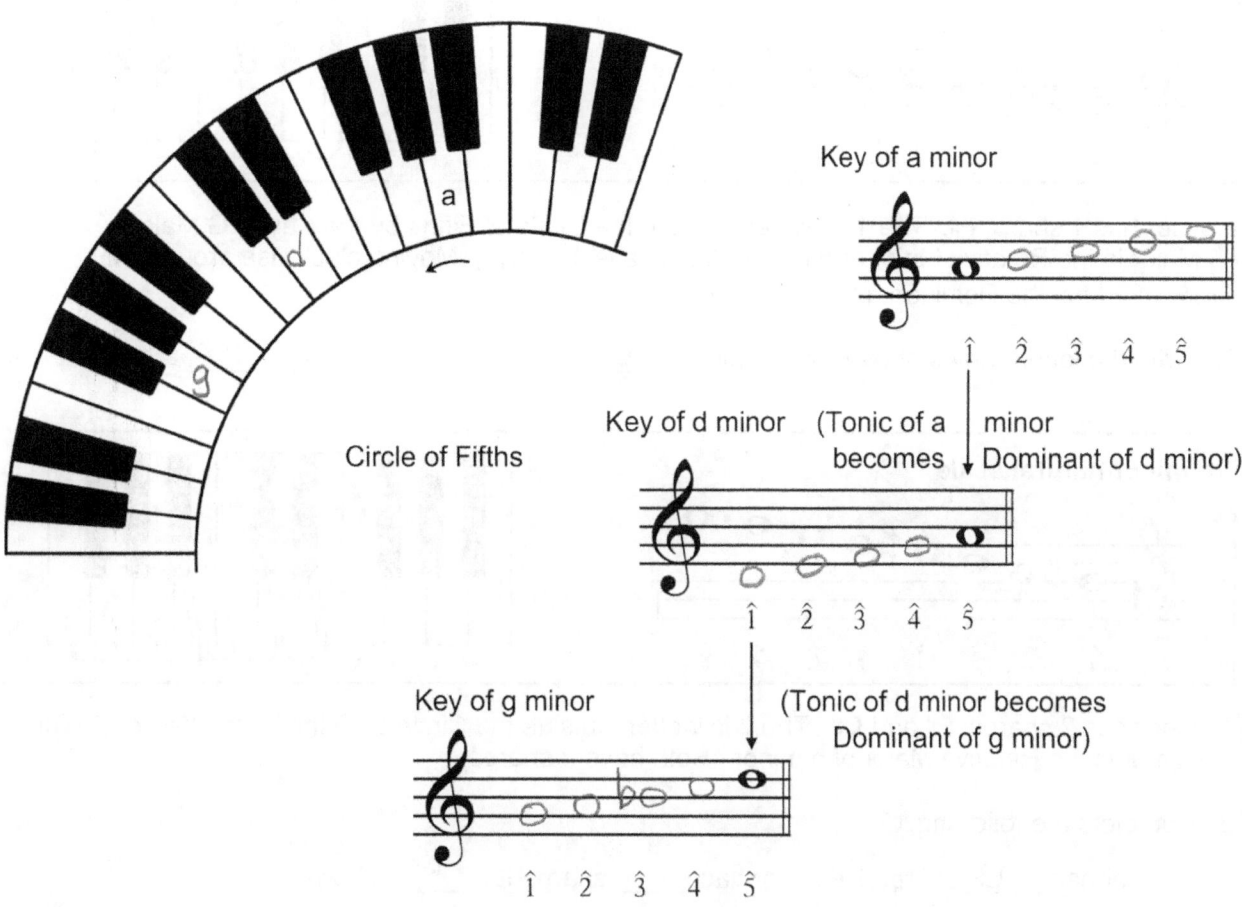

69

NATURAL MINOR SCALES with SHARPS

A **natural minor** scale is a series of 8 notes in a specific pattern:
$\hat{1}$ whole tone $\hat{2}$ semitone $\hat{3}$ whole tone $\hat{4}$ whole tone $\hat{5}$ semitone $\hat{6}$ whole tone $\hat{7}$ whole tone $\hat{8}$ ($\hat{1}$).

The semitones are between degrees $\hat{2}$ and $\hat{3}$, and between degrees $\hat{5}$ and $\hat{6}$ of the natural minor scale. Semitones are indicated by a semitone slur.

♪ **Note:** This pattern will create a NATURAL MINOR SCALE beginning on any note.

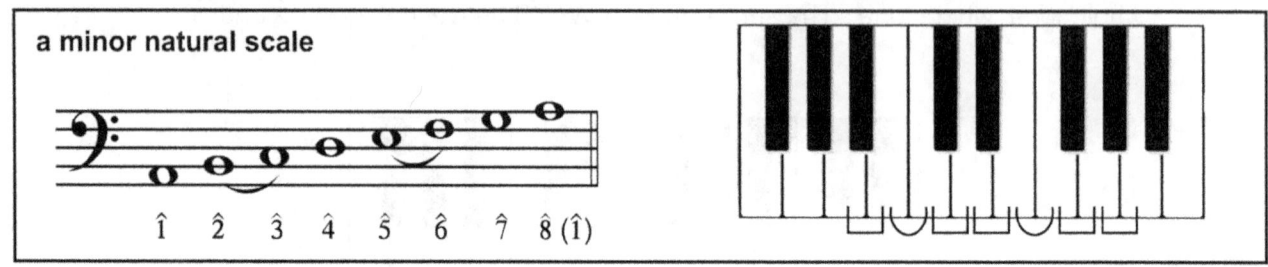

"**a**" minor has **0** (zero) sharps or flats. The **0** is written outside the Circle of Fifths by the Key of C Major. (C Major is the Relative Major of a minor. Both have 0 sharps.) Moving clockwise around the Circle of Fifths, the Dominant of "**a**" minor is E.

1. Write the letter names above the numbers: _A_ _B_ _C_ _D_ _E_
                                                                                            $\hat{1}$ $\hat{2}$ $\hat{3}$ $\hat{4}$ $\hat{5}$

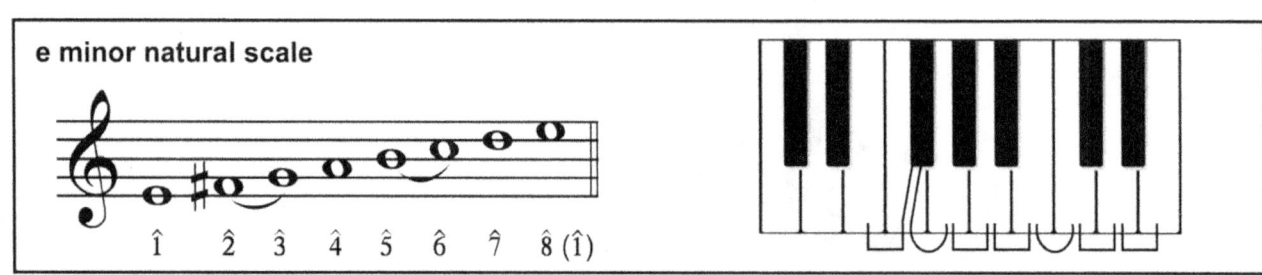

e minor has 1 sharp, **F♯**. The **1** is written outside the Circle of Fifths by the Key of G Major. (G Major is the Relative Major of e minor. Both have 1 sharp.) Moving clockwise around the Circle of Fifths, the Dominant of e minor is B.

2. Write the letter names above the numbers: _E_ _F♯_ _G_ _A_ _B_
                                                                                            $\hat{1}$ $\hat{2}$ $\hat{3}$ $\hat{4}$ $\hat{5}$

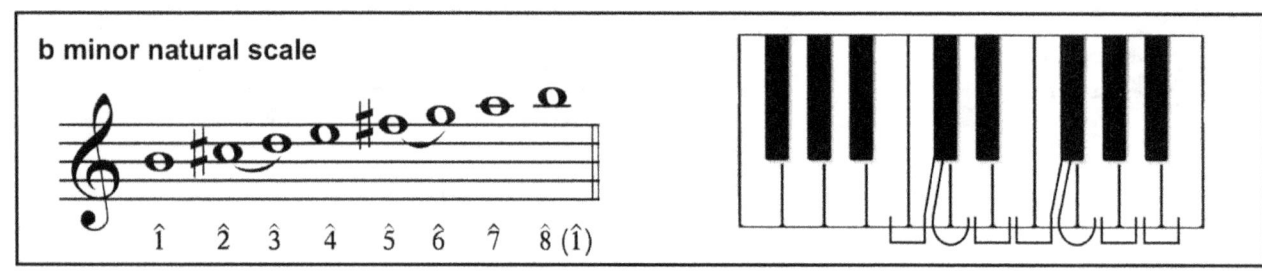

b minor has 2 sharps, **F♯** and **C♯**. The **2** is written outside the Circle of Fifths by the Key of D Major. (D Major is the Relative Major of b minor. Both have 2 sharps).

3. Complete the following.

   a minor has __0__ sharps. e minor has __1__ sharp. It is __F__ sharp.
   b minor has __2__ sharps. They are __F__ sharp and __C__ sharp.

CIRCLE of FIFTHS - MINOR SCALES with SHARPS

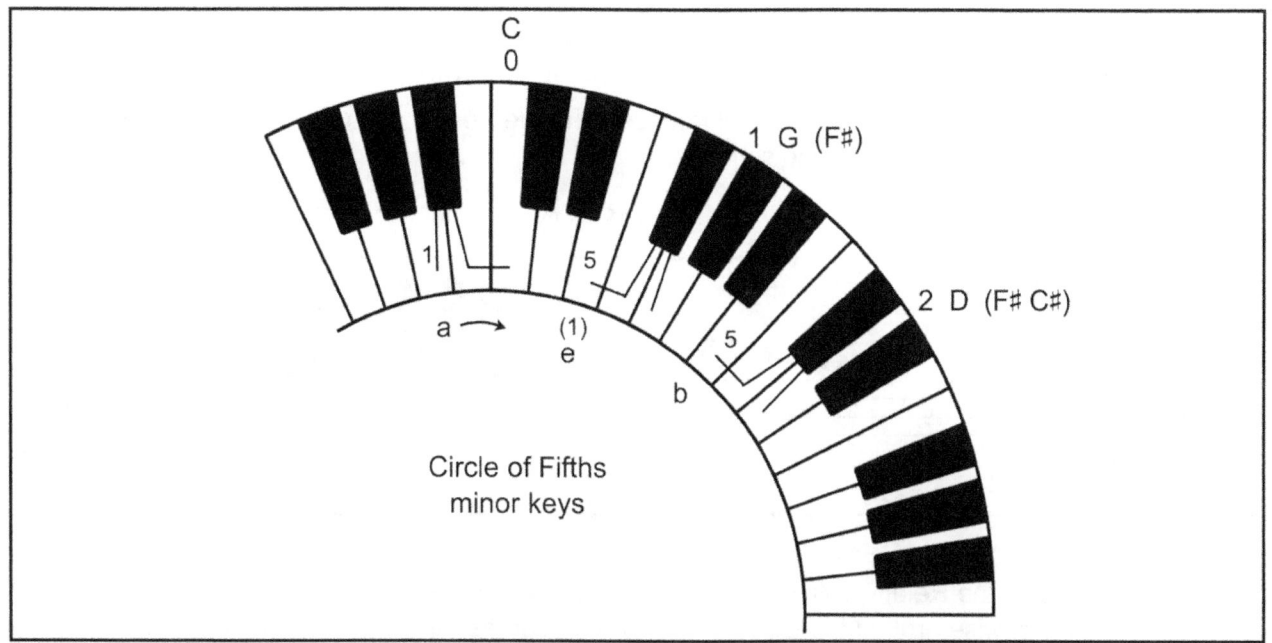

A natural minor scale can be written **WITH** or **WITHOUT** a center bar line.

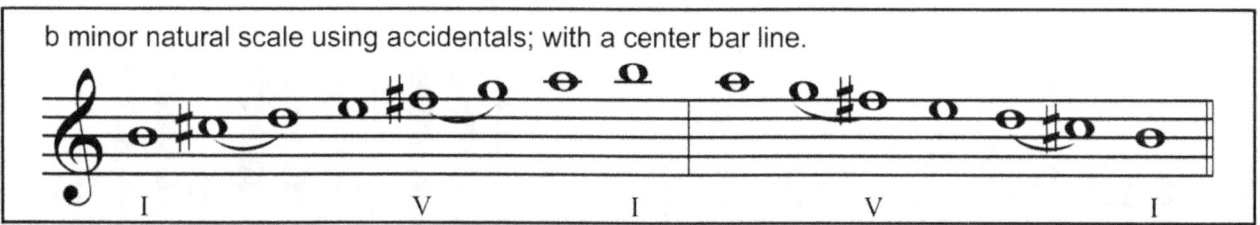

b minor natural scale using accidentals; with a center bar line.

I   V   I   V   I

♪ **Note:** Always write scales in the **SAME WAY**, either **WITH** or **WITHOUT** a center bar line.

1. a) Write the following scales, ascending and descending, in the given clef. Use whole notes. Use accidentals (sharps) when necessary.
   b) Label the Tonic (I) and Dominant (V) notes.

a) a minor natural scale

b) e minor natural scale

c) b minor natural scale

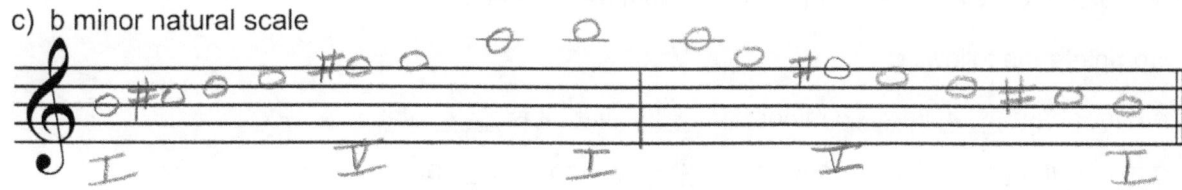

71

NATURAL MINOR SCALES with FLATS

A **natural minor scale** is a series of 8 notes in a specific pattern:
$\hat{1}$ whole tone $\hat{2}$ semitone $\hat{3}$ whole tone $\hat{4}$ whole tone $\hat{5}$ semitone $\hat{6}$ whole tone $\hat{7}$ whole tone $\hat{8}$ ($\hat{1}$).

The semitones are between degrees $\hat{2}$ and $\hat{3}$, and between degrees $\hat{5}$ and $\hat{6}$ of the natural minor scale. Semitones are indicated by a semitone slur.

♪ **Note:** This pattern will create a NATURAL MINOR SCALE beginning on any note.

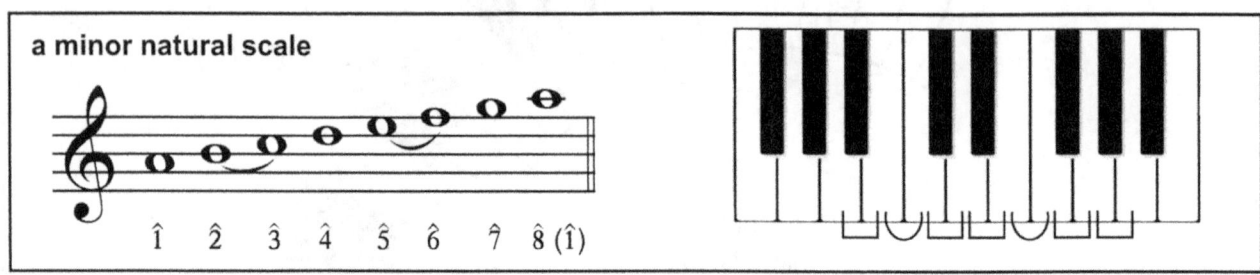

"a" minor has **0** (zero) sharps or flats. The **0** is written outside the Circle of Fifths by the Key of C Major. (C Major is the Relative Major of a minor. Both have 0 sharps.)
Moving counterclockwise around the Circle of Fifths, A becomes the Dominant of d minor.

1. Write the letter names above the numbers: __D__ __E__ __F__ __G__ __A__
                                                                                 $\hat{1}$ $\hat{2}$ $\hat{3}$ $\hat{4}$ $\hat{5}$

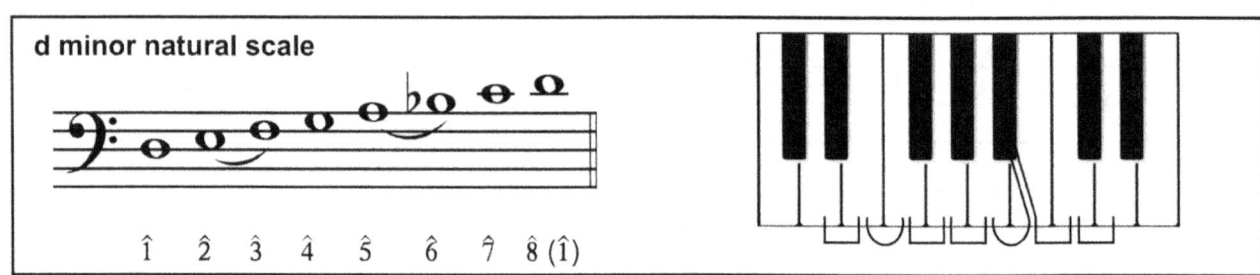

d minor has 1 flat, **B♭**. The **1** is written outside the Circle of Fifths by the Key of F Major.
(F Major is the Relative Major of d minor. Both have 1 flat.)
Moving counterclockwise around the Circle of Fifths, D becomes the Dominant of g minor.

2. Write the letter names above the numbers: __G__ __A__ __B♭__ __C__ __D__
                                                                                 $\hat{1}$ $\hat{2}$ $\hat{3}$ $\hat{4}$ $\hat{5}$

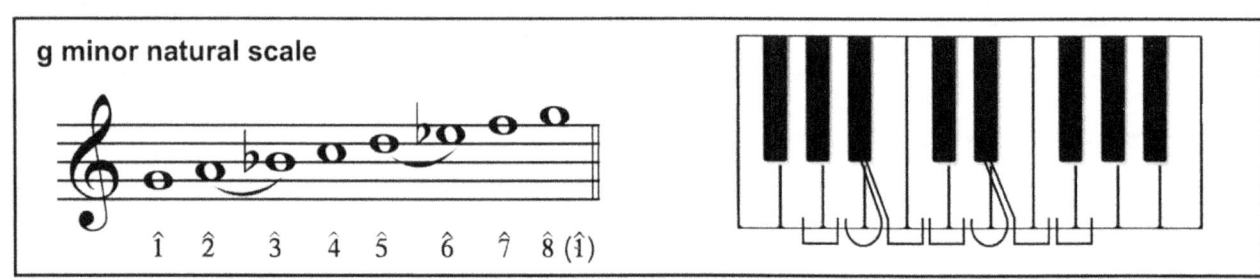

g minor has 2 flats, **B♭** and **E♭**. The **2** is written outside the Circle of Fifths by the Key of B♭ Major. (B♭ Major is the Relative Major of g minor. Both have 2 flats.)

3. Complete the following.

   a minor has __0__ flats. d minor has __1__ flat. It is __B__ flat.
   g minor has __2__ flats. They are __B__ flat and __E__ flat.

CIRCLE of FIFTHS - MINOR KEYS with FLATS

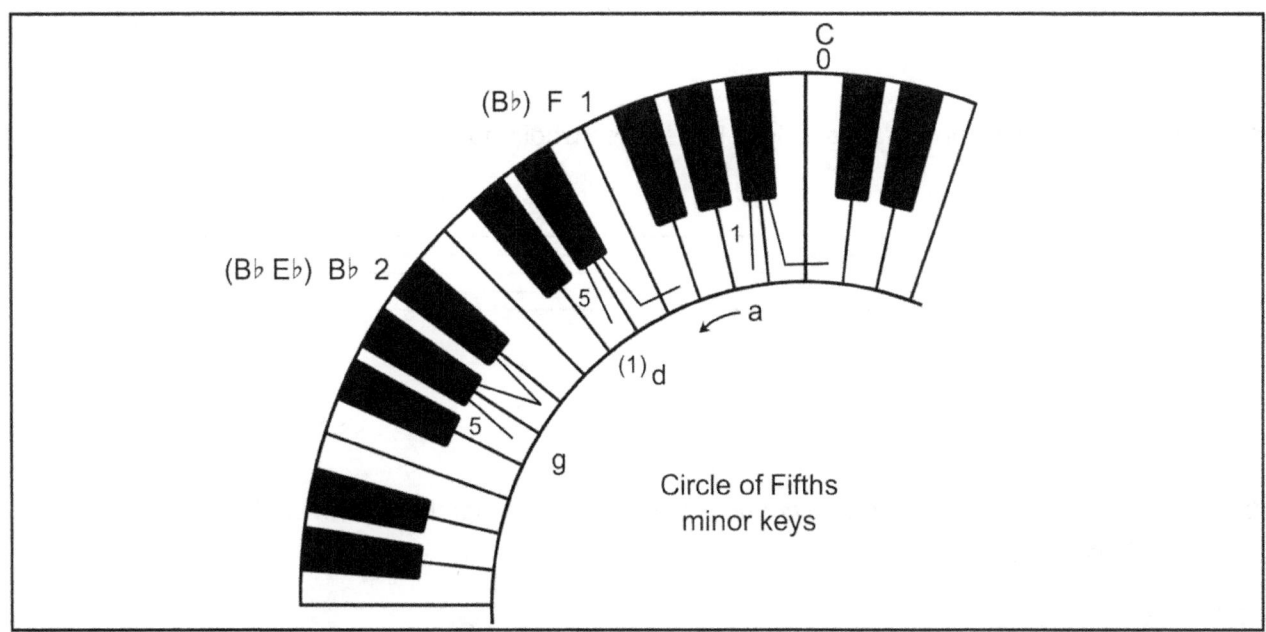

When writing a scale using accidentals **WITH** a center bar line, the accidentals must be repeated in the descending scale. When writing a scale using accidentals **WITHOUT** a center bar line, accidentals are **ONLY** written in the ascending scale.

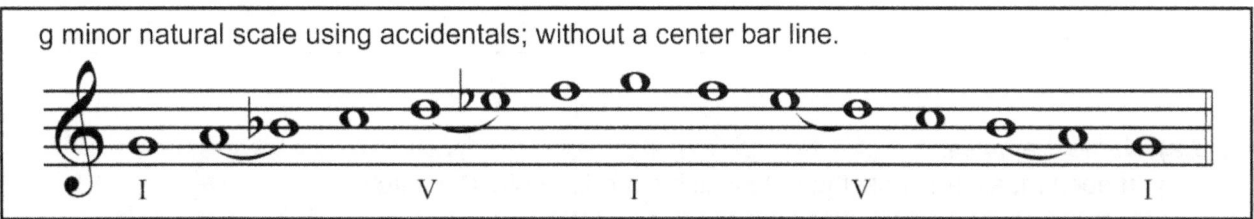

g minor natural scale using accidentals; without a center bar line.

1. a) Write the following scales, ascending and descending, in the given clef. Use whole notes. Use accidentals (flats) when necessary.
   b) Label the Tonic (I) and Dominant (V) notes.

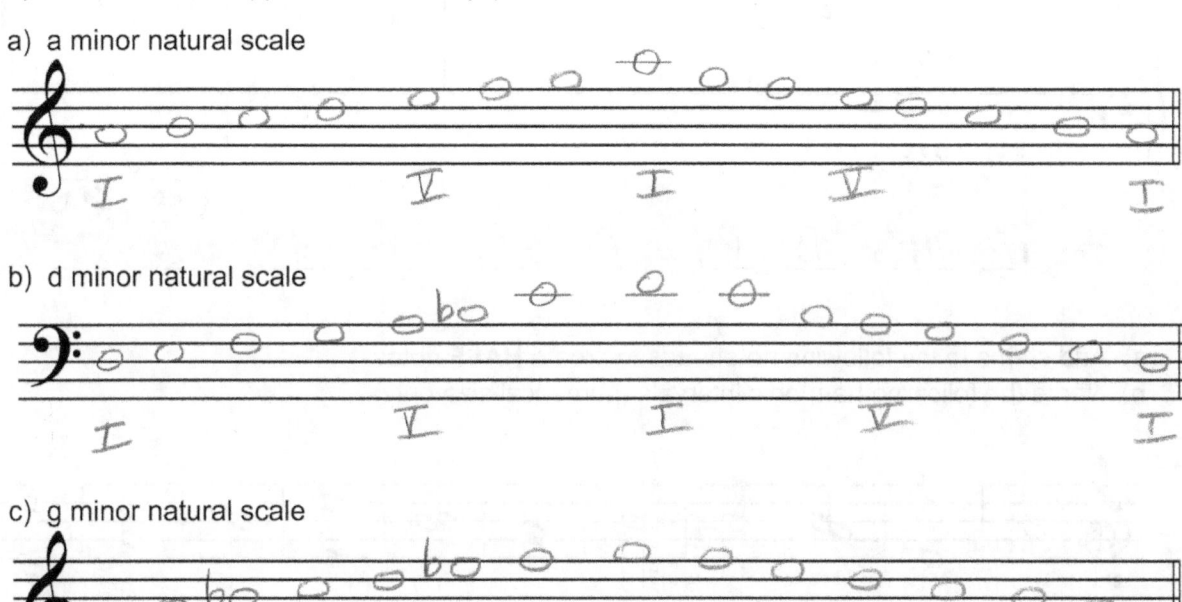

73

Lesson 6 — Review Test

Total Score: ____ / 100

1. Write the following notes. Use **ledger lines**. Use whole notes.

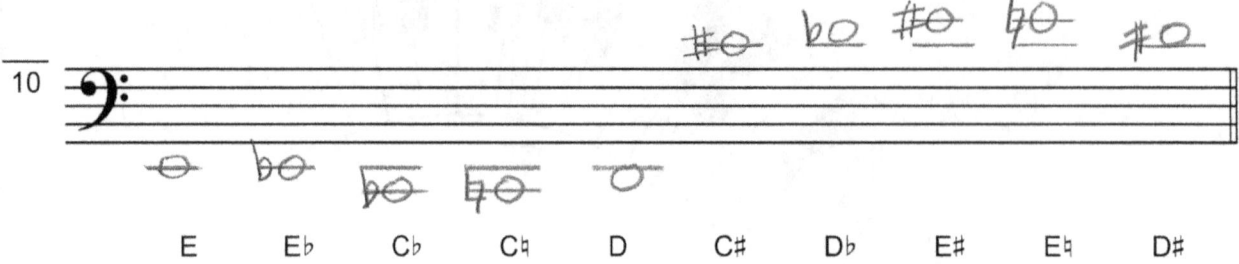

E   Eb   Cb   C♮   D   C#   Db   E#   E♮   D#

2. a) Add **STEMS** and a **BEAM** to create a pair of beamed eighth notes in each measure.
   b) Name the notes.

G A   E F   C D   G A   A F   E B

3. a) Name the notes.
   b) In each measure, circle the note which sounds **LOWER** in pitch.

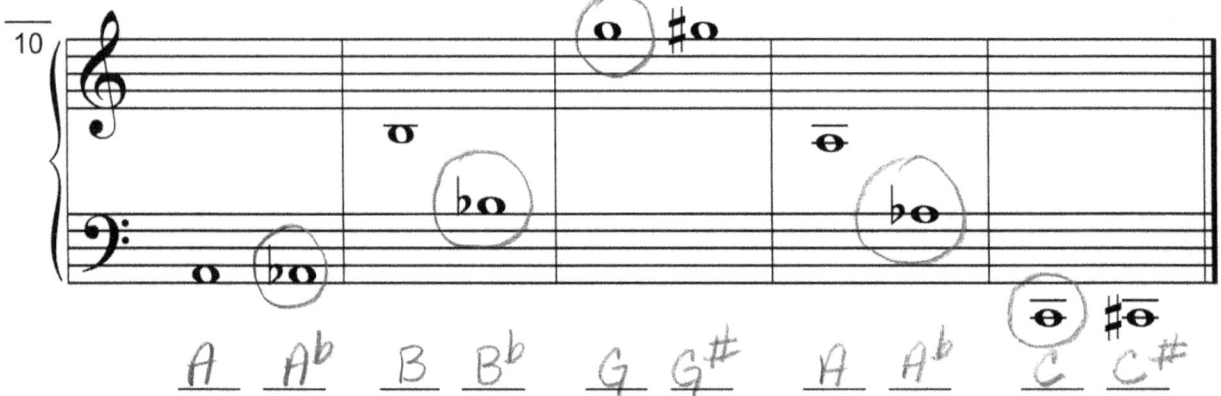

A Ab   B Bb   G G#   A Ab   C C#

4. a) Add stems to the following noteheads to create **HALF** notes.
   b) Name the following harmonic intervals (numerical size only).

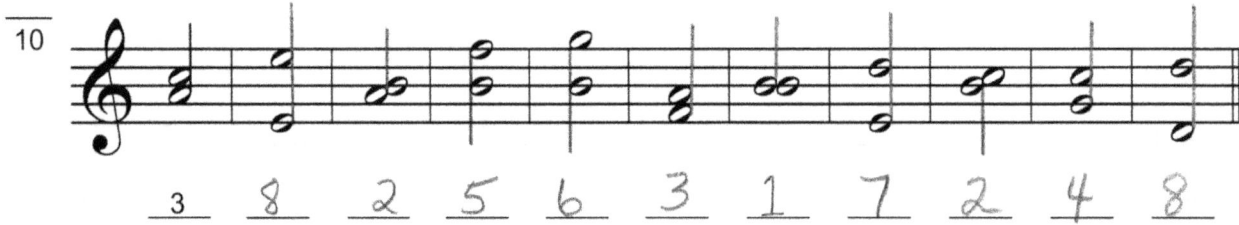

3   8   2   5   6   3   1   7   2   4   8

5. a) **SCOOP** each Basic Beat in each measure.
    b) Write the **PULSE** below each Basic Beat.
    c) Add **RESTS** below each bracket to complete each measure.
    d) Cross off the Basic Beat as each beat is completed.

___
10

6. a) Write the following harmonic intervals above each of the given notes. Use whole notes.
    b) Name the notes. Write the name of the LOWER note first, then the HIGHER note.

___
10

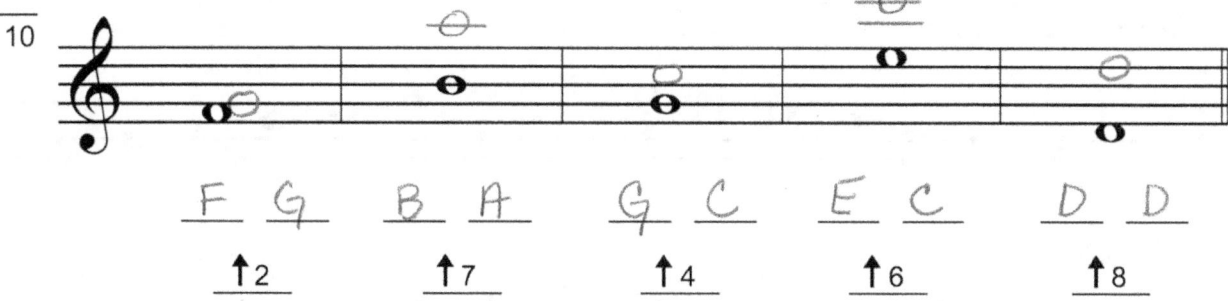

7. a) Name the notes.
    b) Name the melodic interval between the notes. Use an up or a down arrow to indicate direction.

___
10

75

8. a) Complete the Circle of Fifths by adding the Major keys on the outside of the circle and the minor keys on the inside of the circle.

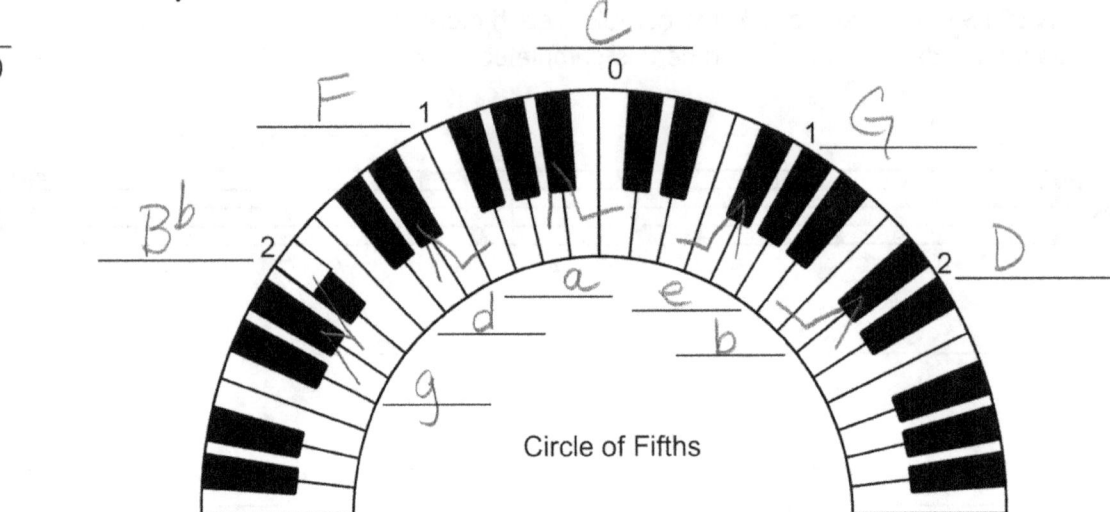

Circle of Fifths

b) Draw the correct clef (Treble Clef or Bass Clef) at the beginning of each staff to form the following scales. Add any necessary accidentals. Observe the center bar line.

C Major scale

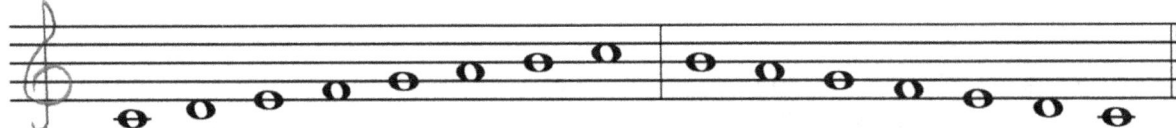

a minor natural scale

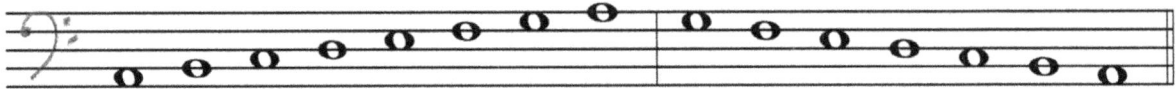

G Major scale

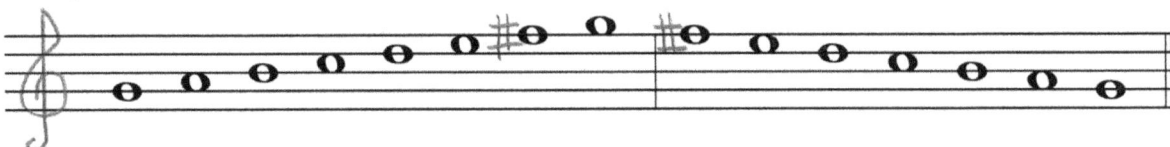

b minor natural scale

F Major scale

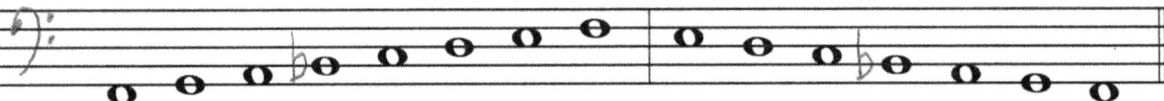

9. Copy the music below in the Bass Staff. (Copy the bar lines first.) Correct any stem direction as necessary.

10. a) Write **TWO TIED notes** which equal the value of the given note. Write the total number of beats given to the tied notes.

𝅗𝅥. = 𝅗𝅥 ⌣ 𝅘𝅥 = __3__ beats

𝅗𝅥 = 𝅘𝅥 ⌣ 𝅘𝅥 = __2__ beats

𝅝 = 𝅗𝅥 ⌣ 𝅗𝅥 = __4__ beats

𝅘𝅥. = 𝅘𝅥 ⌣ 𝅘𝅥𝅮 = __1½__ beats

𝅘𝅥 = 𝅘𝅥𝅮 ⌣ 𝅘𝅥𝅮 = __1__ beat

𝅗𝅥. = 𝅗𝅥 ⌣ 𝅘𝅥 = __3__ beats

b) Write the **MUSICAL SIGN** for each of the following dynamic terms.

piano   _p_

mezzo forte   _mf_

crescendo   <

diminuendo   >

forte   _f_

77

Lesson 7 — Key Signatures

A **KEY SIGNATURE** is a group of sharps or flats that indicates the key.

A **KEY SIGNATURE** is written at the beginning of each staff, after the clef sign and before the Time Signature.

A **Key Signature** is used to simplify reading and writing music. Instead of using accidentals, the sharps or flats are placed in a **specific order** in the Key Signature. The sharps or flats in the Key Signature affect ALL the notes on the staff with the same letter name.

KEY SIGNATURES with SHARPS

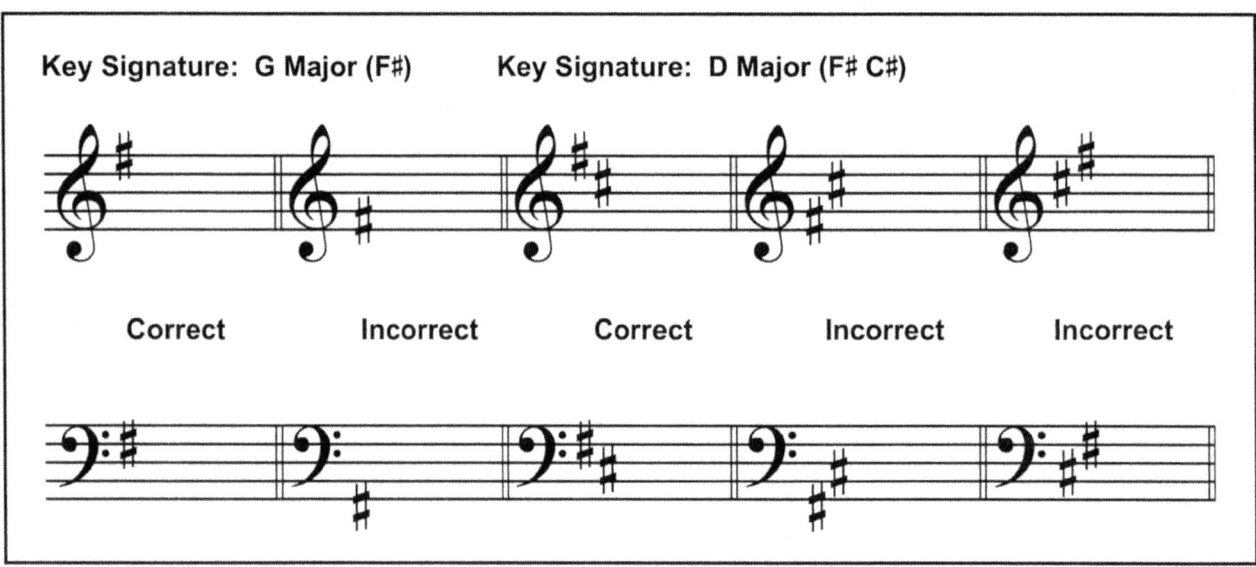

1. Following the examples below, copy the Clef and the Key Signature for G Major and D Major.

KEY SIGNATURES with FLATS

♪ **Note:** The clef sign and Key Signature are written at the beginning of each line of music.

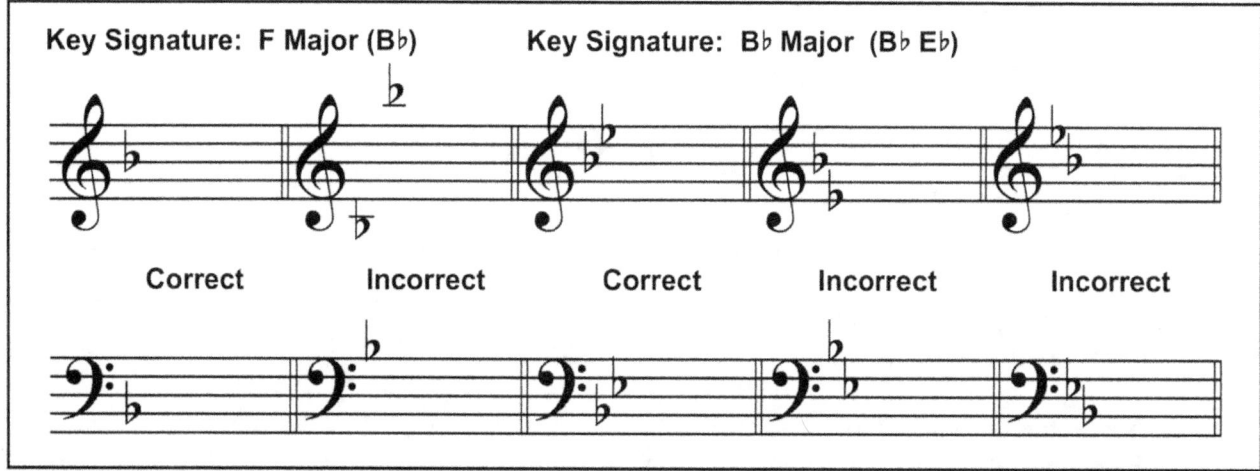

1. Following the examples below, copy the Clef and the Key Signature for F Major and B♭ Major.

♪ **Note:** The Key Signature affects **ALL** the notes on the staff with the same letter name.

2. Name the following notes. Observe the Key Signature.

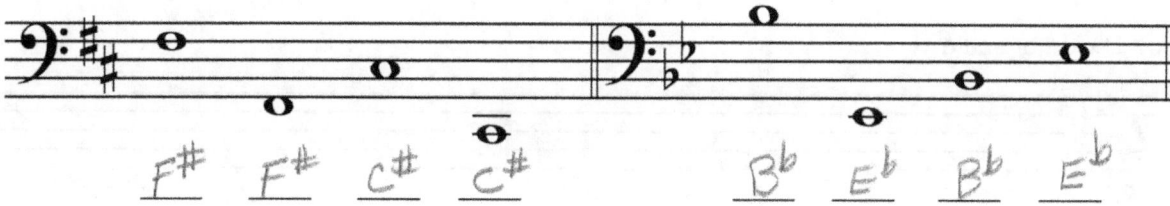

F# F# C# C#   B♭ E♭ B♭ E♭

MAJOR SCALES USING a KEY SIGNATURE

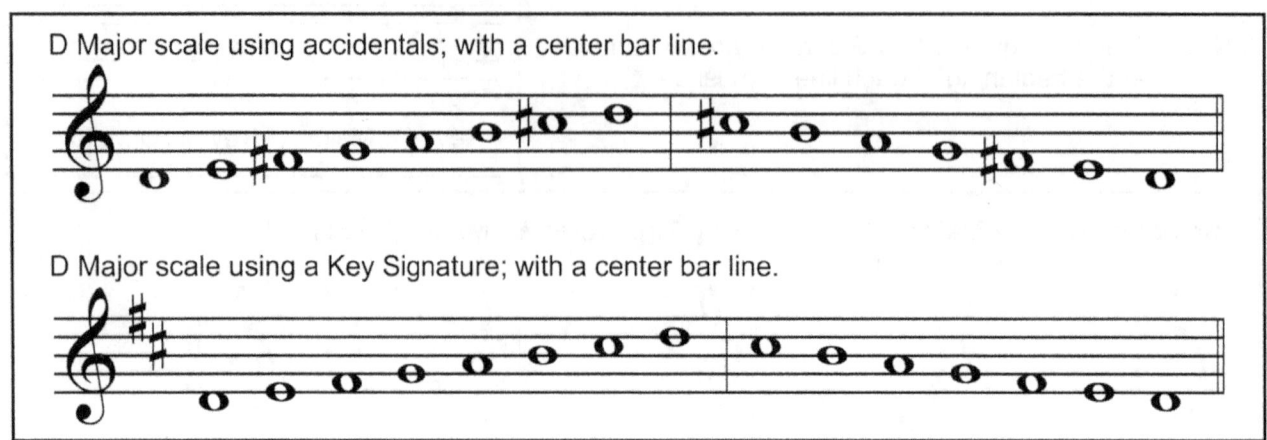

The Circle of Fifths identifies which sharps or flats are in each key.

The number on the outside of the Circle of Fifths indicates how many sharps or flats are in each key.

♪ **Note:** Always write the Key Signature in the correct order on the staff.

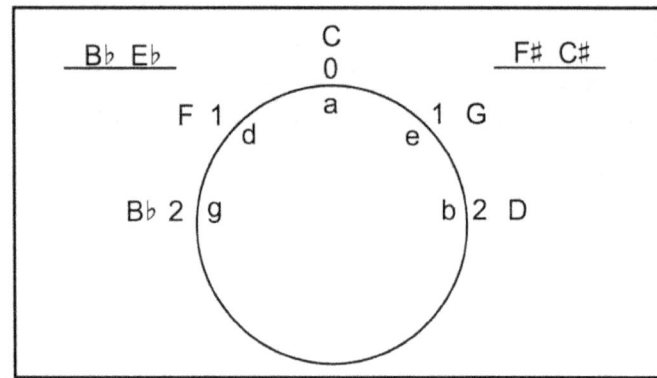

1. Write the following scales, ascending and descending, using a Key Signature. Use whole notes.

   a) G Major scale

   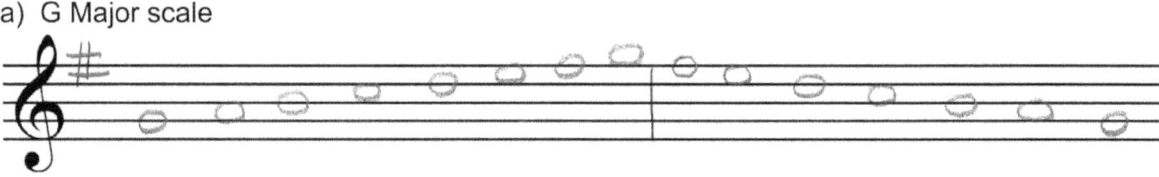

   b) C Major scale

   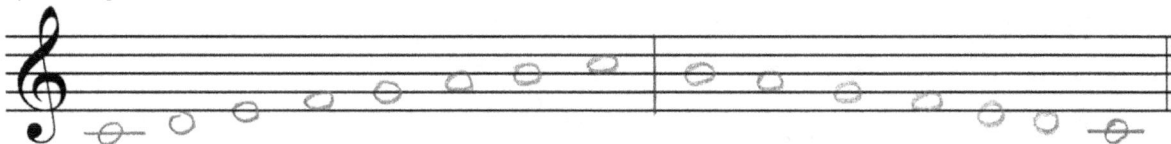

   c) F Major scale

   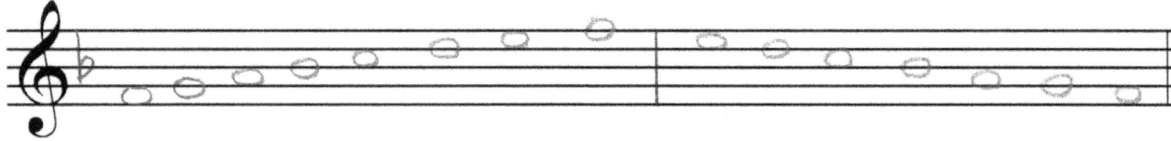

   d) B♭ Major scale

   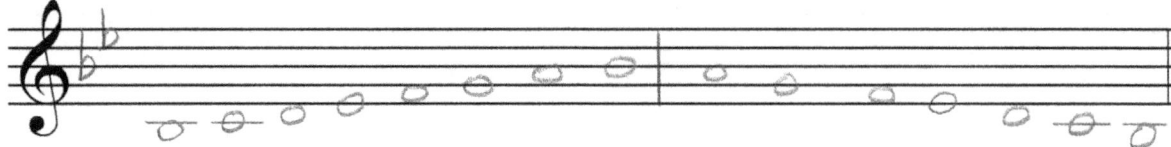

MINOR SCALES USING a KEY SIGNATURE

g minor natural scale using accidentals; without a center bar line.

g minor natural scale using a Key Signature; without a center bar line.

The Circle of Fifths identifies which sharps or flats are in each key.

Major keys and their relative minor keys share the SAME Key Signature.

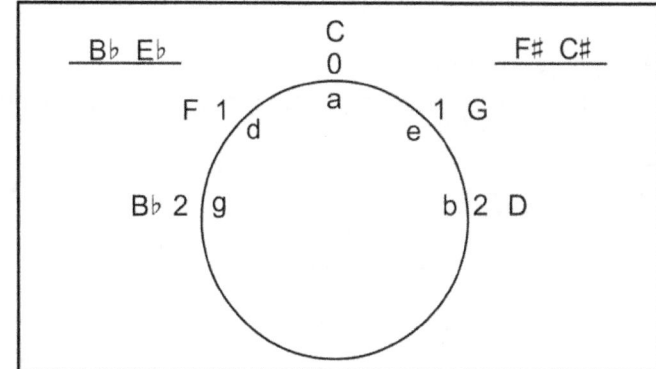

♫ **Note:** Always write the Key Signature in the correct order on the staff.

1. Write the following scales, ascending and descending, using a Key Signature. Use whole notes.

   a) e minor natural scale

   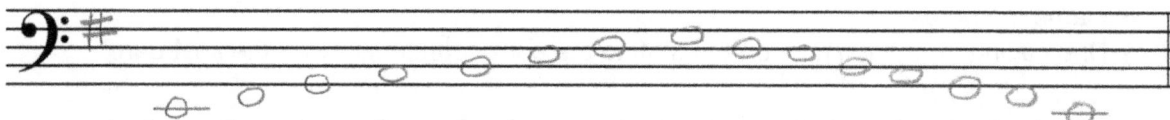

   b) b minor natural scale

   c) d minor natural scale

   d) a minor natural scale

   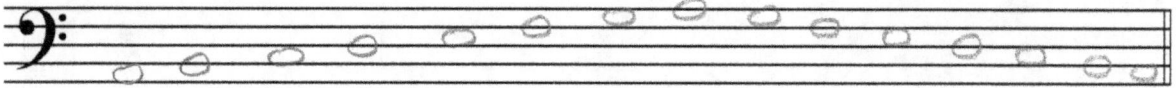

Lesson 7 — Review Test

Total Score: ___ / 100

1. Name the notes. Observe the Key Signature.

F# C# A C# B F# B D C# F#

2. a) Name the notes.
   b) In each measure, circle the note which sounds **HIGHER** in pitch.

A Ab F F# Bb B♮ E♮ Eb C C#

3. a) Add a Treble Clef, Bass Clef and Brace to create the Grand Staff.
   b) Name the notes.
   c) Draw a line from each note on the staff to the corresponding key on the keyboard.

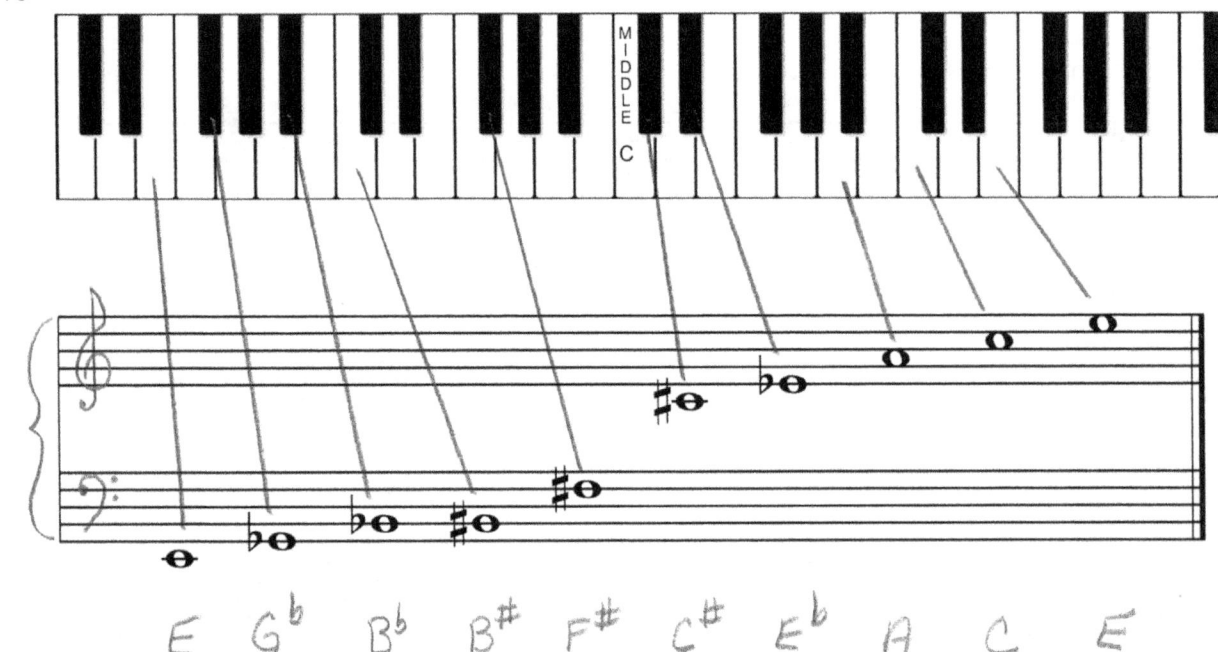

E Gb Bb B# F# C# Eb A C E

4. Identify the distance between the notes in each measure as **WT** (whole tone or whole step) or as **ST** (semitone or half step).

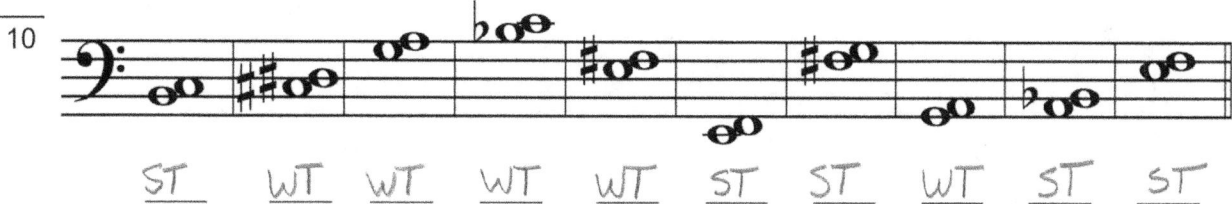

5. a) Write one rest equal in value to the note in each measure.

b) Write the number of beats that the note(s) or rest in each measure receives in $\frac{4}{4}$ time.

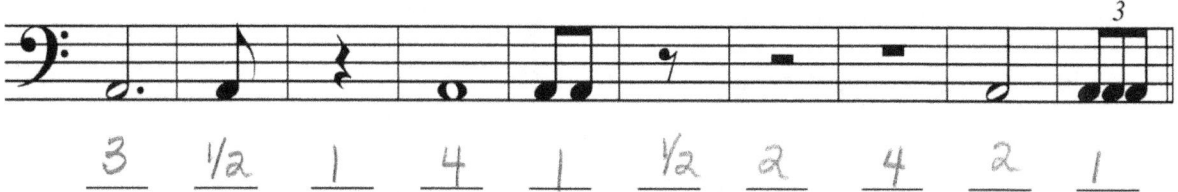

6. a) Name the notes.
   b) Name the melodic interval between the notes in each measure. Use an up or a down arrow to indicate direction.

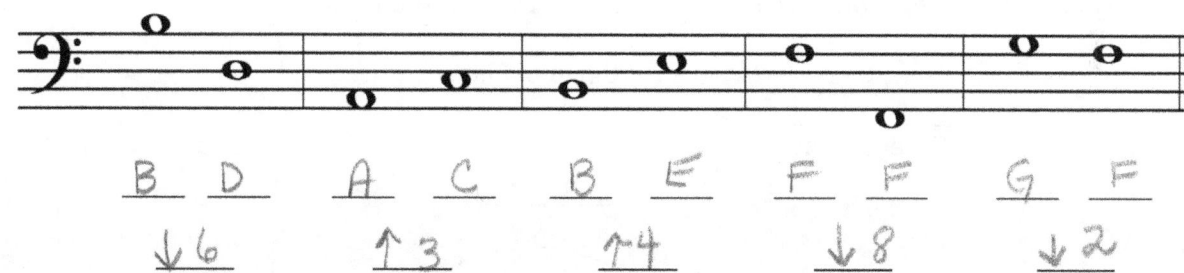

7. Write the following **KEY SIGNATURES** in the Treble Staff.

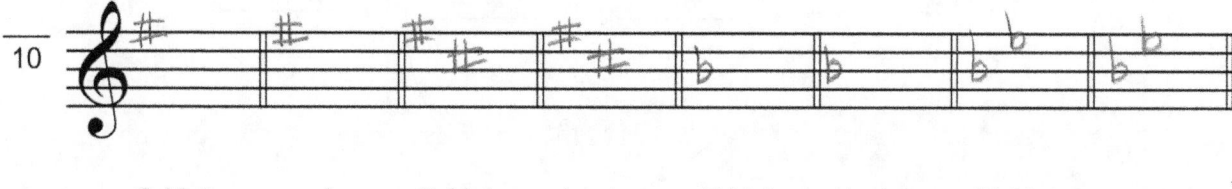

G Major   e minor   D Major   b minor   F Major   d minor   B♭ Major   g minor

8. Analyze the following piece of music by answering the questions below.

a) Add the correct Time Signature directly on the music.
b) Name the key of this piece. __D Major__
c) Locate and circle a whole tone in this piece. Label it as WT.
d) Locate and circle a semitone in this piece. Label it as ST.
e) Name the highest note in this piece. __D__
f) Name the lowest note in this piece. __D__
g) How many measures are in this piece? __4__
h) Explain the dynamic marking in this piece. __gradually louder (cresc.)__
i) Identify the marking at the letter **A** as Tie or Slur. __tie__
j) Identify the marking at the letter **B** as Tie or Slur. __slur__

9. Complete the Circle of Fifths by adding the order of flats on the top left and the order of sharps on the top right. Write the Major keys on the outside of the circle. Use UPPER case letters. Write the minor keys on the inside of the circle. Use lower case letters.

Circle of Fifths

__Bb__ __Eb__
(Order of Flats)

__F#__ __C#__
(Order of Sharps)

C — 0
a
F — 1 — d — e — 1 — G
Bb — 2 — g — b — 2 — D

10. a) Write the following scales, ascending and descending, using a Key Signature. Use whole notes.
  b) Circle 3 **TONIC** notes in each scale. Label them "**I**".

a) F Major scale

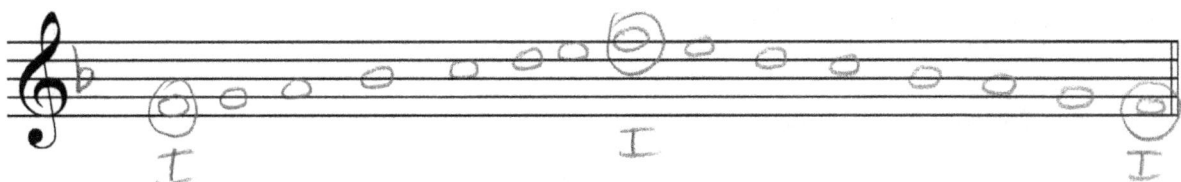

b) d minor natural scale

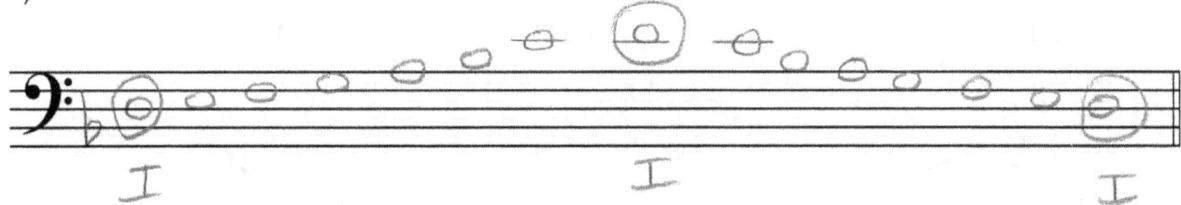

c) C Major scale

d) a minor natural scale

e) G Major scale

Lesson 8 Key Signatures on the Grand Staff

The **KEY SIGNATURE** on the Grand Staff is written in the Treble Staff and in the Bass Staff directly after the clef sign. The Time Signature is written AFTER the Key Signature.

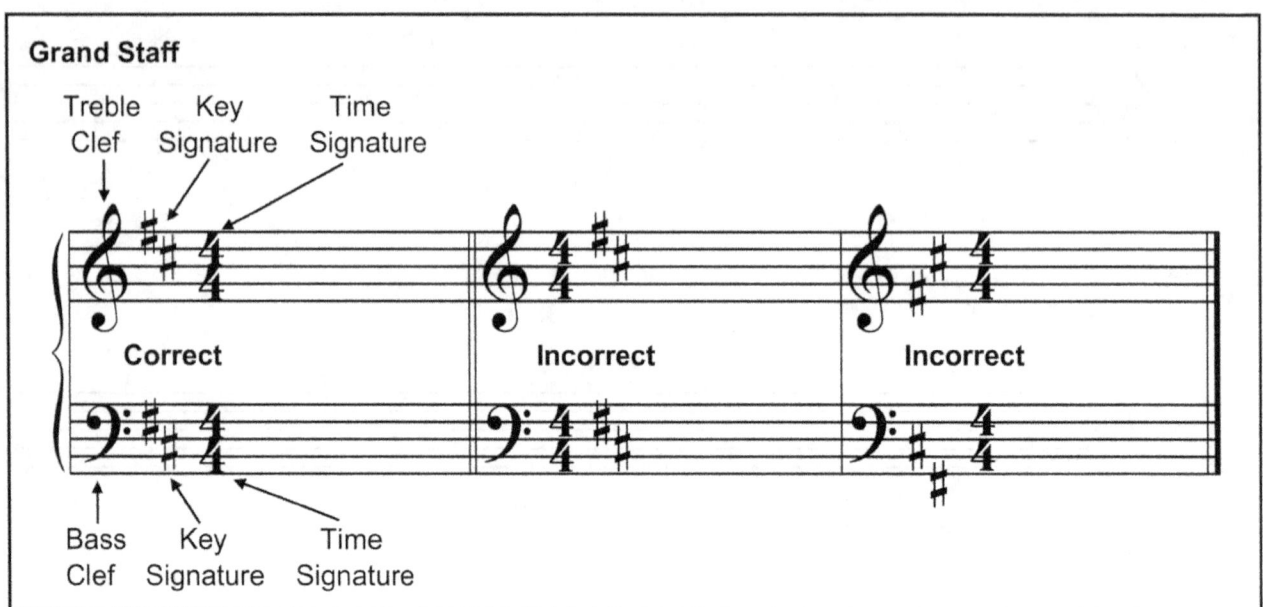

♪ **Note:** This is in alphabetical order: **C**lef, **K**ey and **T**ime.

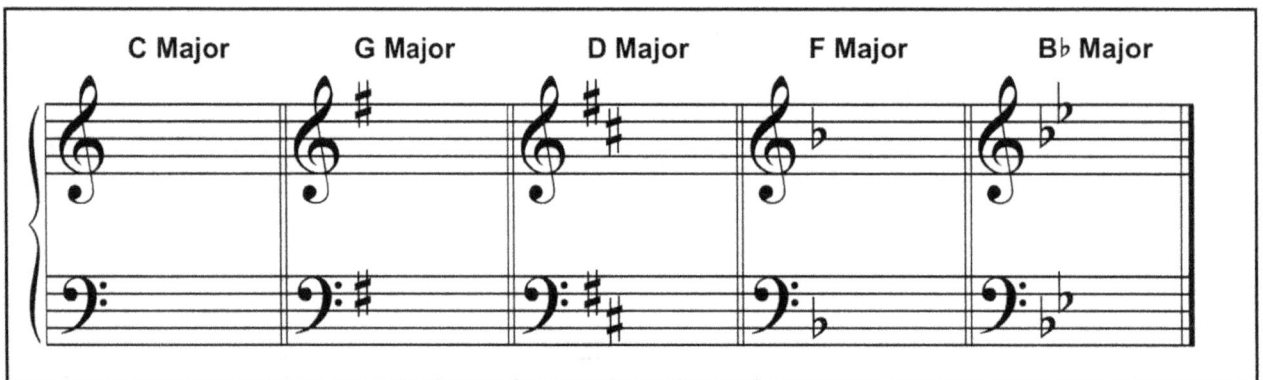

♪ **Note:** The Key of C Major has NO sharps or flats in the Key Signature.

1. Copy the above Key Signatures on the Grand Staff below.

MAJOR and MINOR KEY SIGNATURES

Major keys and their **relative minor** keys share the **SAME** Key Signature.

For Major and minor keys, the sharps or flats in the Key Signature are written in the **SAME** order.

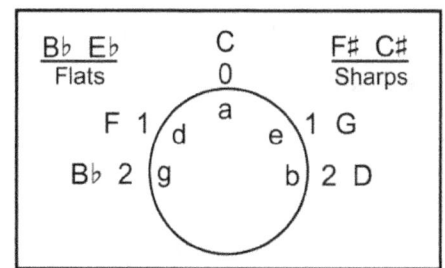

1. Write the Key Signatures for the following **MINOR** keys on the Grand Staff.

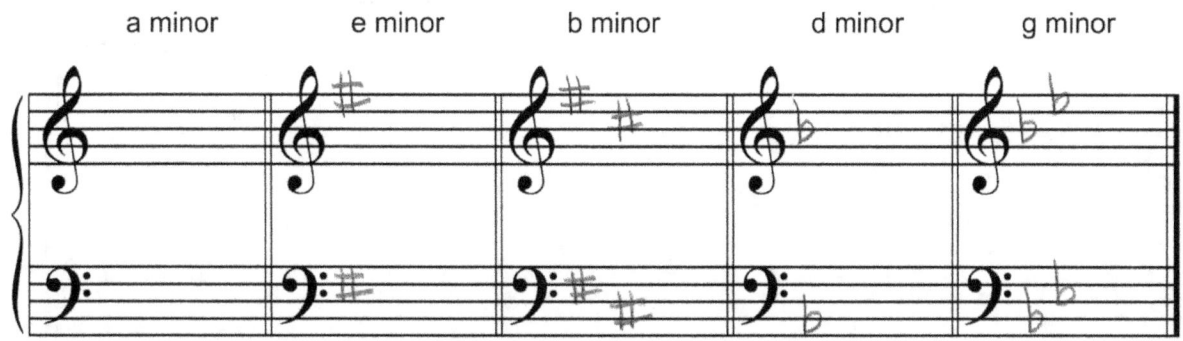

♪ **Note:** The Key Signature is written at the beginning of EVERY line of music.
The Time Signature is written only at the beginning of the first measure.
It is written AFTER the Key Signature in the Treble Staff and in the Bass Staff.

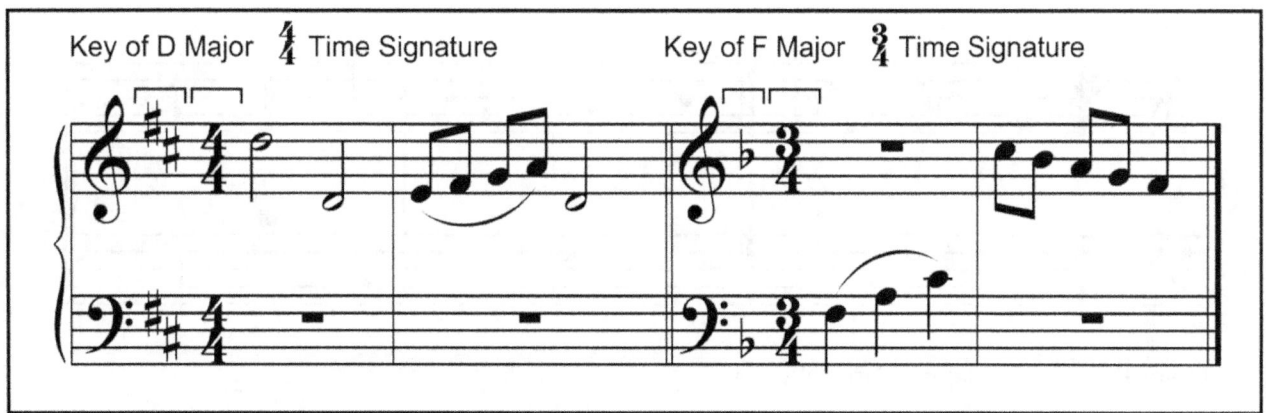

2. Write the Key Signature and Time Signature on the Grand Staff for each of the following melodies.

KEY SIGNATURES, NOTE NAMING and REPEAT SIGNS

Key Signatures on the Grand Staff affect ALL the notes with the same letter name.

A **REPEAT** sign is written as two DOTS (one in space 2 and one in space 3) in front of the final double bar line. A REPEAT sign indicates the music is repeated from the beginning of the piece. When there are TWO repeat signs the music is repeated within the double bar lines.

1. a) Name the Major key.
   b) Name the notes in measures 2 and 3.
   c) Name the sharps or flats in the Key Signature.
   d) When all repeat signs are observed, how many measures are played.

Major Key: _D_ Major   Note Names: _A_ _F#_ _D_   _C#_ _E_ _D_
Key Signature: _F# C#_   Total number of measures played: _6_

Major Key: _F_ Major   Note Names: _Bb_ _A_ _G_   _E_ _C_ _F_
Key Signature: _Bb_   Total number of measures played: _5_

Major Key: _Bb_ Major   Note Names: _Bb_ _D_ _C_   _Eb_ _A_ _Bb_
Key Signature: _Bb Eb_   Total number of measures played: _4_

TEMPO and CHANGES IN TEMPO

"**Tempo**" refers to the rate of speed; how fast or slow the music is played.
TEMPO MARKS are terms used in music to indicate different levels of speed.
The tempo markings are written above the Time Signature.

Term	Definition
largo	very slow
lento	slow
adagio	a slow tempo (slower than *andante* but not as slow as *largo*)
andante	at a moderate walking pace, moderately slow
moderato	at a moderate tempo
allegretto	fairly fast; a little slower than *allegro*
allegro	fast
presto	very fast
prestissimo	as fast as possible

Changes in Tempo

a tempo	return to the original tempo
ritardando, rit.	slowing down gradually
accelerando, accel.	becoming quicker
fermata, 𝄐	pause, hold the note or rest longer than its written value

♪ **Note:** A fermata sign is always written directly above a note or rest and ABOVE the staff.

1. Copy the music below. Include all markings (Tempo, repeat sign, Dynamics and Articulation).

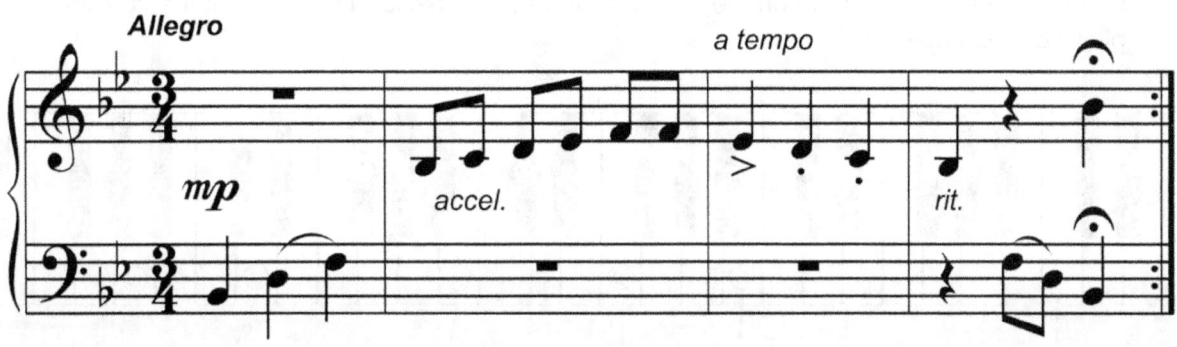

89

Lesson 8 — Review Test

Total Score: ___ / 100

1. Write the following notes in the Bass Staff. Use whole notes.

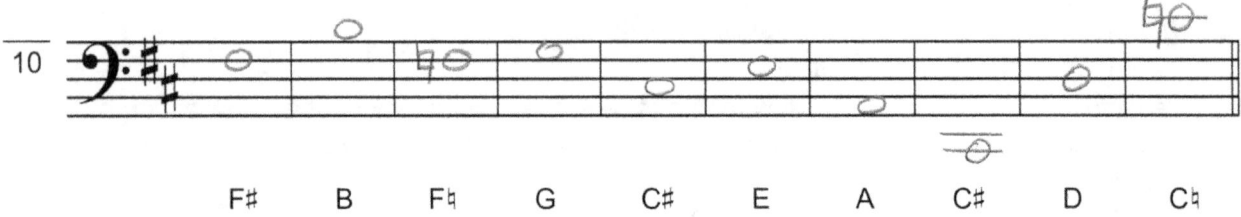

F#   B   F♮   G   C#   E   A   C#   D   C♮

2. a) Add a **DOT** to each of the following notes to create dotted half notes.
   b) Name the notes.

B♭   E♭   A   D   G   A   E♭   G   F   B♭

3. a) Write the notes on the Grand Staff for the keys labelled with a ☺ on the keyboard. Use whole notes.
   b) Name the notes.
   c) Draw a line from each note on the Grand Staff to the corresponding key (at the correct pitch) on the keyboard.

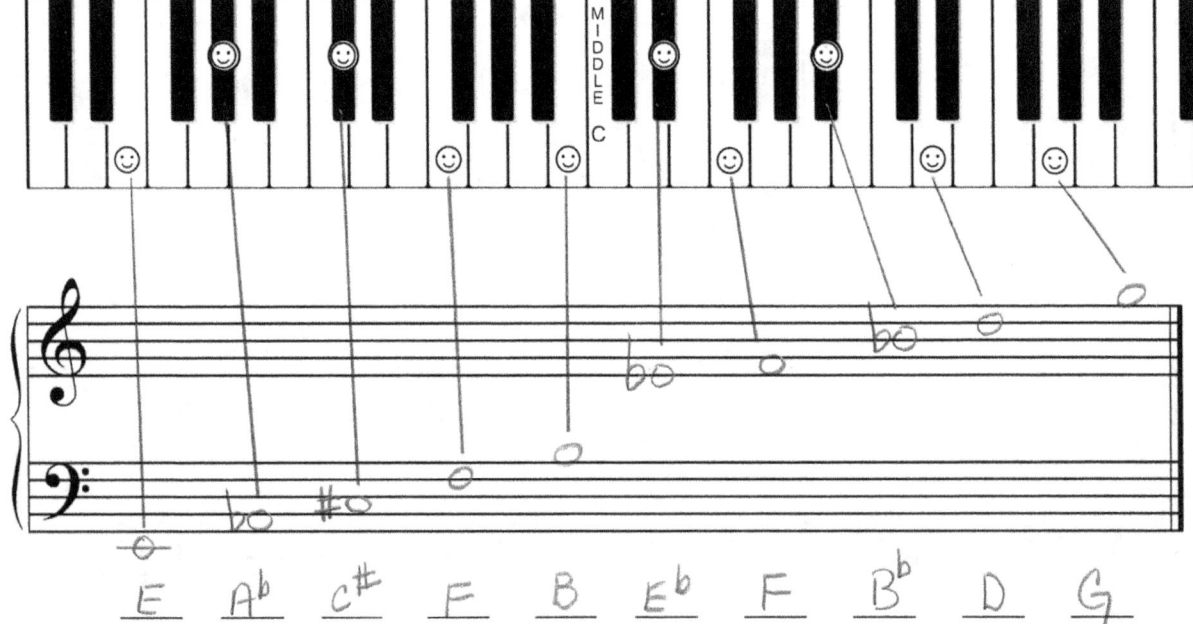

E   A♭   C#   F   B   E♭   F   B♭   D   G

4. Identify the distance between the notes in each measure as **WT** (whole tone or whole step) or as **ST** (semitone or half step).

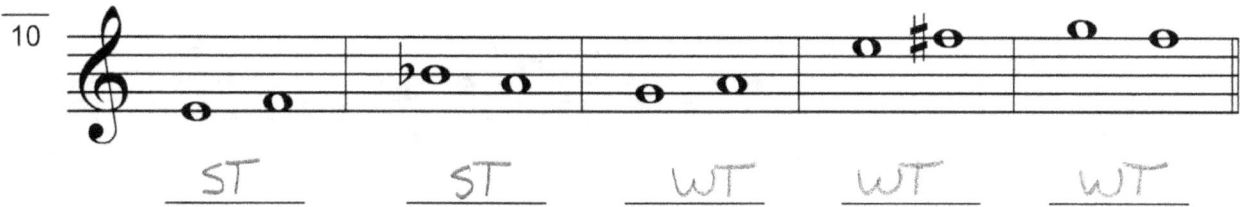

5. Add bar lines to complete the following rhythms. Observe the Time Signatures.

6. a) Name the notes.
   b) Name the melodic interval between the notes in each measure. Use an up or a down arrow to indicate direction.

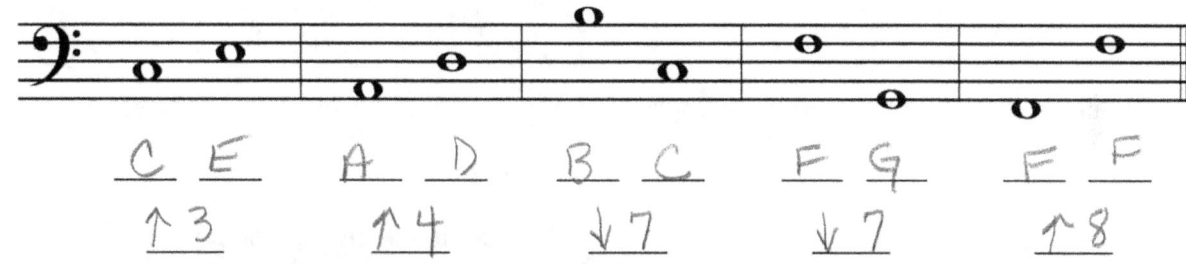

7. a) Write the following **KEY SIGNATURES** in the Treble Staff. (Do NOT repeat the clef sign.)
   b) Write the Tonic note of each key. Use a whole note.

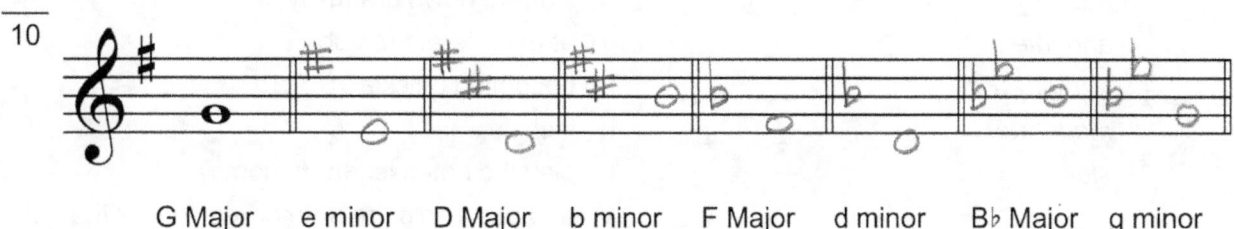

8. Analyze the following piece of music by answering the questions below.

   Adagio

   [music staff with bass clef, mf marking, notes with fermata at A and staccato at B]

   a) Add the correct Time Signature directly on the music.
   b) Name the key of this piece. __B♭ Major__
   c) Explain the tempo of this piece. __Adagio - slow tempo__
   d) Explain the dynamic marking in this piece. __Mezzo forte - Moderately loud__
   e) Name the highest note in this piece. __B♭__
   f) Name the lowest note in this piece. __B♭__
   g) How many measures are in this piece? __4__
   h) Explain the sign at the letter **A**. __fermata - pause, hold longer than its written value__
   i) Explain the sign at the letter **B**. __staccato - detached__
   j) Name the type of note with the longest note value in this piece.
   __dotted half note__

9. Match each musical term with the English definition. (Not all definitions will be used.)

Term		Definition
largo	__e__	a) return to the original tempo
a tempo	__a__	b) moderate walking pace
ritardando, rit.	__f__	c) very fast
allegro	__i__	d) a stressed note
accelerando, accel.	__h__	e) very slow
presto	__c__	f) slowing down gradually
andante	__b__	g) at a moderate tempo
fermata, 𝄐	__k__	h) becoming quicker
moderato	__g__	i) fast
slur	__j__	j) play the notes legato (smooth)
		k) a pause - hold the note or rest longer than its written value

10. Complete the Circle of Fifths by adding the order of flats on the top left and the order of sharps on the top right. Write the Major keys on the outside of the circle. Use UPPER case letters. Write the minor keys on the inside of the circle. Use lower case letters.

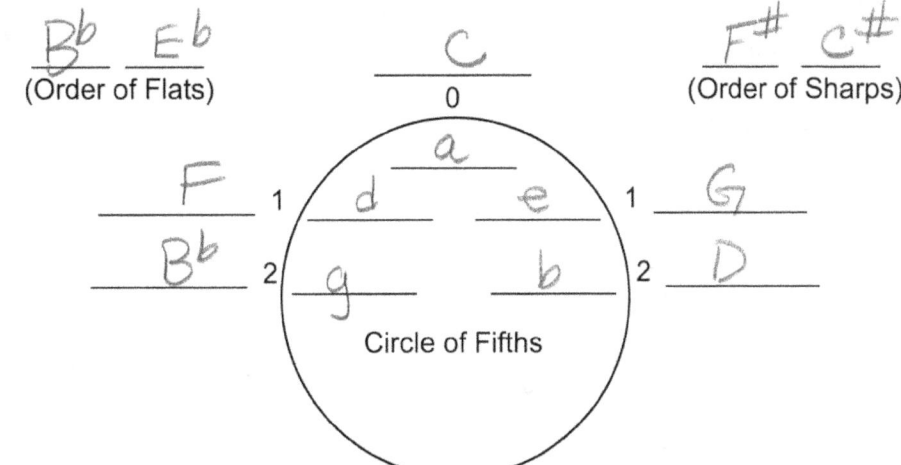

b) Write the following scales **ASCENDING** only, using a Key Signature. Use whole notes.
c) Circle two **TONIC** notes in each scale.

F Major scale

a minor natural scale

D Major scale

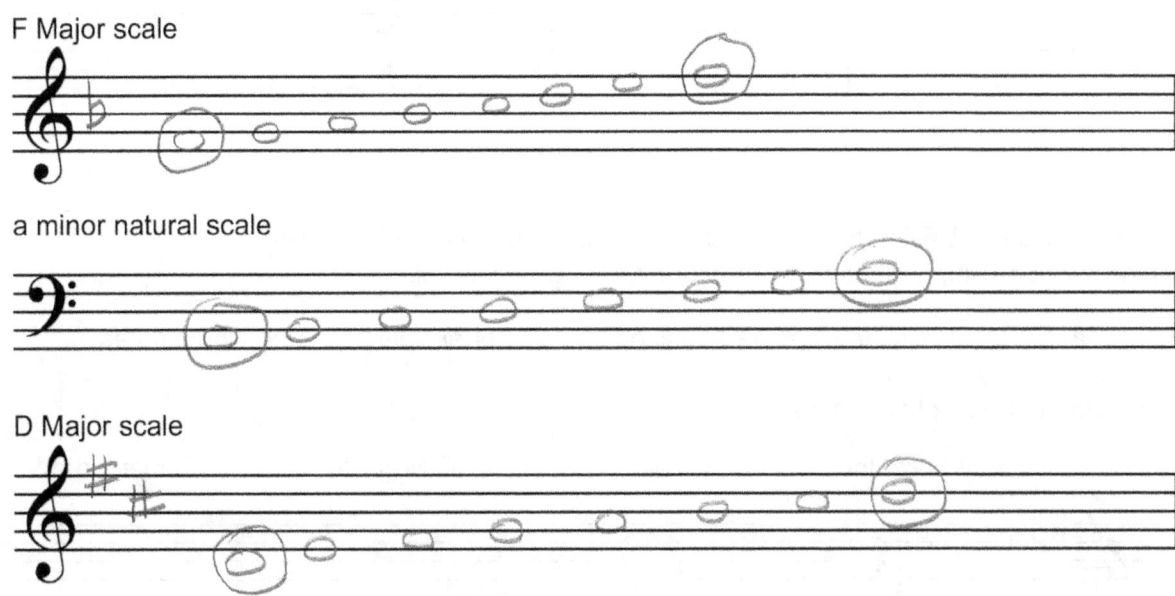

d) Write the following scales **DESCENDING** only, using **ACCIDENTALS** instead of a Key Signature. Use whole notes.
e) Circle two **TONIC** notes in each scale.

e minor natural scale

C Major scale

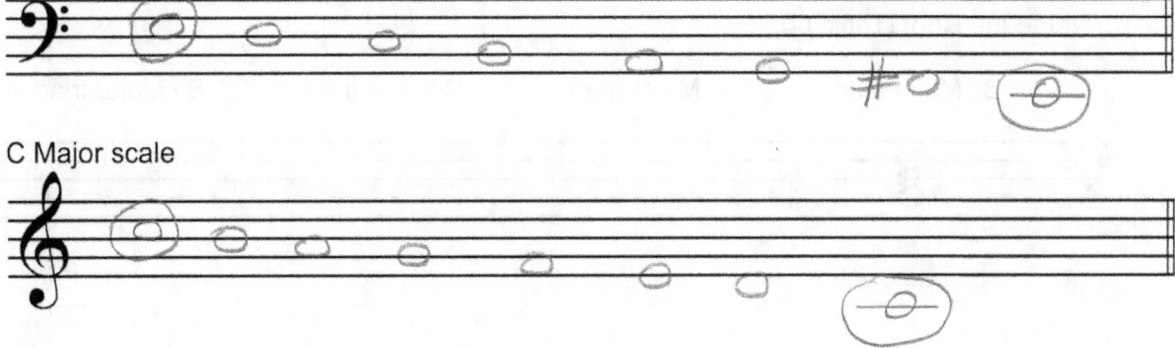

Lesson 9   Major Triads - Solid and Broken

A **MAJOR TONIC TRIAD** is a three note chord built on the first, third and fifth notes (degrees) of a Major scale.

The distance between each note is an interval of a 3rd. (Skipping up pattern.)

The Root (Tonic note) is the lowest note.
The Root names the triad. (Lowest note: **C**, triad: **C Major triad**)

A triad in **ROOT POSITION** is written on **3 LINES** or in **3 SPACES**.

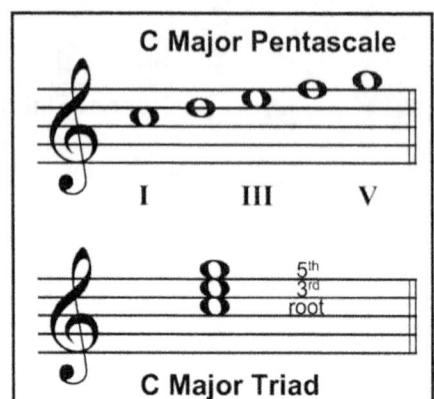

1. a) Copy the following triads.
   b) Name the Root (Tonic note).

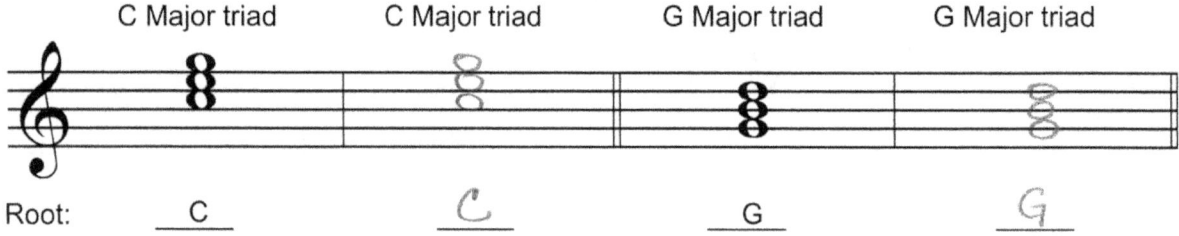

Root: C   C   G   G

The **KEY SIGNATURE** of the Major scale applies to the notes in the Major triad.
Triads may be written with a Key Signature or using accidentals.

2. a) Write the following triads in root position (all lines or all spaces). Use whole notes. Use a Key Signature.
   b) Name the Root (Tonic note).

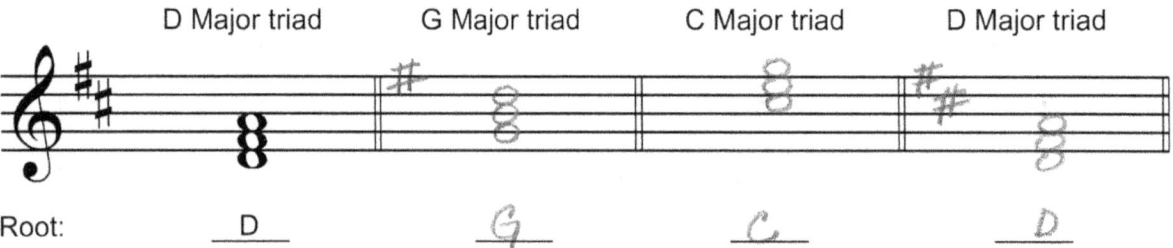

Root: D   G   C   D

3. a) Write the following triads in root position (all lines or all spaces). Use whole notes. Use accidentals when necessary.
   b) Name the Root (Tonic note).

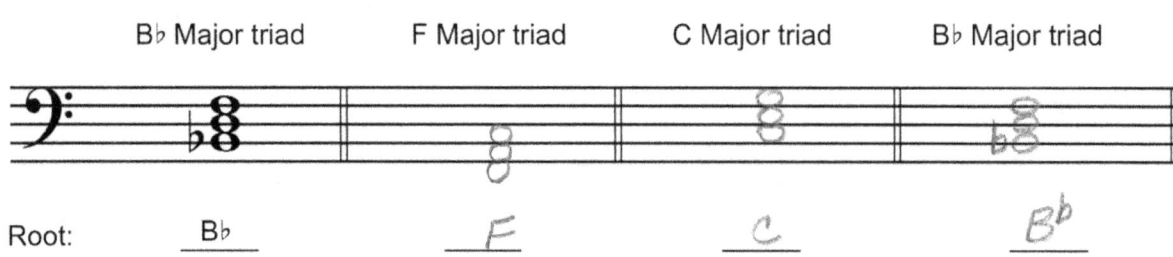

Root: B♭   F   C   B♭

SOLID TRIADS and BROKEN TRIADS

A **SOLID (Blocked) TRIAD** is written one note above the other. All three notes are played at the same time.

A **BROKEN TRIAD** is written one note after the other. The notes are played one note at a time.

Broken triads may be written in the SKIPPING UP (ascending) pattern or the SKIPPING DOWN (descending) pattern.

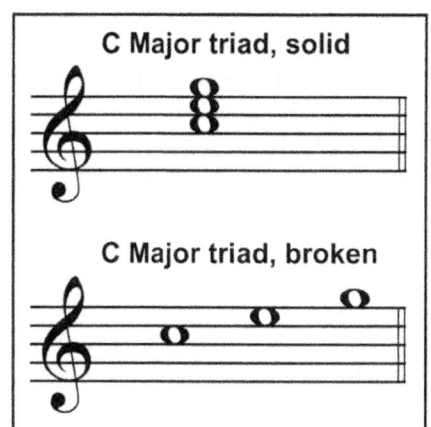

♪ **Note:** The bottom (lowest) note is ALWAYS the Root (Tonic note).

1. a) Copy the following broken triads in root position (all line notes or all space notes).
   b) Name the Root (Tonic note).

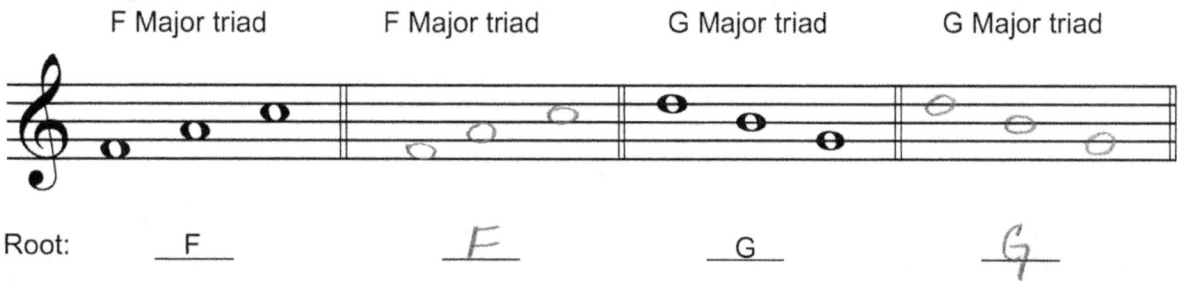

Root: F   F   G   G

2. For each of the following broken triads:
   a) Name the Major triad.
   b) Name the Root (Tonic note).

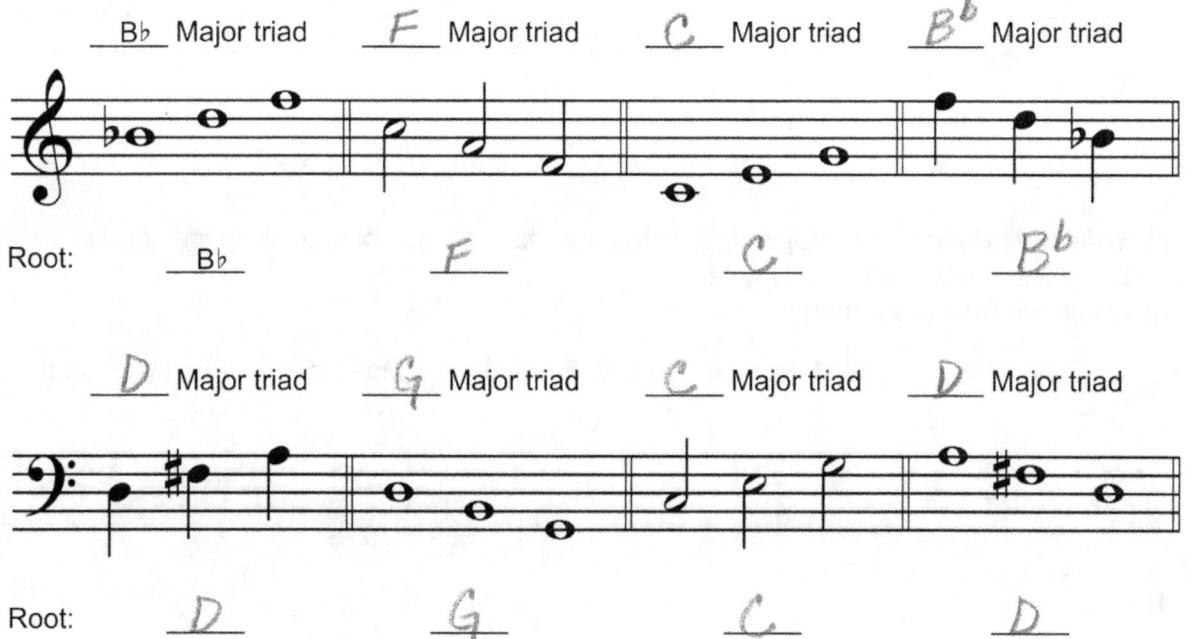

Root: B♭   F   C   B♭

Root: D   G   C   D

95

SOLID (Blocked) TRIAD

A **SOLID (Blocked) TRIAD** is three notes written directly above each other.

Use the Circle of Fifths to identify the Key Signature of the Major key.

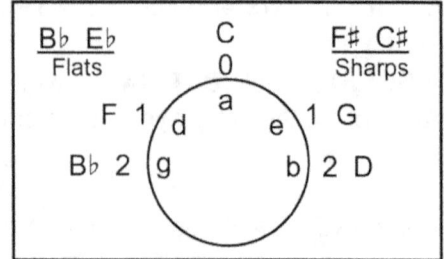

1. a) Write the following solid Major triads in root position (all line notes or all space notes). Use a Key Signature. Use whole notes.
   b) Name the Root (Tonic note).

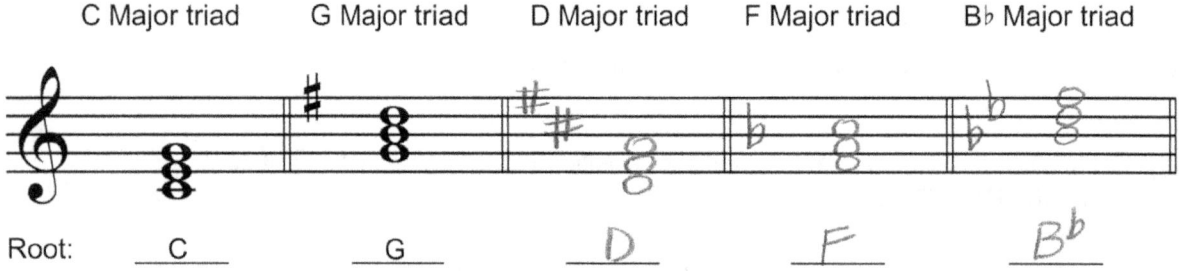

C Major triad — Root: C
G Major triad — Root: G
D Major triad — Root: D
F Major triad — Root: F
B♭ Major triad — Root: B♭

♪ **Note:** When adding stems to a SOLID (blocked) triad, only one stem is used. The stem direction is based on the note furthest away from the middle line.

2. a) Write the following solid Major triads in root position (all line notes or all space notes). Use accidentals. Use half notes.
   b) Name the Root (Tonic note).

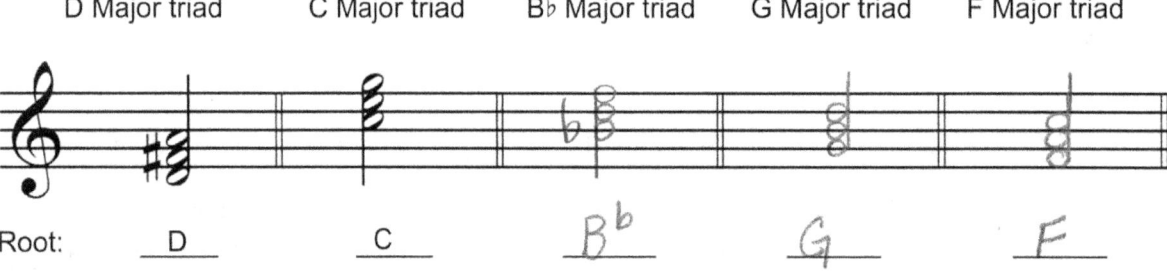

D Major triad — Root: D
C Major triad — Root: C
B♭ Major triad — Root: B♭
G Major triad — Root: G
F Major triad — Root: F

3. a) Write the following solid Major triads in root position (all line notes or all space notes). Use accidentals. Use quarter notes.
   b) Name the Root (Tonic note).

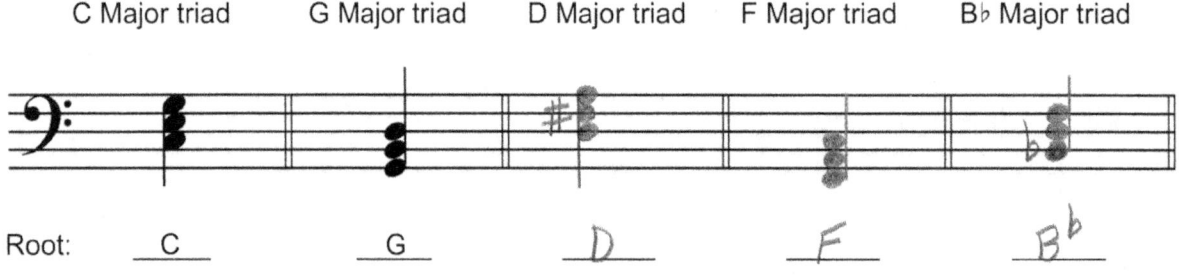

C Major triad — Root: C
G Major triad — Root: G
D Major triad — Root: D
F Major triad — Root: F
B♭ Major triad — Root: B♭

BROKEN TRIAD

A **BROKEN TRIAD** is three notes written **BESIDE** each other.

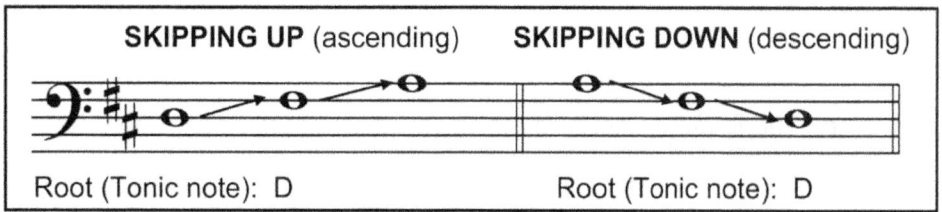

Root (Tonic note): D   Root (Tonic note): D

♪ **Note:** A broken triad can be written in the **SKIPPING UP** (ascending) pattern or in the **SKIPPING DOWN** (descending) pattern.

1. a) Write the following broken Major triads in root position (all line notes or all space notes). Use the skipping up (ascending) pattern. Use a Key Signature. Use whole notes.
   b) Name the Root (Tonic note).

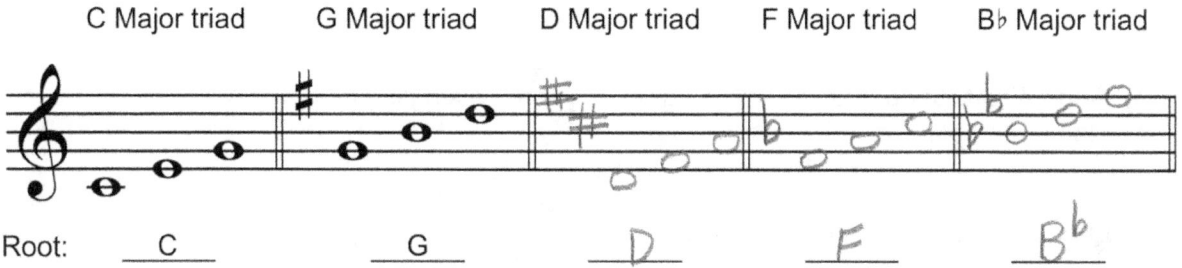

Root: C   G   D   F   B♭

2. a) Write the following broken Major triads in root position (all line notes or all space notes). Use the skipping down (descending) pattern. Use accidentals. Use whole notes.
   b) Name the Root (Tonic note).

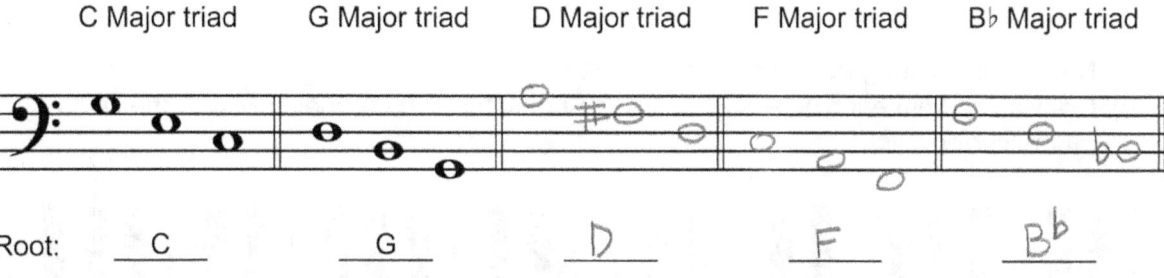

Root: C   G   D   F   B♭

♪ **Note:** A triad written in root position (all line notes or all space notes) is in **CLOSE POSITION**.

3. a) Name the Root (Tonic note) for each Major triad.
   b) Circle Broken or Solid for each of the following Major triads.

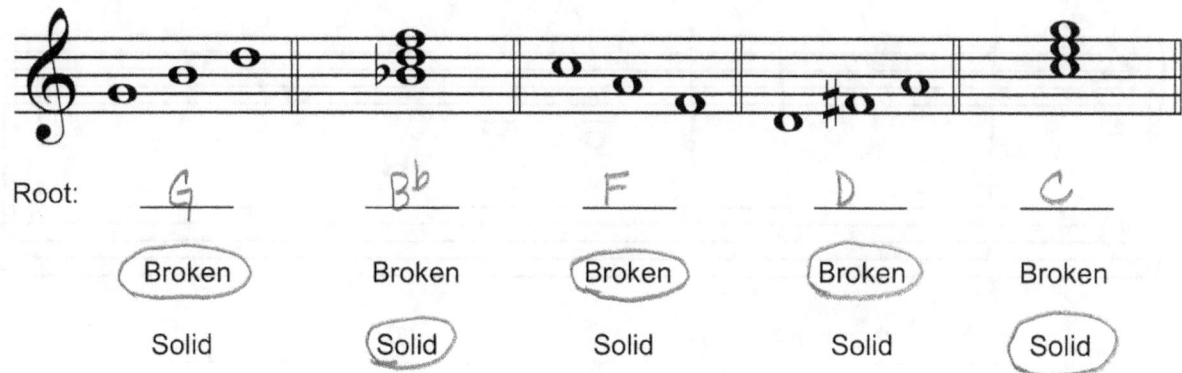

Root: G   B♭   F   D   C

(Broken) Broken (Broken) (Broken) Broken

Solid (Solid) Solid Solid (Solid)

Lesson 9   Review Test

Total Score: ____ / 100

1. Name the following notes in the Bass Clef.

2. a) Add a **FLAG** to each of the following notes to create single eighth notes.
   b) Name the notes.

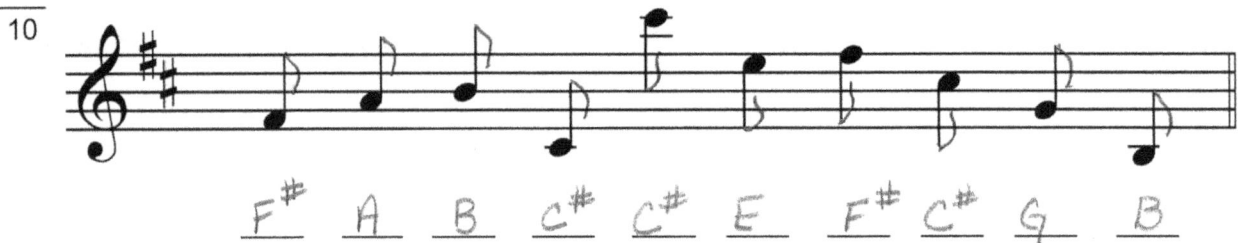

3. a) Name the following notes on the Grand Staff.
   b) Draw a line from each note on the Grand Staff to the corresponding key on the keyboard (at the correct pitch).

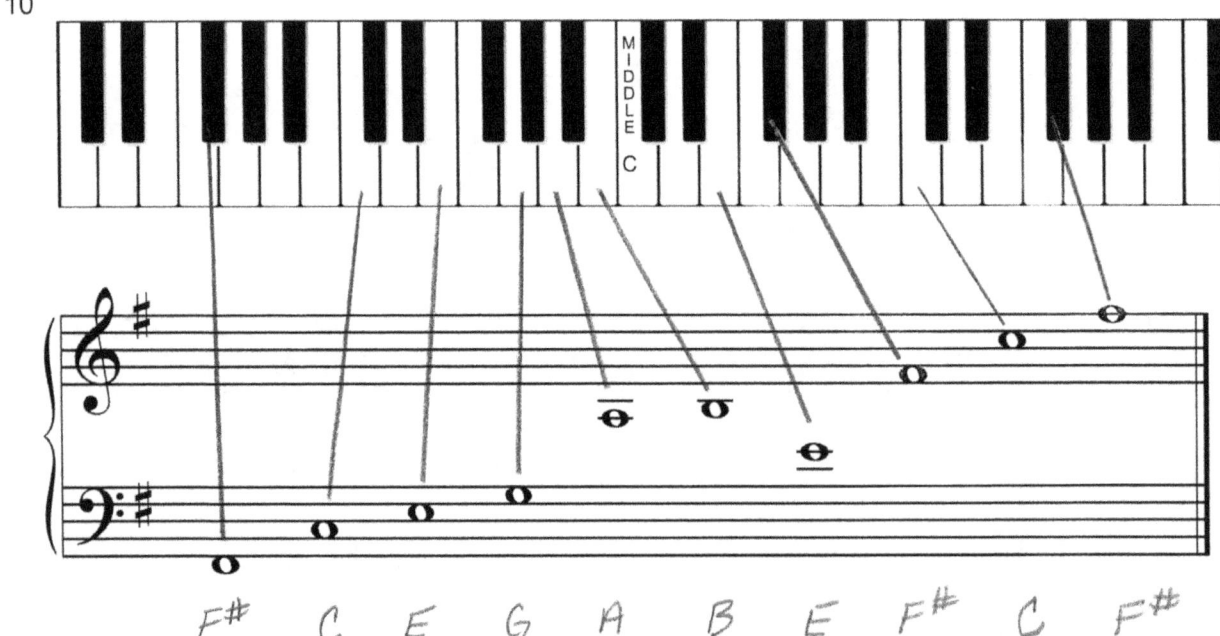

4. Identify the following as **WT** (whole tone) or as **ST** (semitone). Observe the Key Signature.

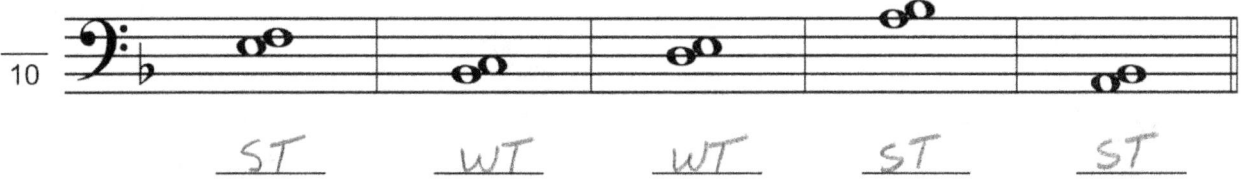

5. a) **SCOOP** each Basic Beat in each measure.
   b) Write the **PULSE** below each Basic Beat.
   c) Add **RESTS** below each bracket to complete each measure.
   d) Cross off the Basic Beat as each beat is completed.

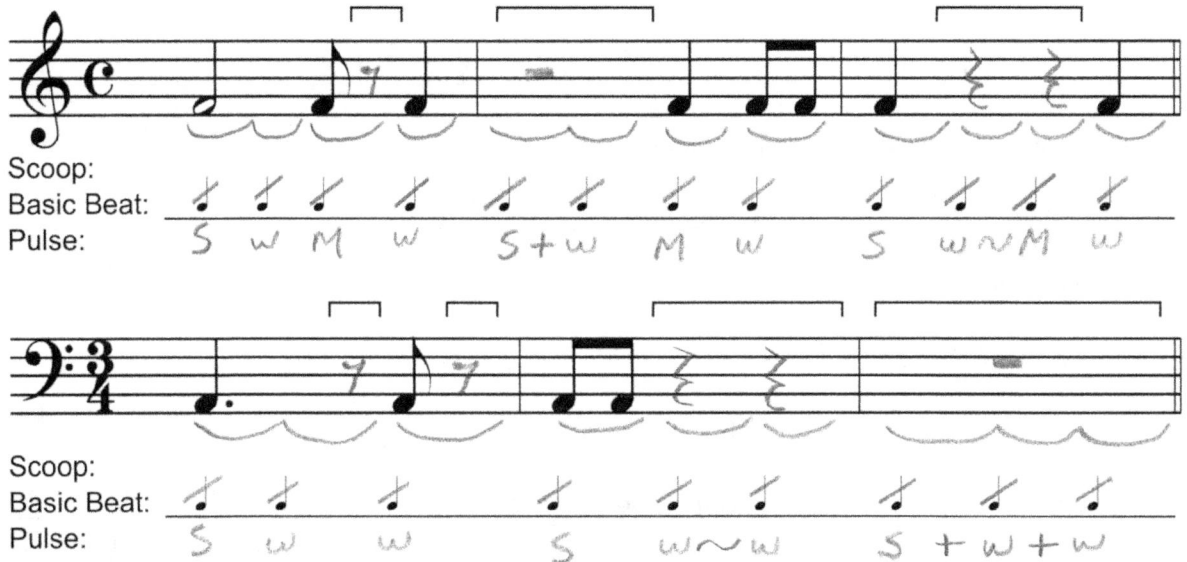

6. a) Name the notes.
   b) Name the melodic interval (numerical size only) in each measure. Use an up or a down arrow to indicate direction.

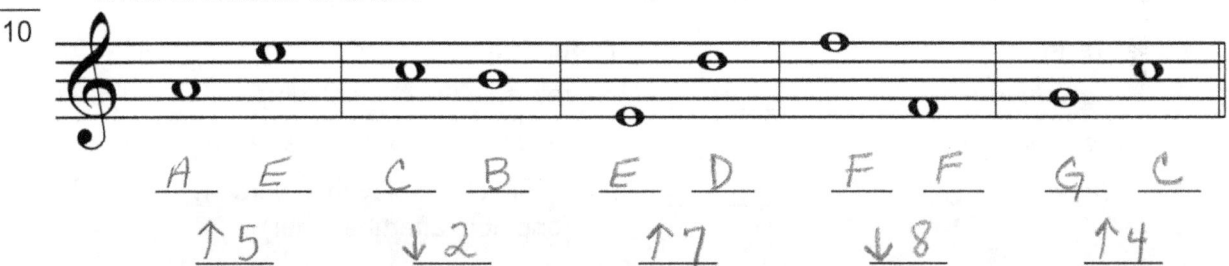

7. a) Write the following **SOLID** Tonic triads in root position. Use accidentals. Use whole notes.
   b) Name the Root (Tonic note).

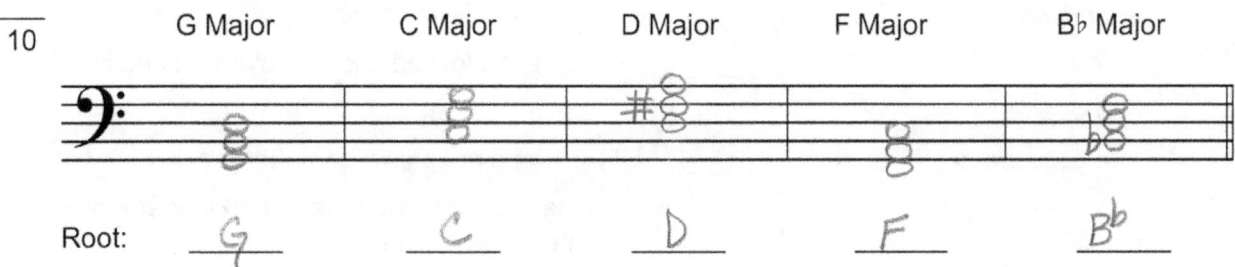

8. Analyze the following piece of music by answering the questions below.

G. St. Germain

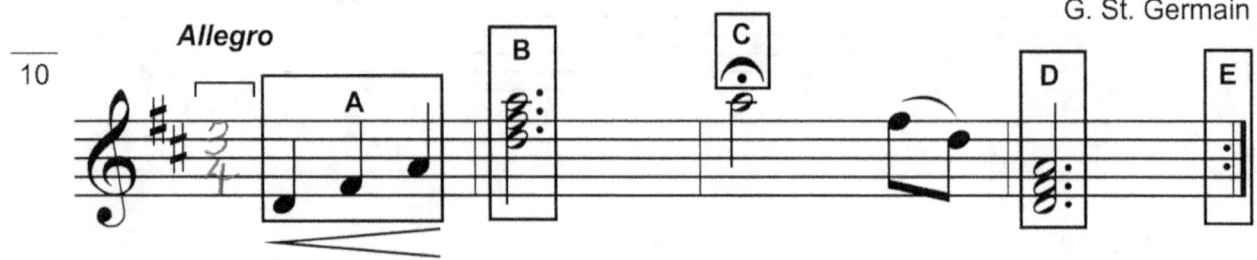

a) Add the correct Time Signature directly on the music.

b) Name the key of this piece. __D Major__

c) Explain the tempo of this piece. __Allegro - fast__

d) Explain the dynamic marking in this piece. __cresc. - gradually louder__

e) Name the root of the triad at the letter **A**. __D__

f) Name the root of the triad at the letter **B**. __D__

g) Name the composer of this piece. __G. St. Germain__

h) Explain the sign at the letter **C**. __fermata - pause, hold longer than its written value.__

i) Identify the triad at the letter **D** as solid or broken. __solid__

j) Explain the sign at the letter **E**. __repeat the music from the beginning__

9. Match each musical term with the English definition. (Not all definitions will be used.)

Term		Definition
solid triad	h	a) return to the original tempo
ritardando, rit.	f	b) moderately slow, at a walking pace
broken triad	c	c) 3 note chord played separately (one note after the other)
allegro	i	d) moderately soft
Key Signature	j	e) very slow
largo	e	f) slowing down gradually
andante	b	g) at a moderate tempo
fermata, ⌒	k	h) 3 note blocked chord (played together)
moderato	g	i) fast
mezzo piano	d	j) sharps or flats written after the clef
		k) pause - hold the note or rest longer than its written value

10. Complete the Circle of Fifths by adding the order of flats on the top left and the order of sharps on the top right. Write the Major keys on the outside of the circle. Use UPPER case letters. Write the minor keys on the inside of the circle. Use lower case letters.

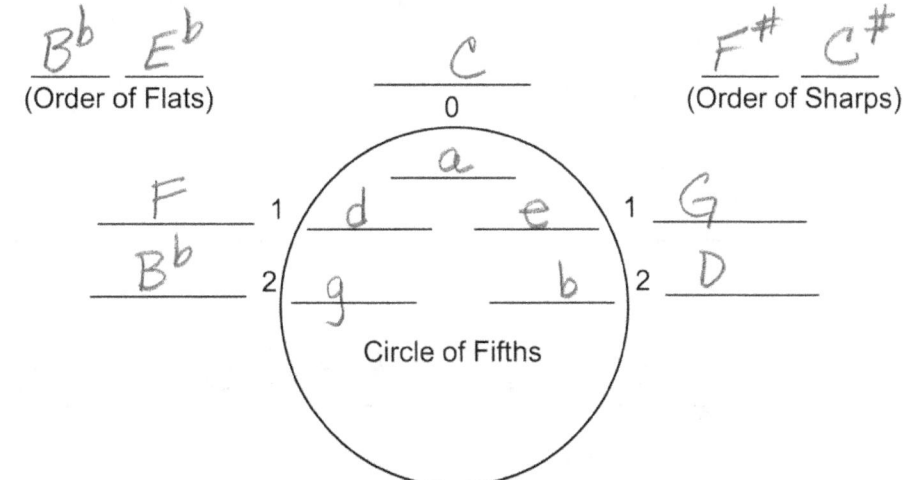

b) Draw the correct clef (Treble Clef or Bass Clef) at the beginning of each staff to form the following scales. Add any necessary accidentals.
c) Circle two TONIC notes in each scale.

D Major scale

e minor natural scale

F Major scale

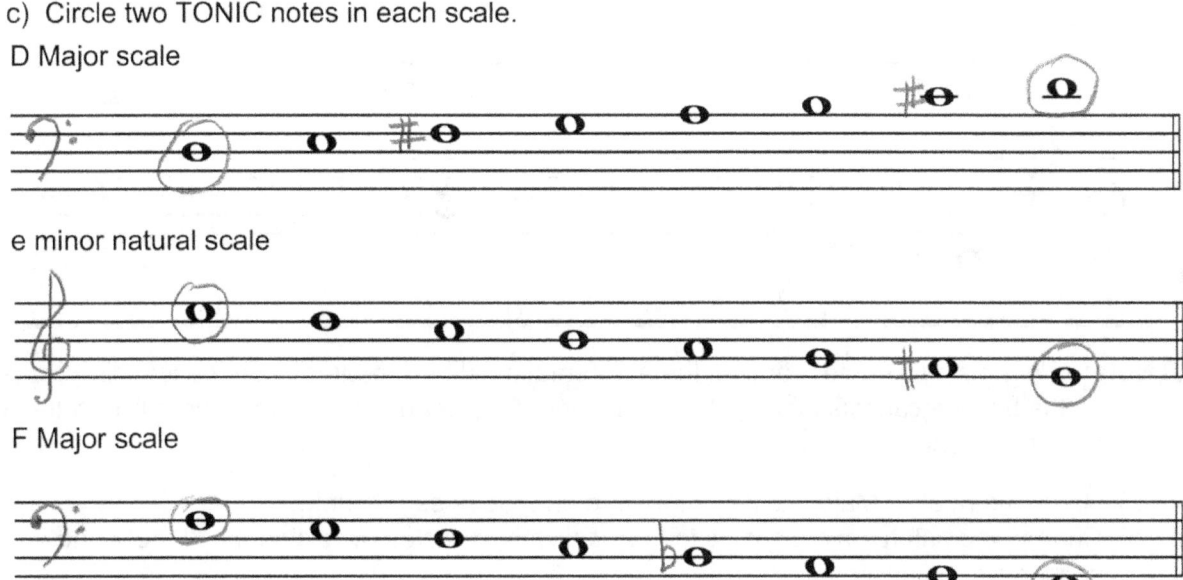

e) Name the following scales.
f) Circle two TONIC notes in each scale.

Scale of G Major

Scale of C Major

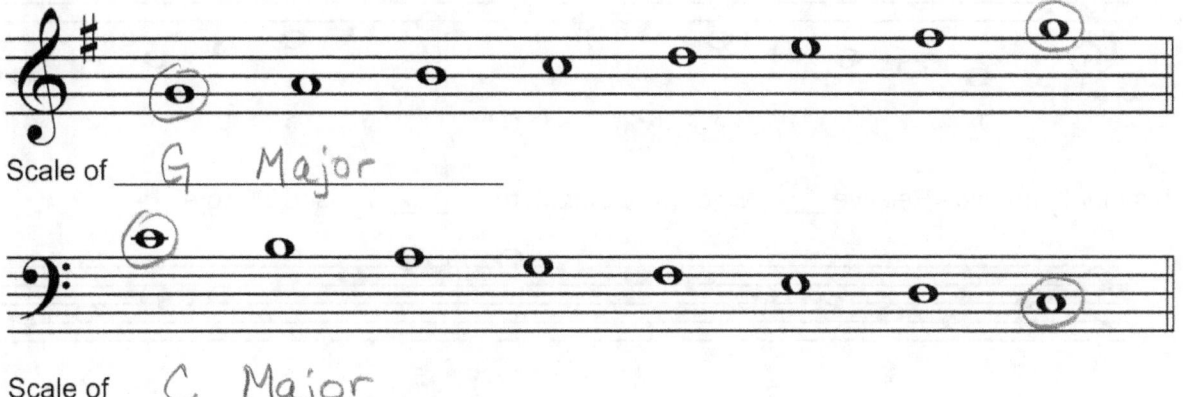

Lesson 10   Harmonic Minor Scales

A **NATURAL MINOR** Scale has the **SAME KEY SIGNATURE** as its **RELATIVE MAJOR**.

As the word **NATURAL** indicates, no accidentals are added.

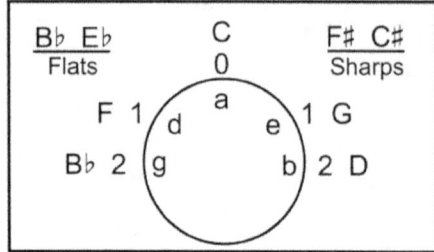

♪ **Note:** Major keys are written on the outside of the Circle of Fifths. Minor keys are written on the inside.

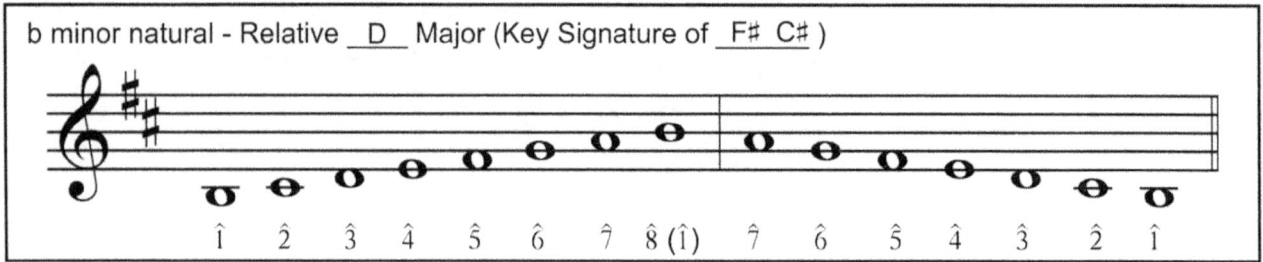

A **HARMONIC MINOR** scale has the SAME Key Signature as its relative Major and RAISES the 7th note one semitone, ascending and descending. The RAISED 7th note is ALWAYS written using an accidental.

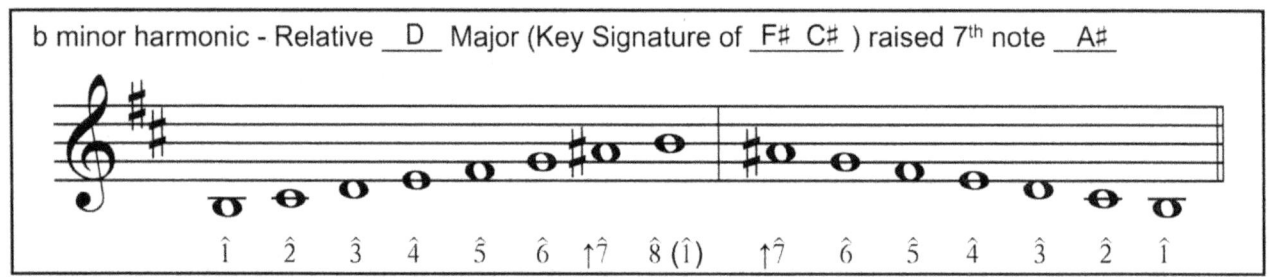

♪ **Note:** When using a center bar line, the accidental must be repeated in the descending scale as the bar line cancels the accidental. Without a center bar line, the accidental is written only in the ascending scale.

1. a) Name the relative Major, its Key Signature and the raised 7th note.
   b) Change the natural minor scales to harmonic minor scales by raising the 7th note one semitone ascending and descending.

e minor harmonic - Relative __G__ Major (Key Signature __F#__) raised 7th note __D#__

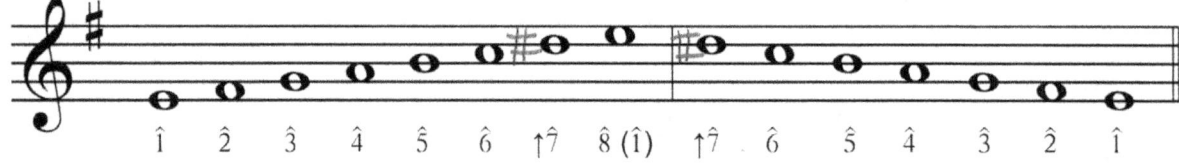

b minor harmonic - Relative __D__ Major (Key Signature __F# C#__) raised 7th note __A#__

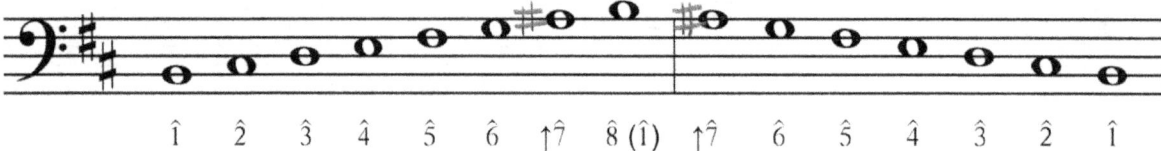

WRITING HARMONIC MINOR SCALES

In a **HARMONIC MINOR SCALE**, the 7th note is raised ascending (going up) and descending (going down). If the 7th note is a flat, it will be raised to a natural. If it is a natural, it will be raised to a sharp.

♪ **Note:** The number **7** is hidden inside the letter **H** for Harmonic.

1. Write the following harmonic minor scales, ascending and descending, using a Key Signature. Use an accidental for the raised 7th note. Use whole notes.

d minor harmonic - Relative __F__ Major (Key Signature __B♭__) raised 7th note __C#__

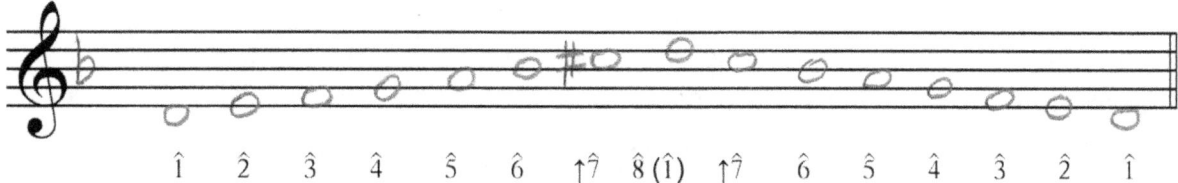

g minor harmonic - Relative __B♭__ Major (Key Signature __B♭ E♭__) raised 7th note __F#__

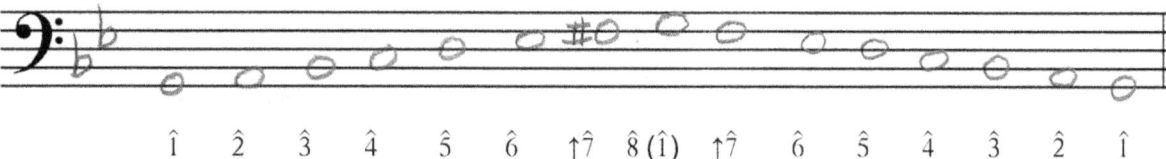

When writing harmonic minor scales using **ACCIDENTALS** instead of a Key Signature, accidentals are needed for the sharps or flats from the Key Signature as well as for the raised 7th note.

♪ **Note:** Always write scales the same way: either **WITH** a center bar line or **WITHOUT** a center bar line.

2. Write the following harmonic minor scales, ascending and descending, using accidentals instead of a Key Signature. Use an accidental for the raised 7th note. Use whole notes.

a minor harmonic - Relative __C__ Major (Key Signature __—__) raised 7th note __G#__

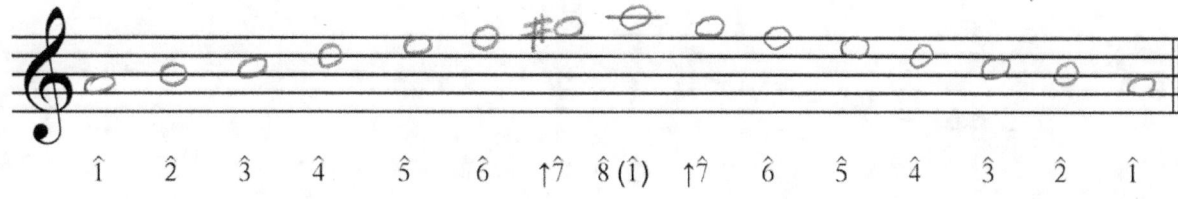

e minor harmonic - Relative __G__ Major (Key Signature __F#__) raised 7th note __D#__

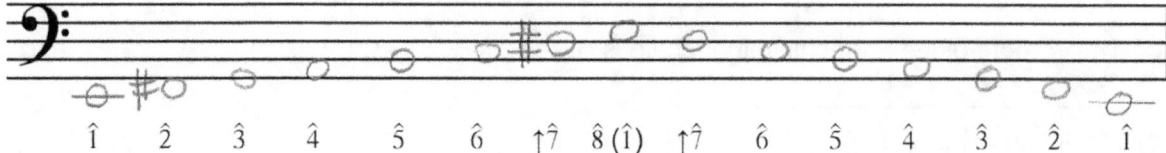

WRITING NATURAL AND HARMONIC MINOR SCALES

When writing a harmonic minor scale using a Key Signature, it will be necessary to also use accidentals for the raised 7th note.

1. Write d minor natural scale, ascending and descending, using a Key Signature. Use whole notes.

   d minor natural - Relative __F__ Major (Key Signature __Bb__)

2. Write d minor harmonic scale, ascending and descending, using a Key Signature and any necessary accidentals. Use whole notes.

   d minor harmonic - Relative __F__ Major (Key Signature __Bb__) raised 7th note __C#__

3. Write e minor natural scale, ascending and descending, using accidentals instead of a Key Signature. Use whole notes.

   e minor natural - Relative __G__ Major (Key Signature __F#__)

4. Write e minor harmonic scale, ascending and descending, using accidentals instead of a Key Signature. Use whole notes.

   e minor harmonic - Relative __G__ Major (Key Signature __F#__) raised 7th note __D#__

5. Fill in the blanks.

   a) A natural minor has the SAME Key Signature as its __relative__ Major.
   b) A harmonic minor scale has a RAISED __7th__ note.
   c) The 7th note of the harmonic minor scale is raised __ascending__ and __descending__.
   d) A bar line cancels an __accidental__.

Lesson 10   Review Test

Total Score: ____ / 100

1. Write the following notes in the Treble Clef. Use whole notes.

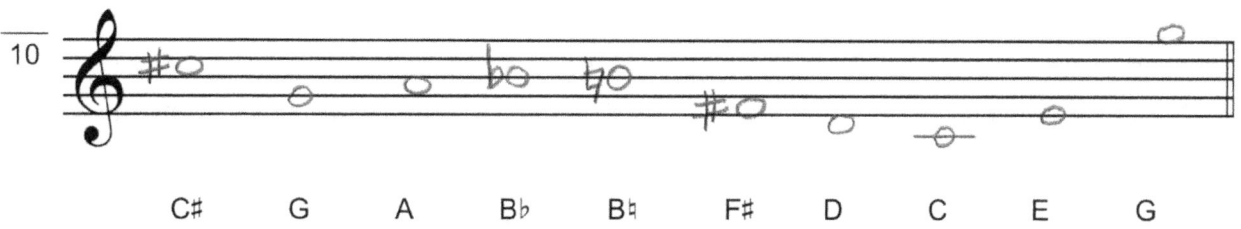

     C#   G   A   B♭   B♮   F#   D   C   E   G

2. a) Add a **STEM** to each of the following noteheads to create half notes.
   b) Name the notes. Observe the Key Signature.

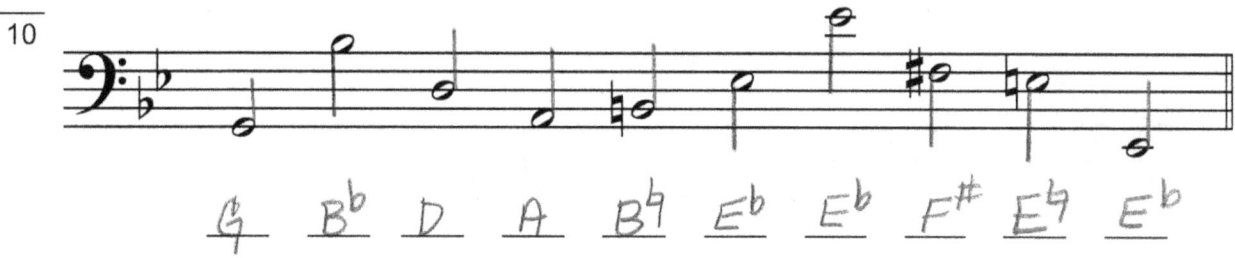

    G   B♭   D   A   B♮   E♭   E♭   F#   E♮   E♭

3. a) Name the following notes on the Grand Staff.
   b) Draw a line from each note on the Grand Staff to the corresponding key on the keyboard (at the correct pitch).

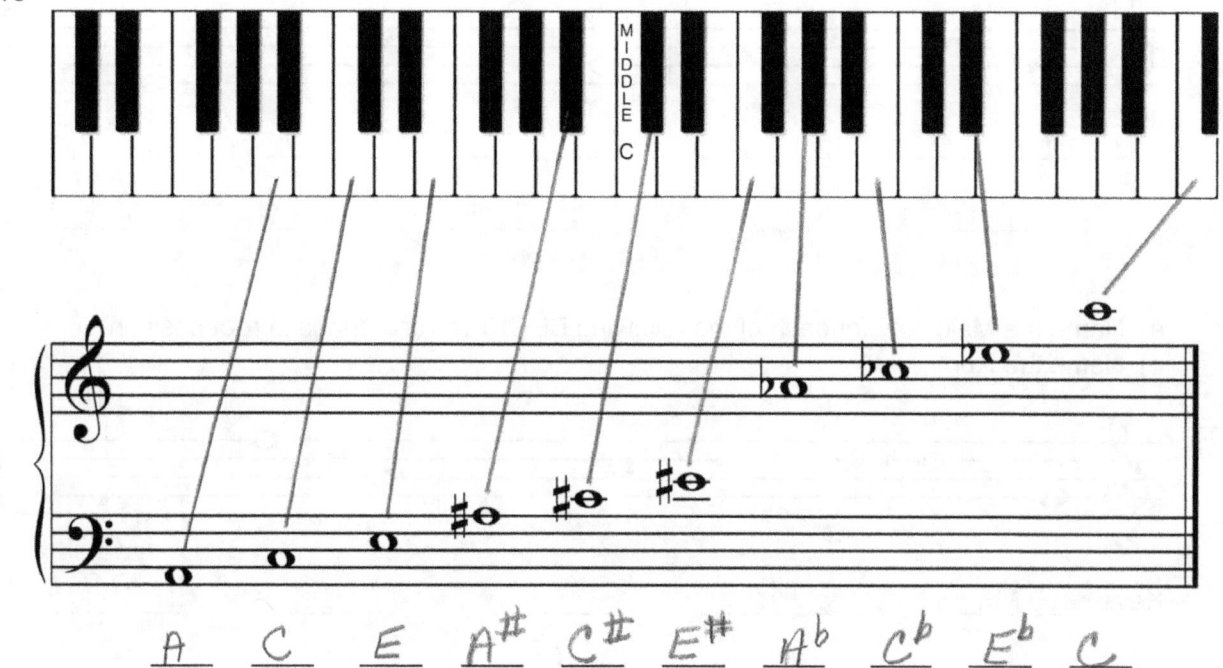

    A   C   E   A#   C#   E#   A♭   C♭   E♭   C

4. Write the following **SOLID** Tonic triads in root position. Use the note values indicated. Use accidentals when necessary.

Triad:	B♭ Major	G Major	C Major	F Major	D Major
Notes:	whole notes	quarter notes	half notes	whole notes	half notes

5. Add the correct Time Signature directly below each bracket.

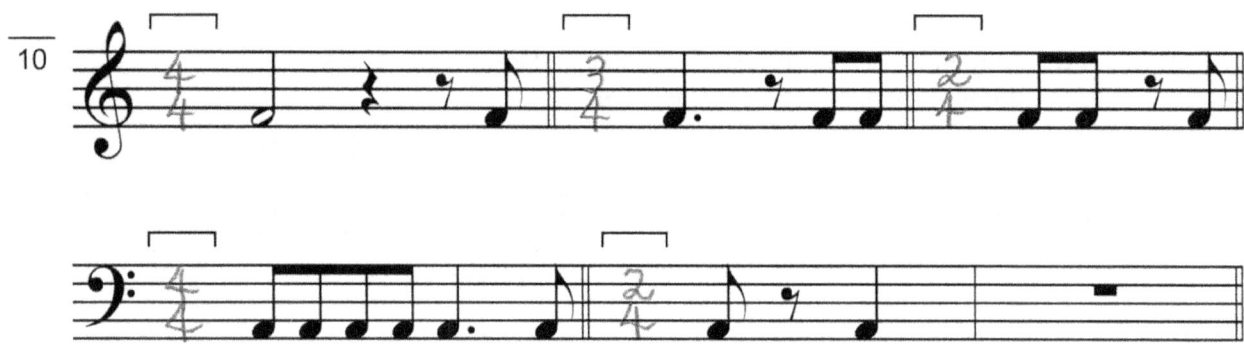

6. a) Name the notes.
   b) Name the melodic interval between the notes in each measure. Use an up or a down arrow to indicate direction.

F B   E A   G F   C A   E F
↑4   ↓5   ↑7   ↓3   ↑2

7. a) Name the Major key for each of the following BROKEN Tonic triads in root position.
   b) Name the Root.

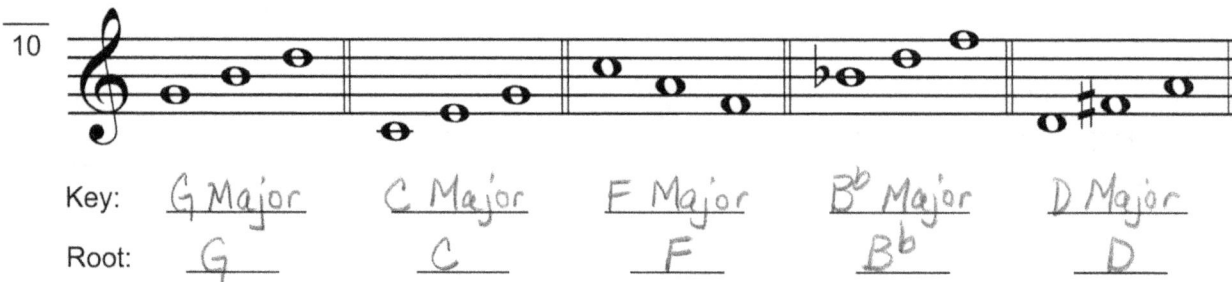

Key: G Major   C Major   F Major   B♭ Major   D Major
Root: G   C   F   B♭   D

8. Analyze the following piece of music by answering the questions below.

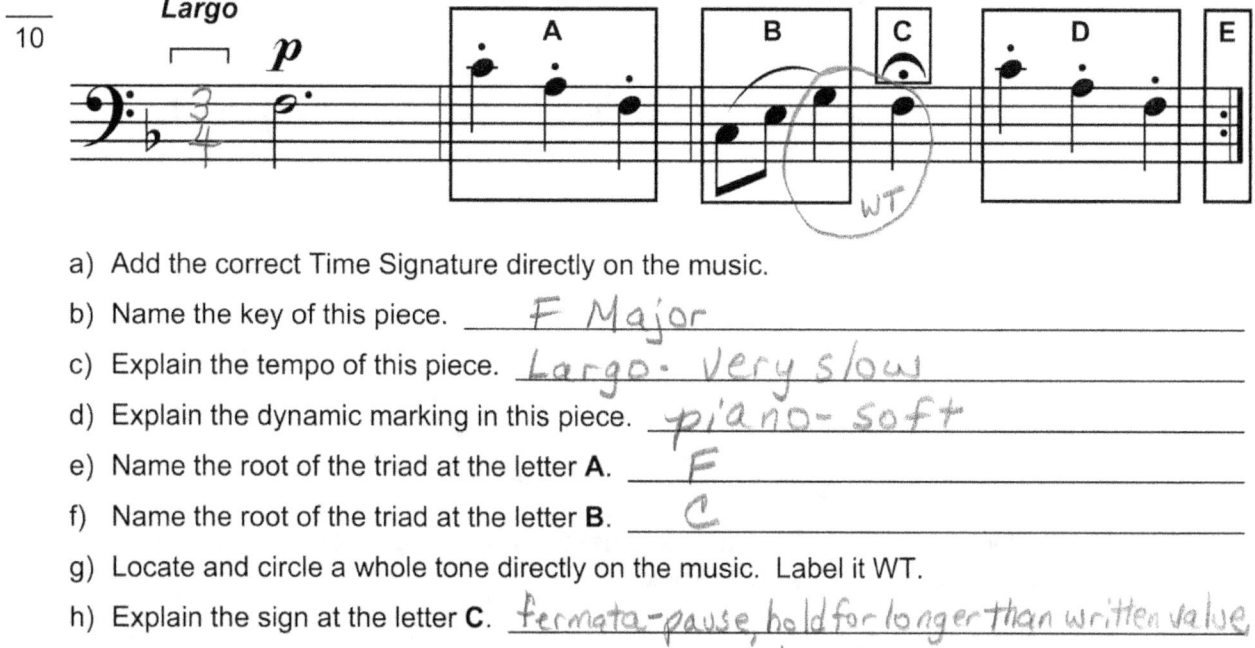

a) Add the correct Time Signature directly on the music.
b) Name the key of this piece. __F Major__
c) Explain the tempo of this piece. __Largo - very slow__
d) Explain the dynamic marking in this piece. __piano - soft__
e) Name the root of the triad at the letter **A**. __F__
f) Name the root of the triad at the letter **B**. __C__
g) Locate and circle a whole tone directly on the music. Label it WT.
h) Explain the sign at the letter **C**. __fermata - pause, hold for longer than written value__
i) Identify the triad at the letter **D** as solid or broken. __broken__
j) Explain the sign at the letter **E**. __repeat the music from the beginning__

9. Match each musical sign with the English definition. (Not all definitions will be used.)

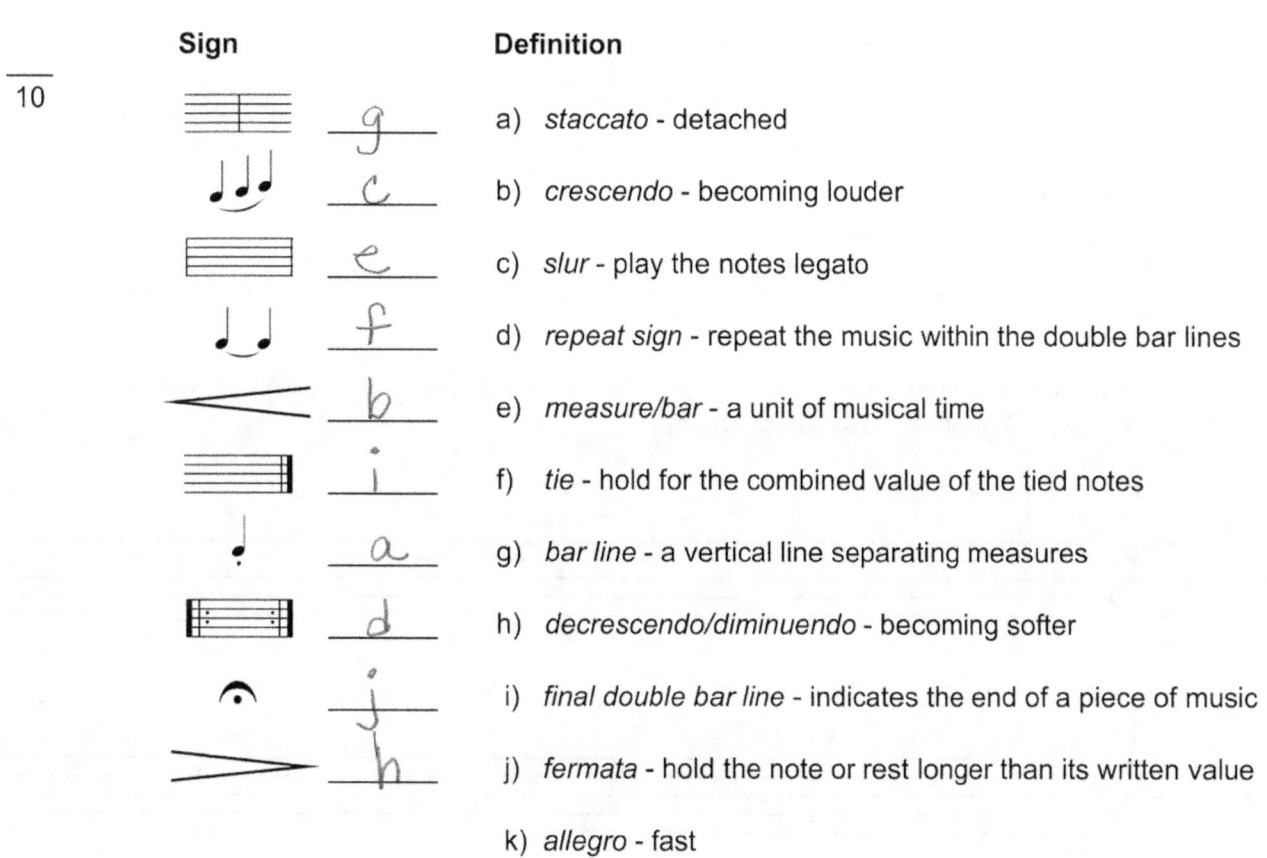

a) *staccato* - detached
b) *crescendo* - becoming louder
c) *slur* - play the notes legato
d) *repeat sign* - repeat the music within the double bar lines
e) *measure/bar* - a unit of musical time
f) *tie* - hold for the combined value of the tied notes
g) *bar line* - a vertical line separating measures
h) *decrescendo/diminuendo* - becoming softer
i) *final double bar line* - indicates the end of a piece of music
j) *fermata* - hold the note or rest longer than its written value
k) *allegro* - fast

10. Complete the Circle of Fifths by adding the order of flats on the top left and the order of sharps on the top right. Write the Major keys on the outside of the circle. Use UPPER case letters. Write the minor keys on the inside of the circle. Use lower case letters.

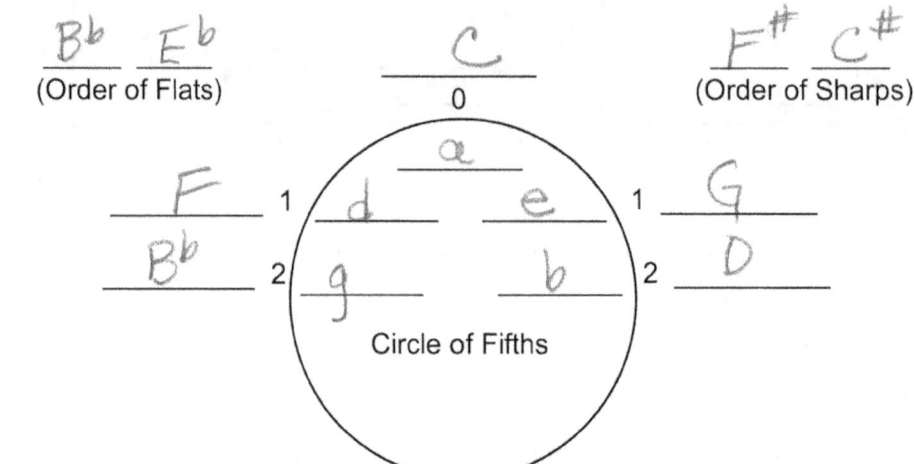

b) Write the following scales, ascending and descending, using a Key Signature. Use accidentals when necessary. Use whole notes.

C Major scale

e minor harmonic scale

G Major scale

c) Write the following scales, ascending and descending, using ACCIDENTALS instead of a Key Signature. Use whole notes.

a minor harmonic scale

F Major scale

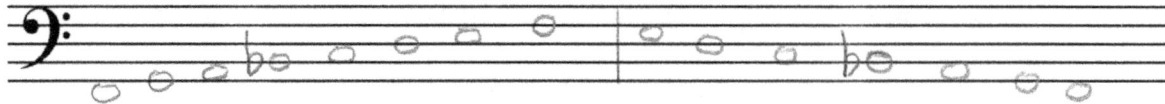

Lesson 11 — Melodic Minor Scales

A **NATURAL MINOR** Scale has the **SAME KEY SIGNATURE** as its **RELATIVE MAJOR**.

As the word **NATURAL** indicates, no accidentals are added.

♪ **Note:** Major keys are written on the outside of the Circle of Fifths. Minor keys are written on the inside.

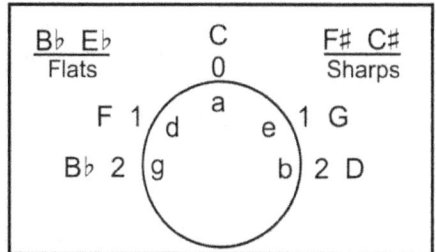

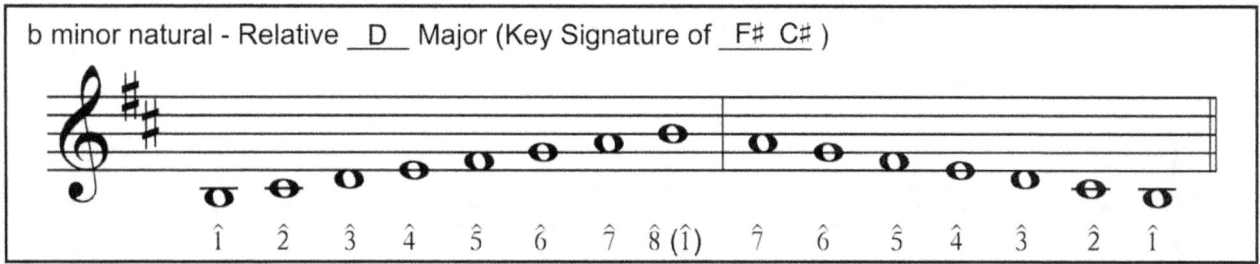

b minor natural - Relative __D__ Major (Key Signature of __F♯ C♯__)

A **MELODIC MINOR** scale has the SAME Key Signature as its relative Major. In a melodic minor scale, the 6th and 7th notes are RAISED one semitone ascending and LOWERED one semitone descending. The RAISED 6th and 7th notes are ALWAYS written using accidentals.

♪ **Note:** A bar line cancels an accidental, but NOT a Key Signature. When using a Key Signature and the center bar line, no accidentals are needed to lower the 6th and 7th notes in the descending melodic minor scale.

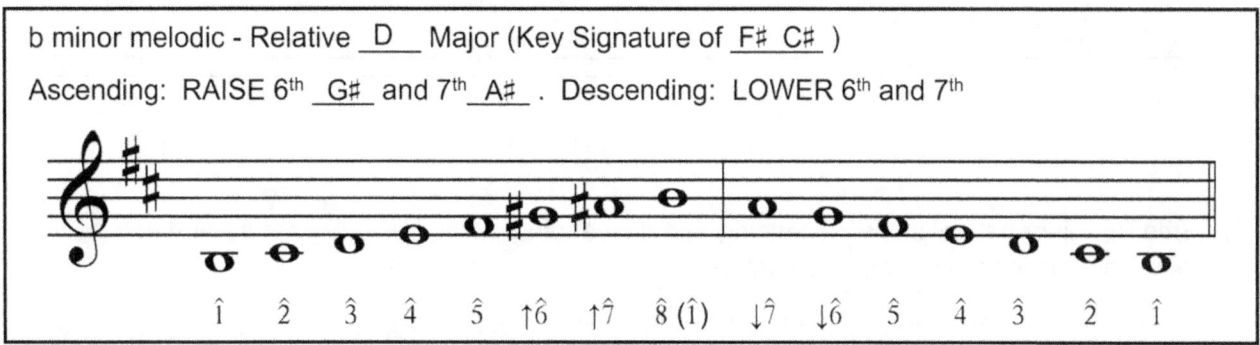

b minor melodic - Relative __D__ Major (Key Signature of __F♯ C♯__)
Ascending: RAISE 6th __G♯__ and 7th __A♯__ . Descending: LOWER 6th and 7th

♪ **Note:** When using a Key Signature without a center bar line, accidentals are needed to raise the 6th and 7th notes in the ascending melodic minor scale and to lower the 6th and 7th notes in the descending melodic minor scale.

1. a) Name the relative Major, its Key Signature and the raised 6th and 7th notes.
   b) Change the natural minor scale to a melodic minor scale by RAISING the 6th and 7th notes one semitone ascending, and by LOWERING the 6th and 7th notes one semitone descending.

   e minor harmonic - Relative __G__ Major (Key Signature __F♯__)
   Ascending: RAISE 6th __C♯__ and 7th __D♯__ . Descending: LOWER 6th and 7th

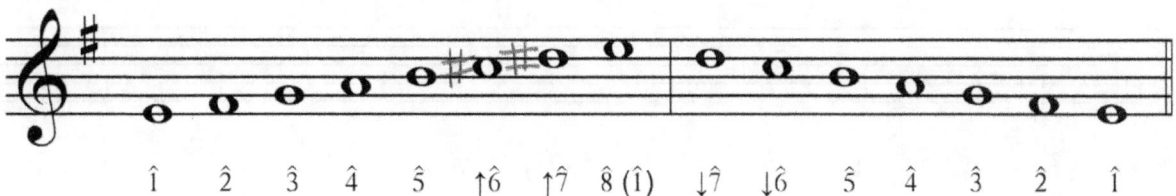

WRITING MELODIC MINOR SCALES

In a **MELODIC MINOR SCALE**, the 6th and 7th notes are raised ascending (going up) and lowered descending (going down). In the ascending scale, if either note is a flat, it will be raised to a natural. If either note is a natural, it will be raised to a sharp.

♪ **Note:** The numbers **6** and **7** are hidden inside the letter **M** for melodic.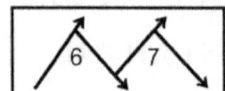

1. Write the following melodic minor scales, ascending and descending, using a Key Signature. Use accidentals for the raised 6th and 7th notes. Use whole notes.

    d minor melodic - Relative _F_ Major (Key Signature of _B♭_)
    Ascending: RAISE 6th _B♮_ and 7th _C♯_. Descending: LOWER 6th and 7th

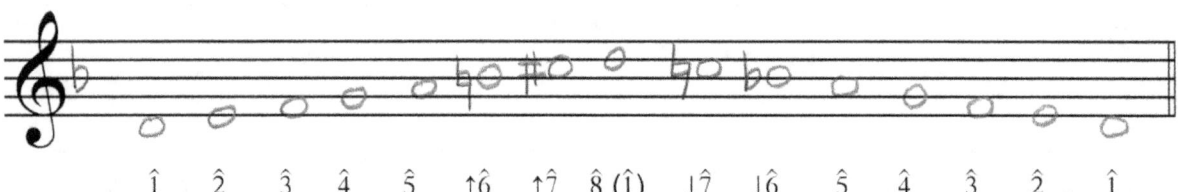

    g minor melodic - Relative _B♭_ Major (Key Signature of _B♭ E♭_)
    Ascending: RAISE 6th _E♮_ and 7th _F♯_. Descending: LOWER 6th and 7th

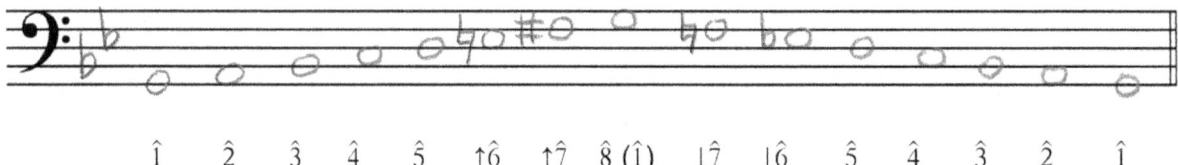

2. Write "a" minor natural scale, ascending and descending, using a Key Signature and any necessary accidentals. Use whole notes.

    a minor natural - Relative _C_ Major (Key Signature of _—_)

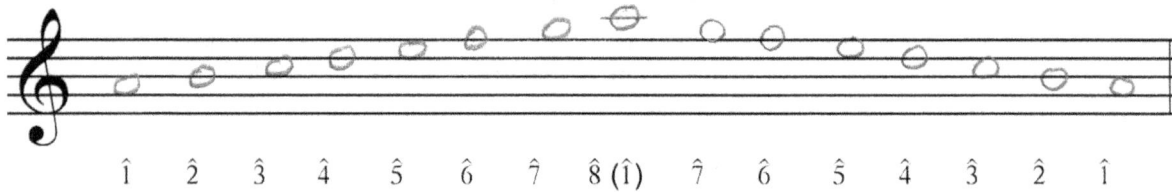

3. Write "a" minor melodic scale, ascending and descending, using accidentals instead of a Key Signature. Use whole notes.

    a minor melodic - Relative _C_ Major (Key Signature of _—_) raised 6th _F♯_ 7th _G♯_

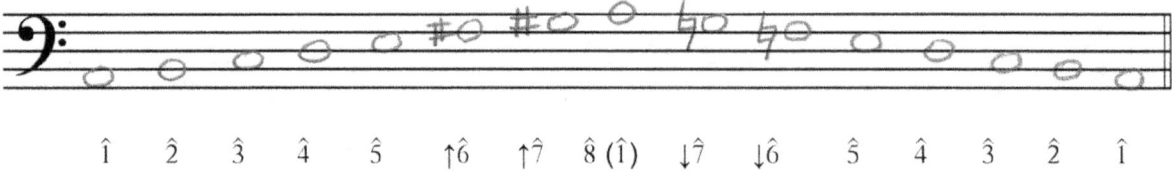

WRITING NATURAL and MELODIC MINOR SCALES

When writing a melodic minor scale using a Key Signature, it will be necessary to also use accidentals for the raised 6th and 7th notes.

1. Write d minor natural scale, ascending and descending, using a Key Signature. Use whole notes.

   d minor natural - Relative __F__ Major (Key Signature __B♭__)

2. Write d minor melodic scale, ascending and descending, using a Key Signature. Use accidentals for the raised 6th and 7th notes. Use whole notes.

   d minor melodic - Relative __F__ Major (Key Signature __B♭__) raised 6th __B♮__ 7th __C♯__

♪ **Note:** When using a center bar line, the accidentals for the raised 6th and 7th note are cancelled by the bar line. No further accidentals are needed to lower them.

3. Write e minor natural scale, ascending and descending, using accidentals. Use whole notes.

   e minor natural - Relative __G__ Major (Key Signature __F♯__)

4. Write e minor melodic scale, ascending and descending, using accidentals. Use whole notes.

   e minor melodic - Relative __G__ Major (Key Signature __F♯__) raised 6th __C♯__ 7th __D♯__

5. Fill in the blanks:

   a) A natural minor has the same Key Signature as its __relative__ Major.
   b) A melodic minor scale has a raised __6th__ note and raised __7th__ note.
   c) The 6th and 7th notes of the melodic minor scale are __raised__ in the ascending scale and __lowered__ in the descending scale.

Lesson 11 — Review Test

Total Score: ___ / 100

1. Write the following notes. Use **ledger lines**. Use whole notes.

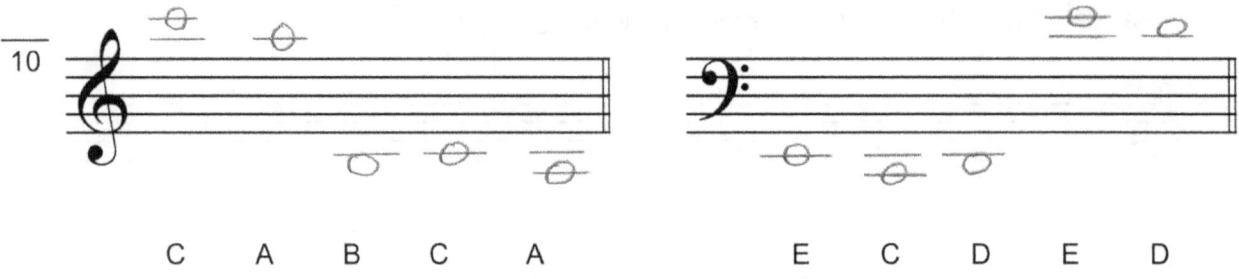

C A B C A   E C D E D

2. a) Add **STEMS** and a **BEAM** to create a pair of beamed eighth notes in each measure.
   b) Name the notes. Observe the Key Signature.

Bb C   Bb Eb   D Eb   D A   Eb Bb

3. a) Name the following notes on the Grand Staff.
   b) Draw a line from each note on the Grand Staff to the corresponding key on the keyboard (at the correct pitch).

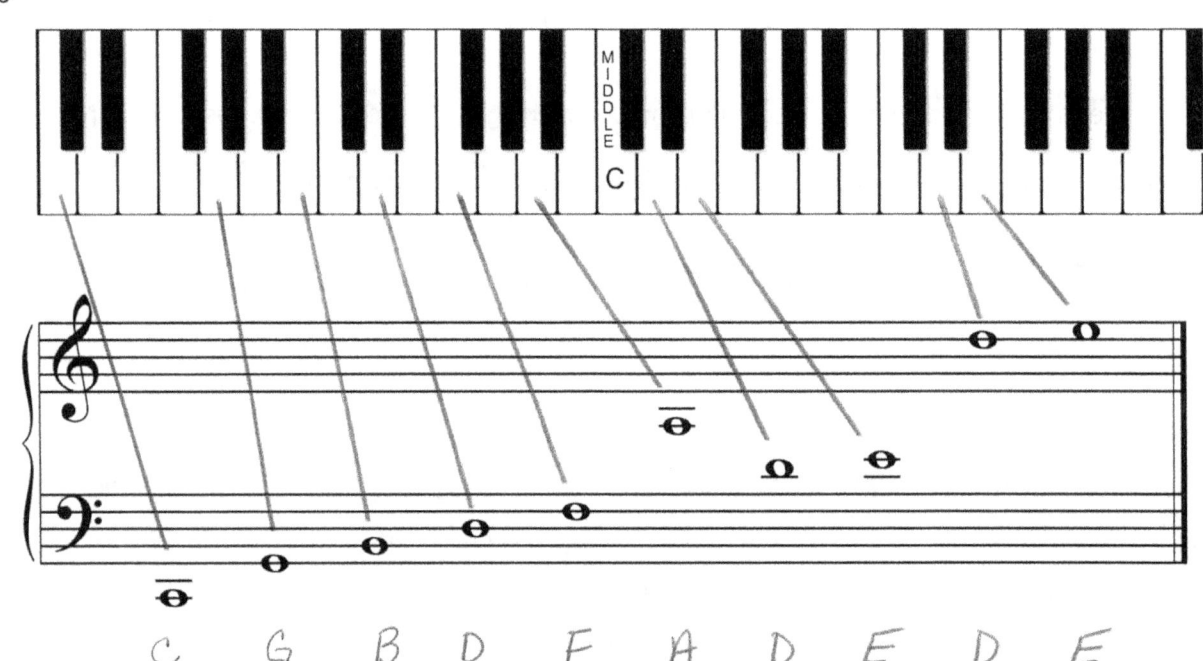

C G B D F A D E D E

4. Identify the following as **WT** (whole tone) or as **ST** (semitone). Observe the Key Signature.

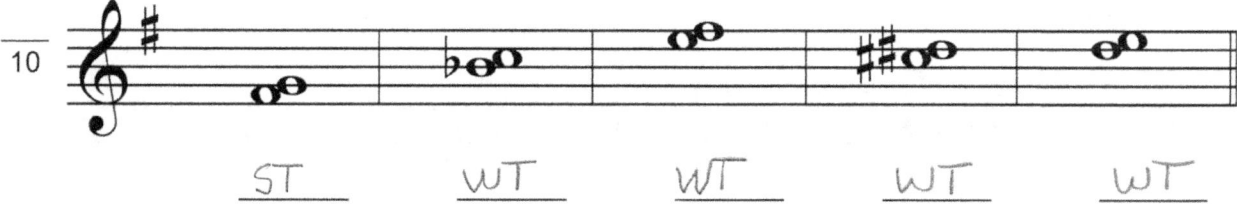

   ST   WT   WT   WT   WT

5. a) **SCOOP** each Basic Beat in each measure.
   b) Write the **PULSE** below each Basic Beat.
   c) Add **RESTS** below each bracket to complete each measure.
   d) Cross off the Basic Beat as each beat is completed.

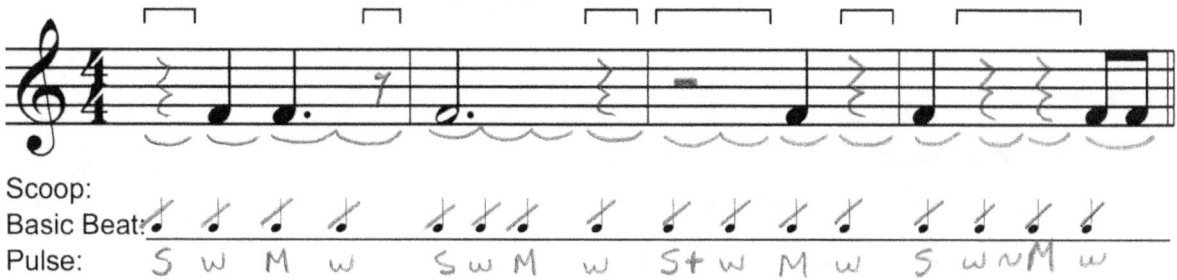

Scoop:
Basic Beat:
Pulse: S W M W   S w M W   S t W M W   S W N M W

   e) Add the correct time signature below each bracket for the following measures.

6. Name the size of the boxed melodic intervals (number size only). Use an up, down or across arrow to indicate direction.

   ↑4   ↓2   →1   ↑5   ↓6

7. Name the ROOT of the following Tonic Major triads. Circle Solid or Broken for each.

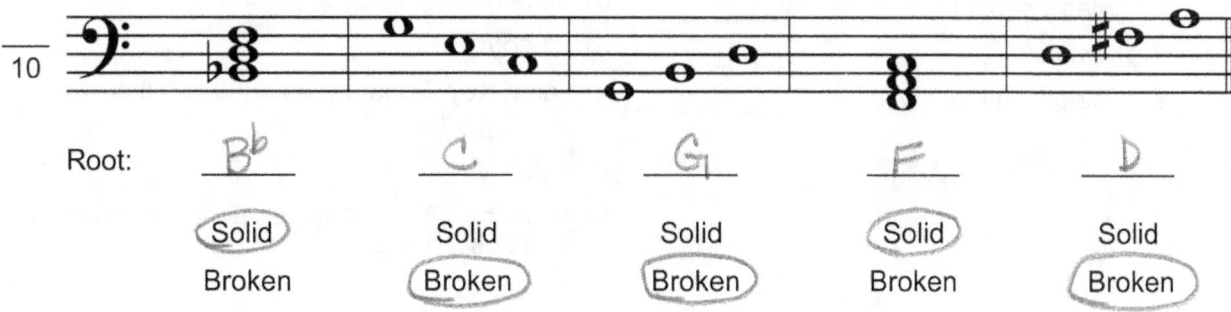

Root: B♭   C   G   F   D

        (Solid) Solid   Solid   Solid   Solid
         Broken (Broken)(Broken)(Broken)(Broken)

8. Analyze the following piece of music by answering the questions below.

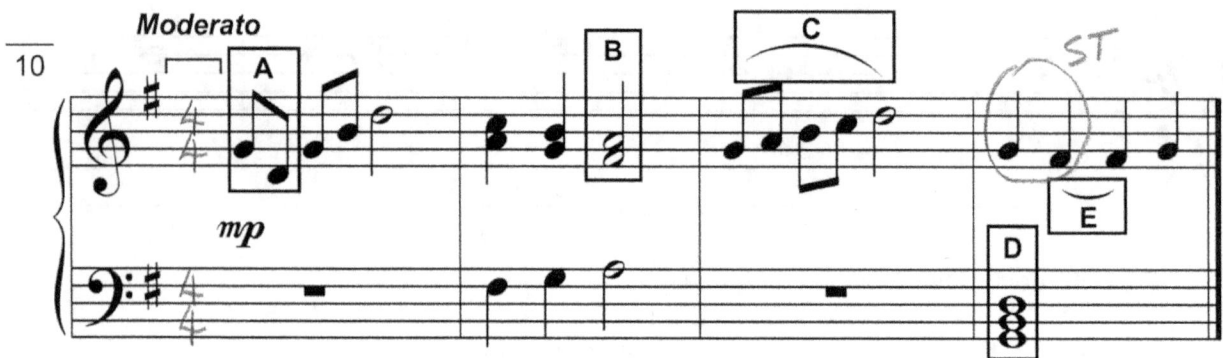

a) Add the correct Time Signature directly on the music.
b) Name the key of this piece. __G Major__
c) Explain the tempo of this piece. __Moderato - moderate tempo__
d) Explain the dynamic marking in this piece. __Mezzo piano - moderately soft__
e) Name the melodic interval at the letter **A**. __4__
f) Name the harmonic interval at the letter **B**. __3__
g) Locate and circle a semitone directly on the music. Label it ST.
h) Explain the sign at the letter **C**. __slur - play legato (smooth)__
i) Identify the triad at the letter **D** as solid or broken. __solid__
j) Explain the sign at the letter **E**. __tie - hold for combined value of the tied notes__

9. Match each musical term with the English definition. (Not all definitions will be used.)

Term **Definition**

piano, *p* __j__ a) return to the original tempo
diminuendo, dim. __f__ b) slowing down gradually
a tempo __a__ c) raise the 6th and 7th notes one semitone ascending and lower one semitone descending
natural minor scale __i__
mezzo forte, *mf* __d__ d) moderately loud
harmonic minor scale __k__ e) very slow
legato __h__ f) becoming softer
ritardando, rit. __b__ g) detached
staccato __g__ h) smooth
melodic minor scale __c__ i) same Key Signature as relative Major, with nothing added
j) soft
k) raise the 7th note one semitone ascending and descending

10. Complete the Circle of Fifths by adding the order of flats on the top left and the order of sharps on the top right. Write the Major keys on the outside of the circle. Use UPPER case letters. Write the minor keys on the inside of the circle. Use lower case letters.

B♭ E♭ (Order of Flats)
C 0
F♯ C♯ (Order of Sharps)

F 1 d a e 1 G
B♭ 2 g b 2 D

Circle of Fifths

b) Write the following scales, ascending and descending, using a Key Signature and any necessary accidentals. Use whole notes.

D Major scale

g minor natural scale

e minor harmonic scale

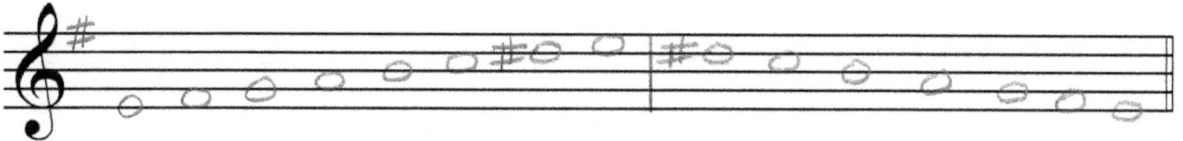

c) Write the following scales, ascending and descending, using accidentals instead of a Key Signature. Use whole notes.

a minor melodic scale

d minor natural scale

Lesson 12　　　Analysis and Musical Terms

ANALYSIS of a musical piece is the process of examining the details of the composition before beginning to learn or perform the piece.

TITLE - written at the top center of the music.
TEMPO - (speed at which the piece is performed) written on the top left above the Time Signature.
COMPOSER - (name of person who wrote the music) written on the top right of the piece.
TIME SIGNATURE - written in BOTH the Treble Clef and the Bass Clef.
MEASURE NUMBERS - can be written inside a small box above the top left of the measure.
DYNAMICS - written on the Grand Staff in between the Treble Clef and the Bass Clef.

1. Analyze the following piece of music by answering the questions below.

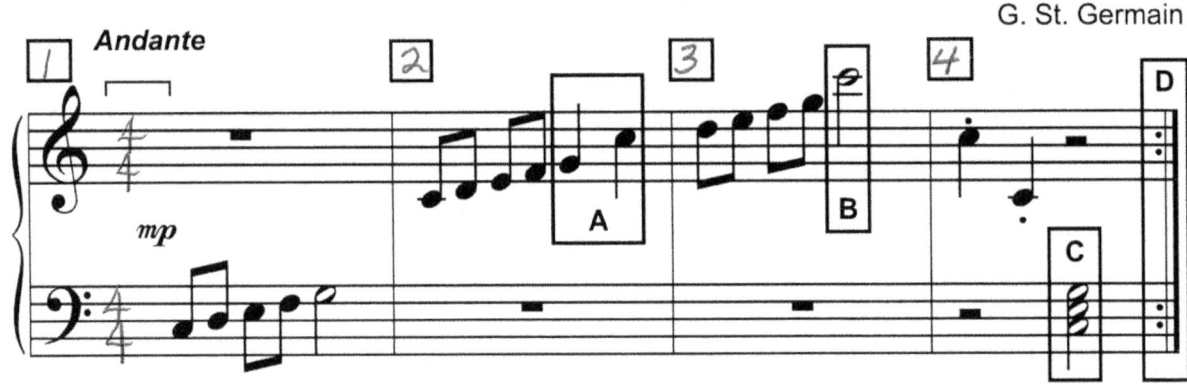

a) Name the title of this piece. _The Bike Ride_

b) What is the tempo of this piece? _Andante - Moderately slow, walking pace_

c) Name the composer of this piece. _G. St. Germain_

d) Number the measures in the boxes provided above each measure.

e) Add the correct Time Signature directly on the music.

f) Name the interval at the letter **A**. _4_

g) Name the note at the letter **B**. _C_

h) Name the root of the triad at the letter **C**. _C_

i) Explain the sign at the letter **D**. _repeat the music from the beginning_

j) When the repeat sign is followed, how many measures are played? _8_

MUSICAL TERMS - DYNAMICS, TEMPO and ARTICULATION

DYNAMICS - the varying degrees of loudness or softness.

Term	Symbol or Sign	Definition
crescendo	cresc. or <	becoming louder
decrescendo	decresc. or >	becoming softer
diminuendo	dim. or >	becoming softer
fortissimo	*ff*	very loud
forte	*f*	loud
mezzo forte	*mf*	moderately loud, medium loud
mezzo piano	*mp*	moderately soft, medium soft
piano	*p*	soft
pianissimo	*pp*	very soft

1. Write the sign for the following dynamics.

pp	*mf*	*f*	*p*	*mp*
very soft	moderately loud	loud	soft	moderately soft

TEMPO - the rate of speed; how fast or slow the music is played.

Terms	Definition
largo	very slow
lento	slow
adagio	fairly slow
andante	at a moderate walking pace, moderately slow
moderato	at a moderate tempo
allegretto	fairly fast; a little slower than allegro
allegro	fast
presto	very fast
prestissimo	as fast as possible

Changes in Tempo

a tempo	return to the original tempo
accelerando, accel.	becoming quicker
fermata, 𝄐	pause, hold the note or rest longer than its written value
ritardando, rit.	slowing down gradually

ARTICULATION - the different types of sound created by using different articulation (touch).

Term	Definition	Articulation Mark
accent	a stressed note	>
fermata	pause, hold for longer than the given value	𝄐
legato	smooth	
staccato	detached	♩ ♩
slur	play notes legato (smooth)	♩ ♩
tenuto	hold for the full value of the note	
tie	hold for the combined value of the tied notes	♩ ♩

Lesson 12   Final Prep 2 Exam

Total Score: ____ / 100

1. Draw a Bass Clef on the staff below. Name the notes.

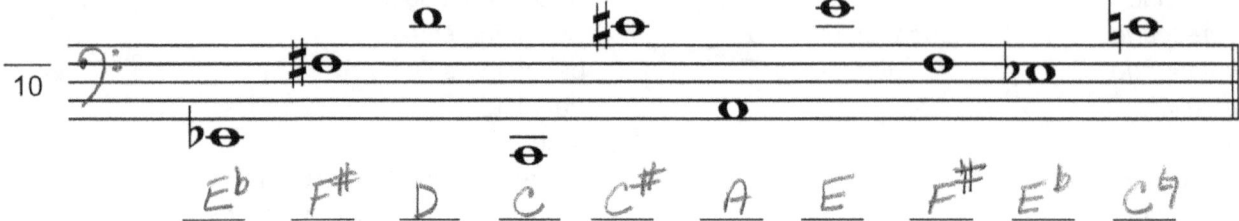

Eb   F#   D   C   C#   A   E   F#   Eb   C♮

2. Write the TONIC note for the following Major keys. Use a Key Signature. Use quarter notes.

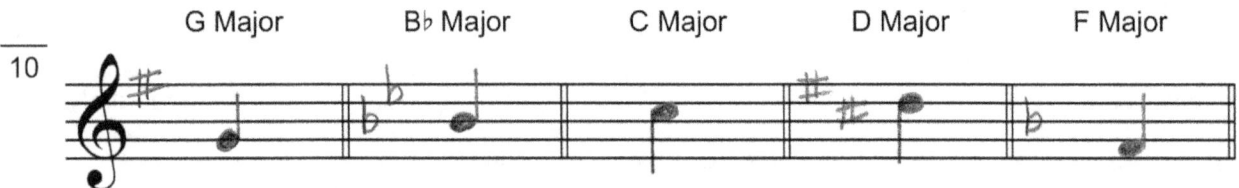

3. a) Write the notes on the Grand Staff for the keys labelled with a ☺ on the keyboard. Use whole notes.
   b) Name the notes.
   c) Draw a line from each note on the Grand Staff to the corresponding key on the keyboard.

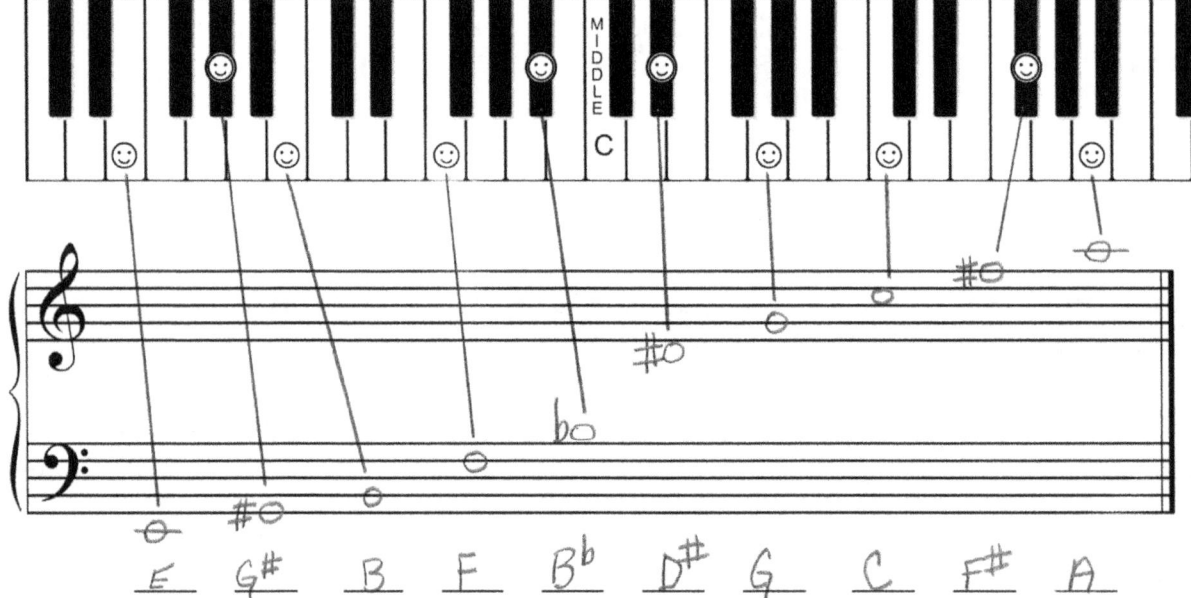

E   G#   B   F   Bb   D#   G   C   F#   A

4. Identify the following as WT (whole tone) or as ST (semitone). Observe the Key Signature.

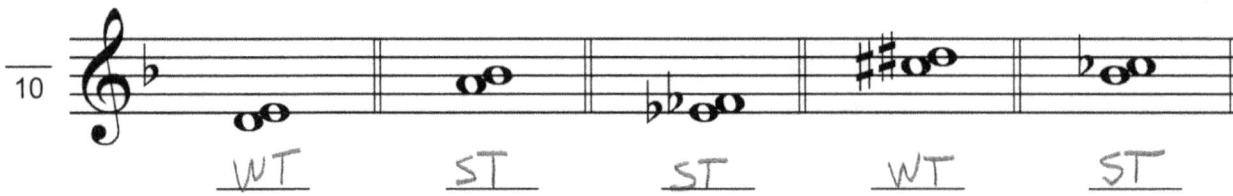

WT   ST   ST   WT   ST

5. Add the correct Time Signature below each bracket for the following measures.

6. a) Identify the interval as harmonic (H) or melodic (M).
   b) Name the interval (numerical size only) between the notes in each measure.

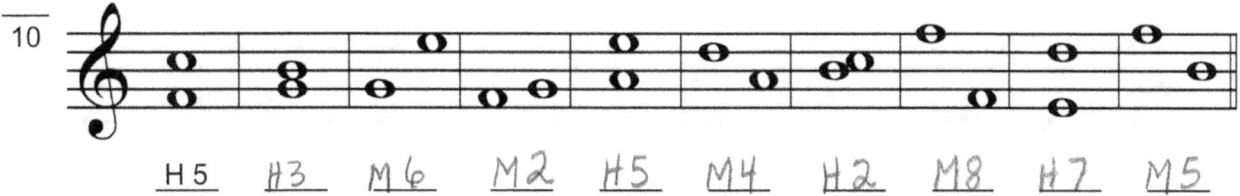

H5   H3   M6   M2   H5   M4   H2   M8   H7   M5

7. a) Write the following **SOLID** Tonic triads in root position. Use accidentals. Use half notes.
   b) Name the Root.

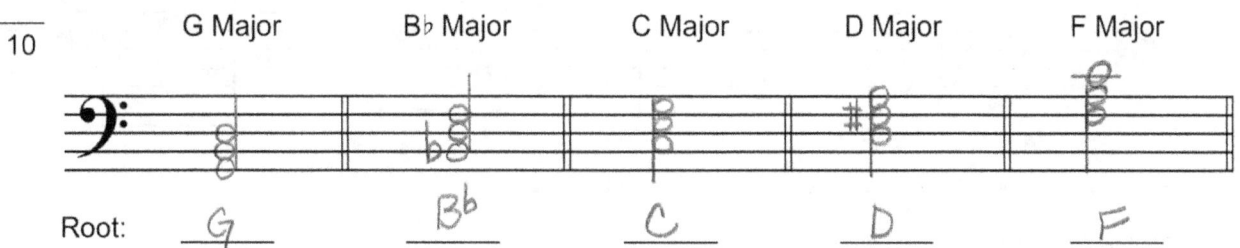

Root: G   Bb   C   D   F

8. Match each musical term with the English definition. (Not all definitions will be used.)

Term		Definition
staccato	b	a) a unit of musical time
crescendo	g	b) detached
fermata	h	c) becoming softer
double bar line	e	d) a vertical line separating measures
slur	f	e) indicates the end of a piece of music
measure/bar	a	f) play the notes legato
bar line	d	g) becoming louder
tie	k	h) hold the note or rest longer than its written value
decrescendo	c	i) repeat the music
repeat sign	i	j) slowing down gradually
		k) hold for the combined value of the tied notes

119

9. a) Identify the following scales as Major or minor: natural, harmonic or melodic.
    b) Name the Tonic note of each scale.

Tonic note: **B♭**   Scale: **B♭ Major**

Tonic note: **B**   Scale: **b minor harmonic**

Tonic note: **E**   Scale: **e minor natural**

10. Analyze the following piece of music by answering the questions below.

    a) Add the correct Time Signature directly on the music.
    b) Name the key of this piece. **C Major**
    c) Explain the tempo of this piece. **Allegro - fast**
    d) Explain the dynamic marking in this piece. **mezzo piano - moderately soft**
    e) Name the root of the triad at the letter **A**. **C**
    f) Name the root of the triad at the letter **B**. **G**
    g) Locate and circle a whole tone directly on the music. Label it WT.
    h) Explain the sign at the letter **C**. **staccato - detached**
    i) Identify the triad at the letter **D** as solid or broken. **broken**
    j) Explain the sign at the letter **E**. **fermata - pause, hold longer than written value**

UltimateMusicTheory.com

Ultimate Music Theory Certificate

_____

has successfully completed all the requirements of the

Prep 2 Rudiments

_____   _____
Music Teacher   *Date*

Enriching Lives Through Music Education

ULTIMATE MUSIC THEORY GUIDE - PREP 2

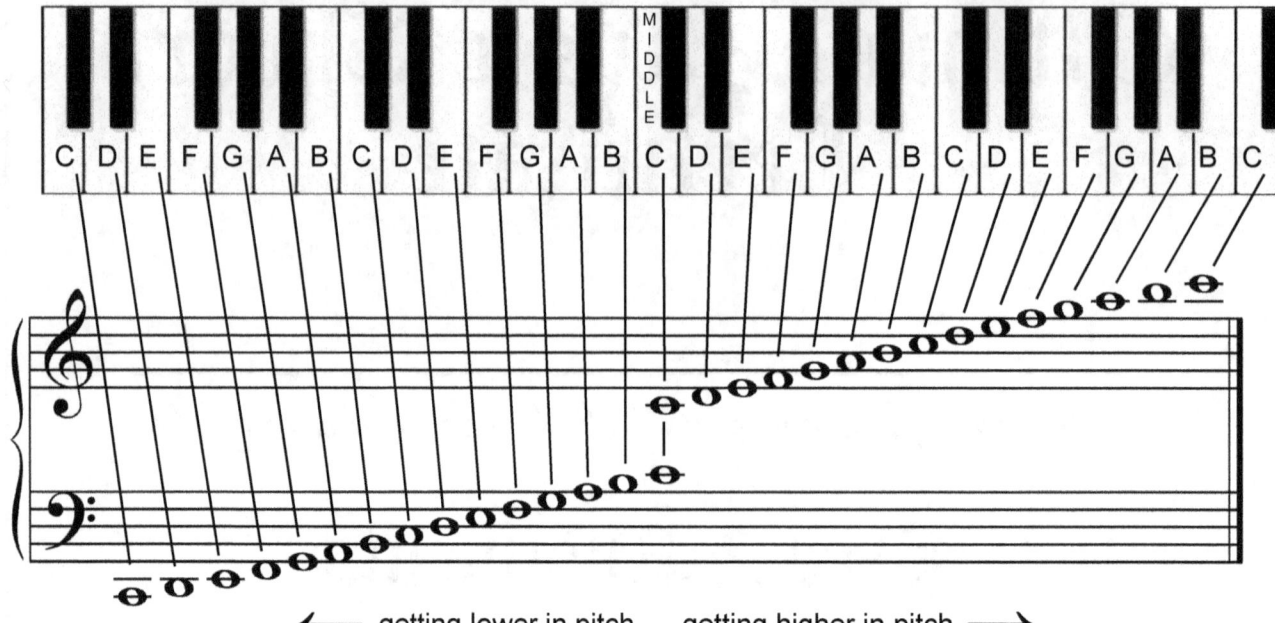

← getting lower in pitch   getting higher in pitch →

An **ACCIDENTAL** is a sign that lowers or raises the pitch one semitone (half step).

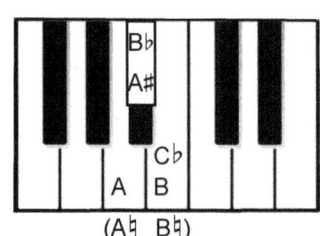

♭ **FLAT - LOWERS** a note one semitone (half step). B to B♭

♯ **SHARP - RAISES** a note one semitone (half step). A to A♯

♮ **NATURAL - CANCELS** a flat or a sharp. B♭ to B♮ or A♯ to A♮

ENHARMONIC EQUIVALENT - same pitch, different letter name. B♭ and A♯ or B♮ and C♭

An **INTERVAL** is the distance in pitch between two notes.

HARMONIC Interval - **H** is for Harmony.
Two notes - one ABOVE the other (together).

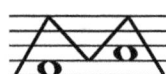

MELODIC Interval - **M** is for Melody.
Two notes - one BESIDE the other (separate).

C Major Pentascale

Scale Degree:	1̂	whole tone	2̂	whole tone	3̂	semitone	4̂	whole tone	5̂
Roman Numeral:	I		II		III		IV		V
Technical Name:	Tonic		Supertonic		Mediant		Subdominant		Dominant

UltimateMusicTheory.com

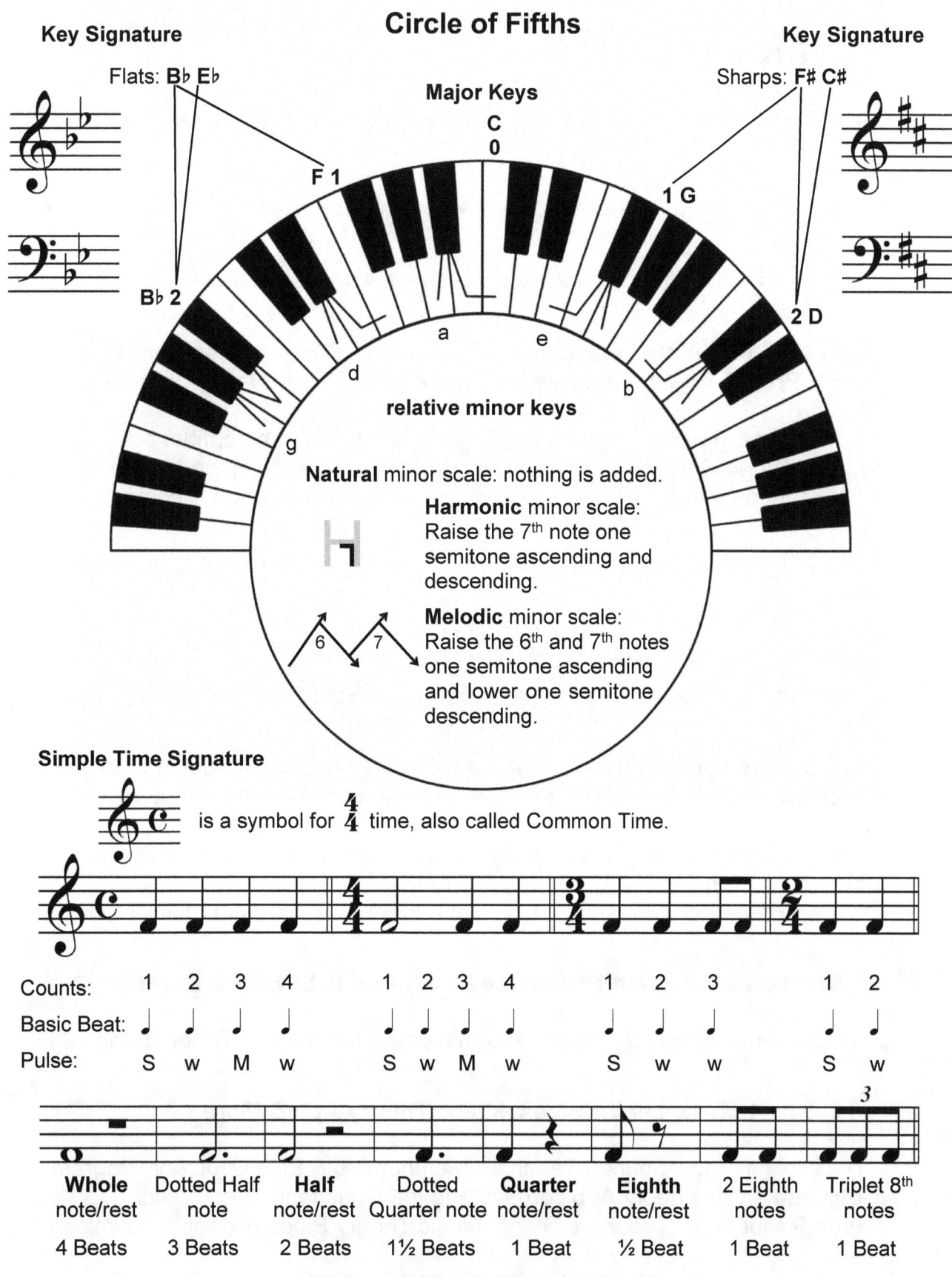

 **Workbooks, Exams, Answers, Online Courses, App & More!**

A Proven Step-by-Step System to Learn Theory Faster - from Beginner to Advanced.

Innovative techniques designed to develop a complete understanding of music theory, to enhance sight reading, ear training, creativity, composition and musical expression.

All UMT Series have matching Answer Books!

The UMT Rudiments Series - Beginner A, Beginner B, Beginner C, Prep 1, Prep 2, Basic, Intermediate, Advanced & Complete (All-In-One)

- ♪ 12 Lessons, Review Tests, and a Final Exam to develop confidence
- ♪ Music Theory Guide & Chart for fast and easy reference of theory concepts
- ♪ 80 Flashcards for fun drills to dramatically increase retention & comprehension

Rudiments Exam Series - Preparatory, Basic, Intermediate & Advanced

- ♪ 8 Exams plus UMT Tips on How to Score 100% on Theory Exams

Each Rudiments Workbook correlates to a Supplemental Workbook.

The UMT Supplemental Series - Prep Level, Level 1, Level 2, Level 3, Level 4, Level 5, Level 6, Level 7, Level 8 & Complete (All-In-One) Level

- ♪ Form & Analysis and Music History - Composers, Eras & Musical Styles
- ♪ Melody Writing using ICE - Imagine, Compose & Explore
- ♪ 12 Lessons, Review Tests, Final Exam and 80 Flashcards for quick study

Supplemental Exam Series - Level 5, Level 6, Level 7 & Level 8

- ♪ 8 Exams to successfully prepare for nationally recognized Theory Exams

UMT Online Courses, Music Theory App & More

- ♪ UMT Certification Course, Teachers Membership & Elite Educator Program
- ♪ Ultimate Music Theory App correlates to the Rudiments Workbooks
- ♪ Free Resources - Teachers Guide, Music Theory Blogs, videos & downloads

Go To: UltimateMusicTheory.com

Flashcards are two-sided: Question is on one side, and the Answer in square box is on the flip side.

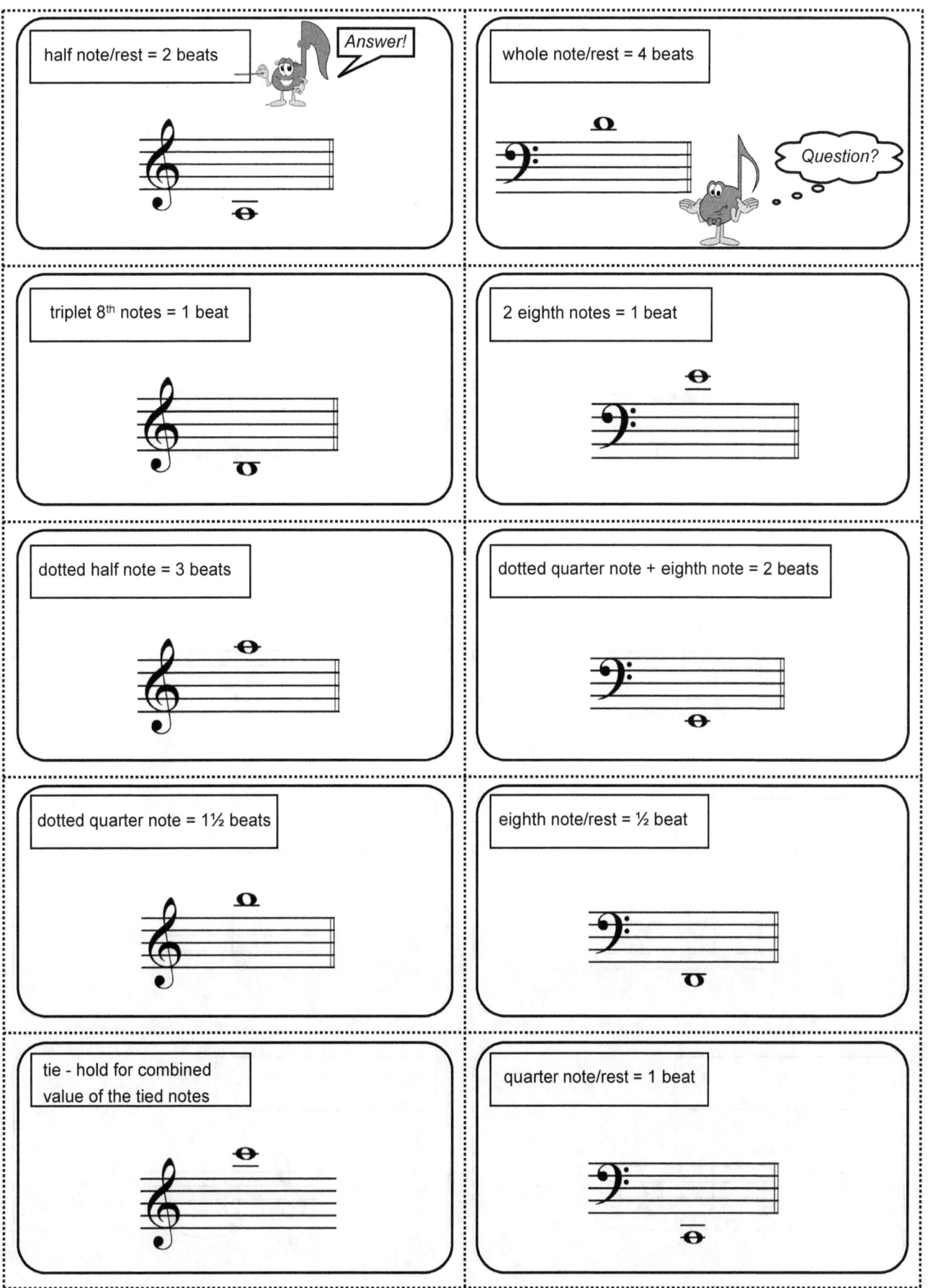

Study by cutting out the Flashcards, or by turning each page to check the answer on the other side.

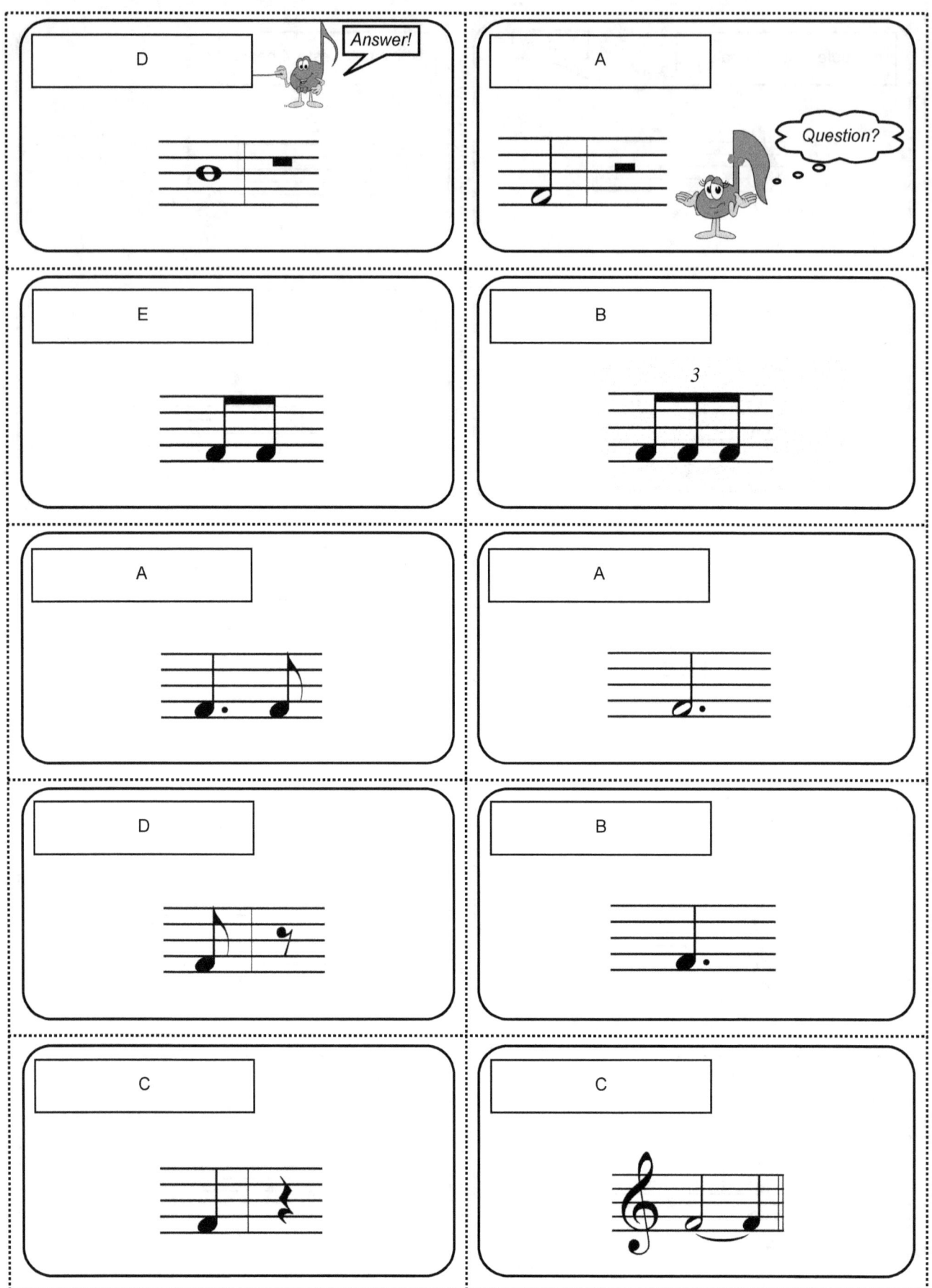

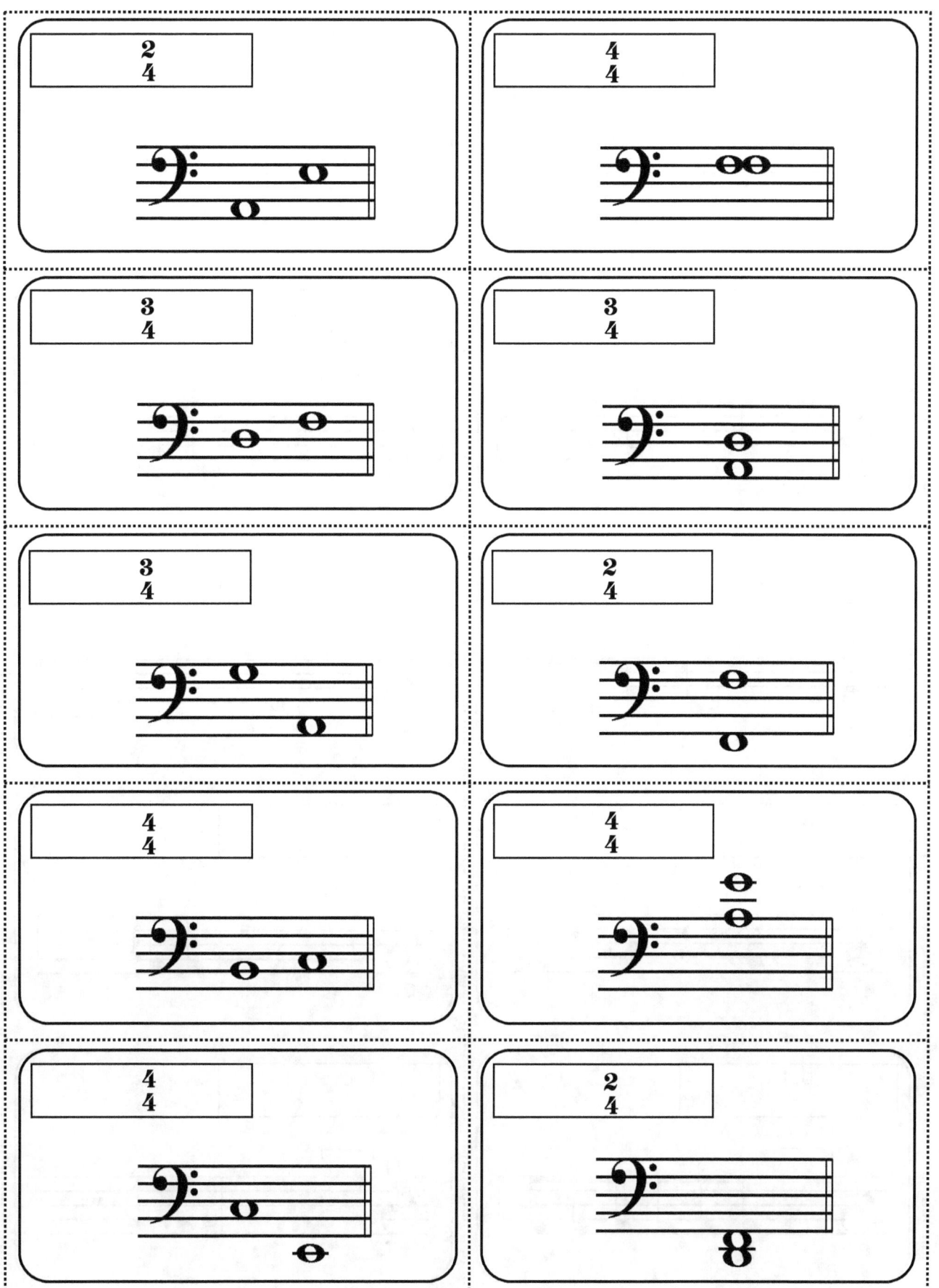

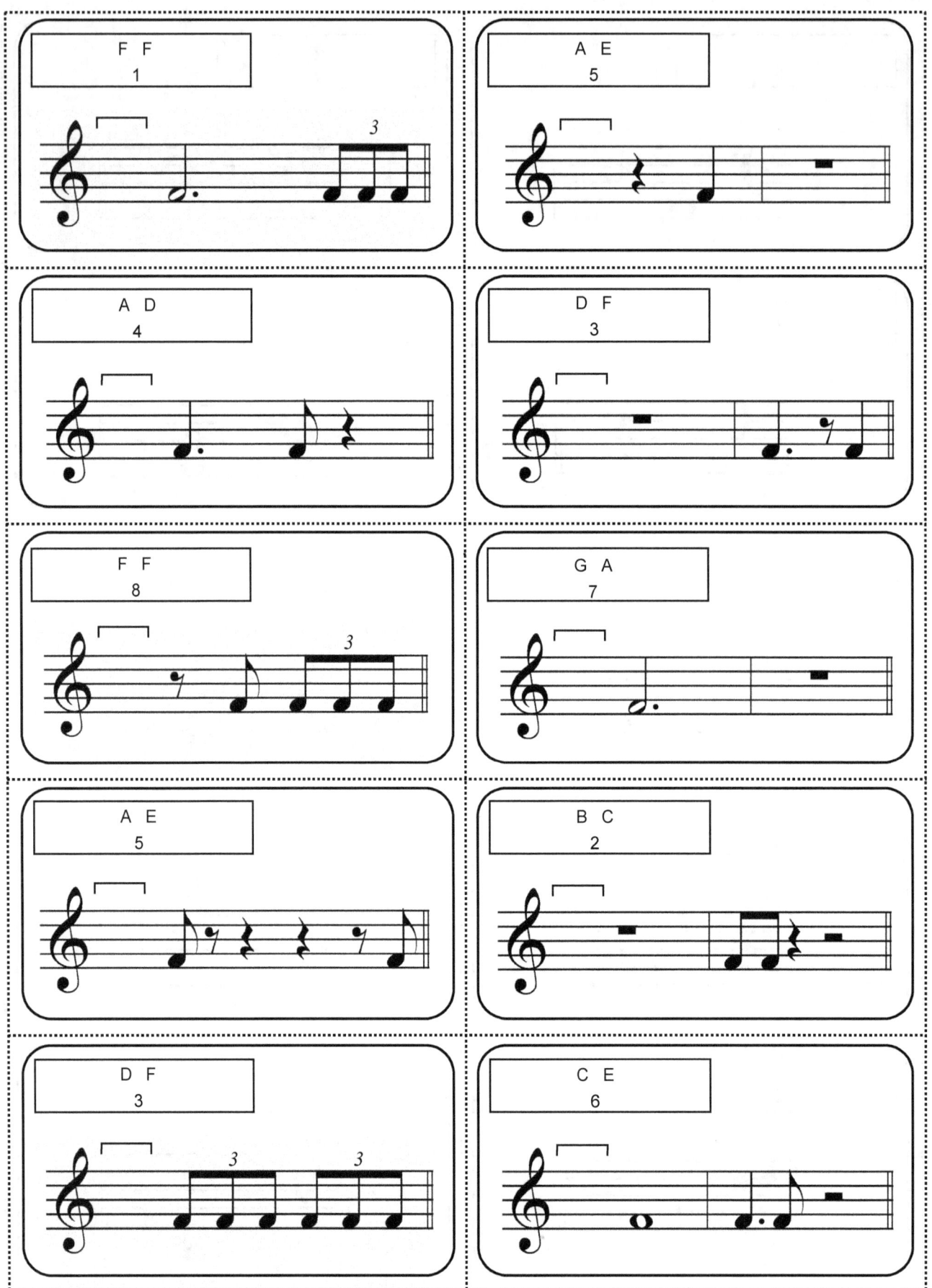

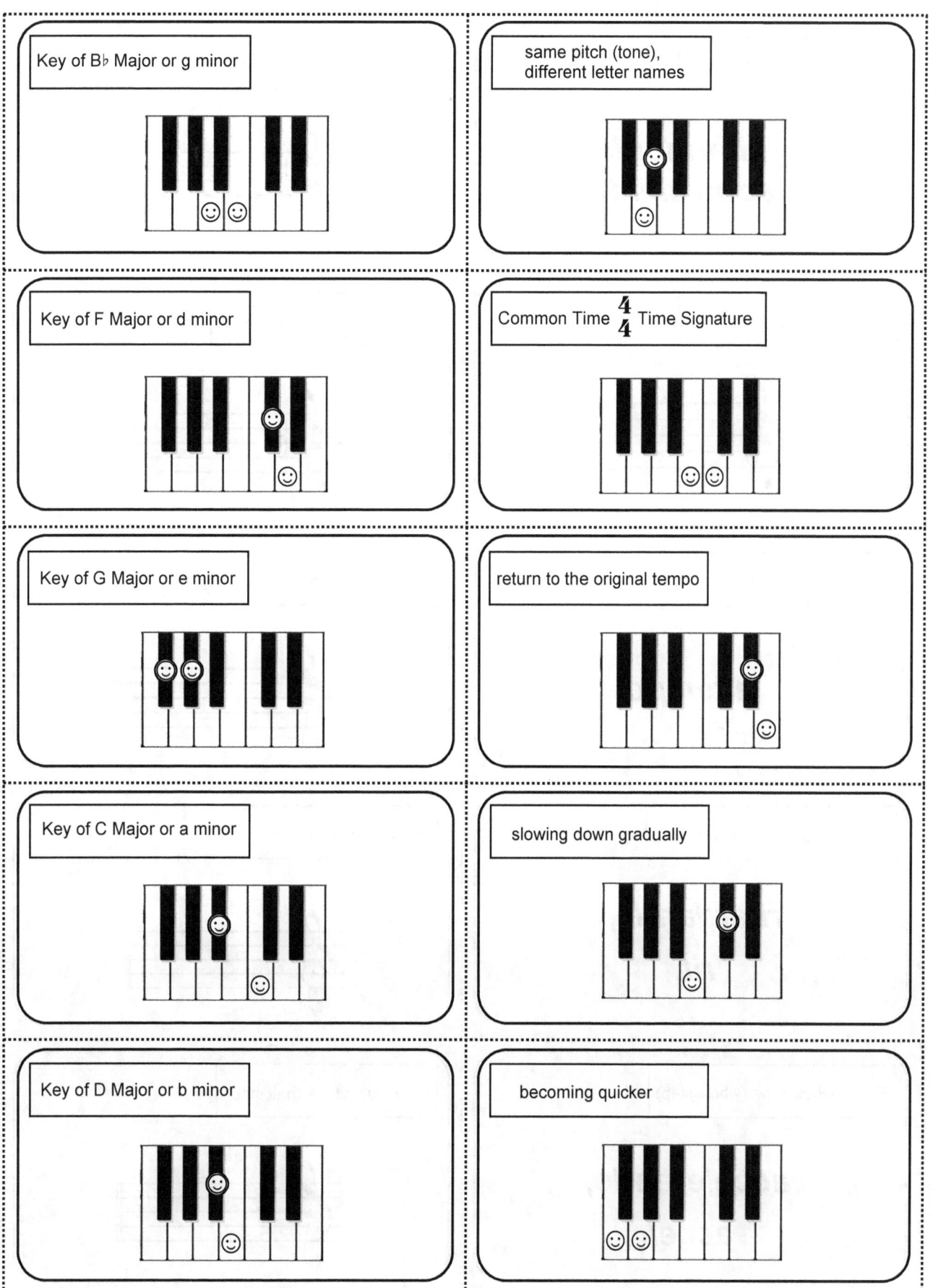

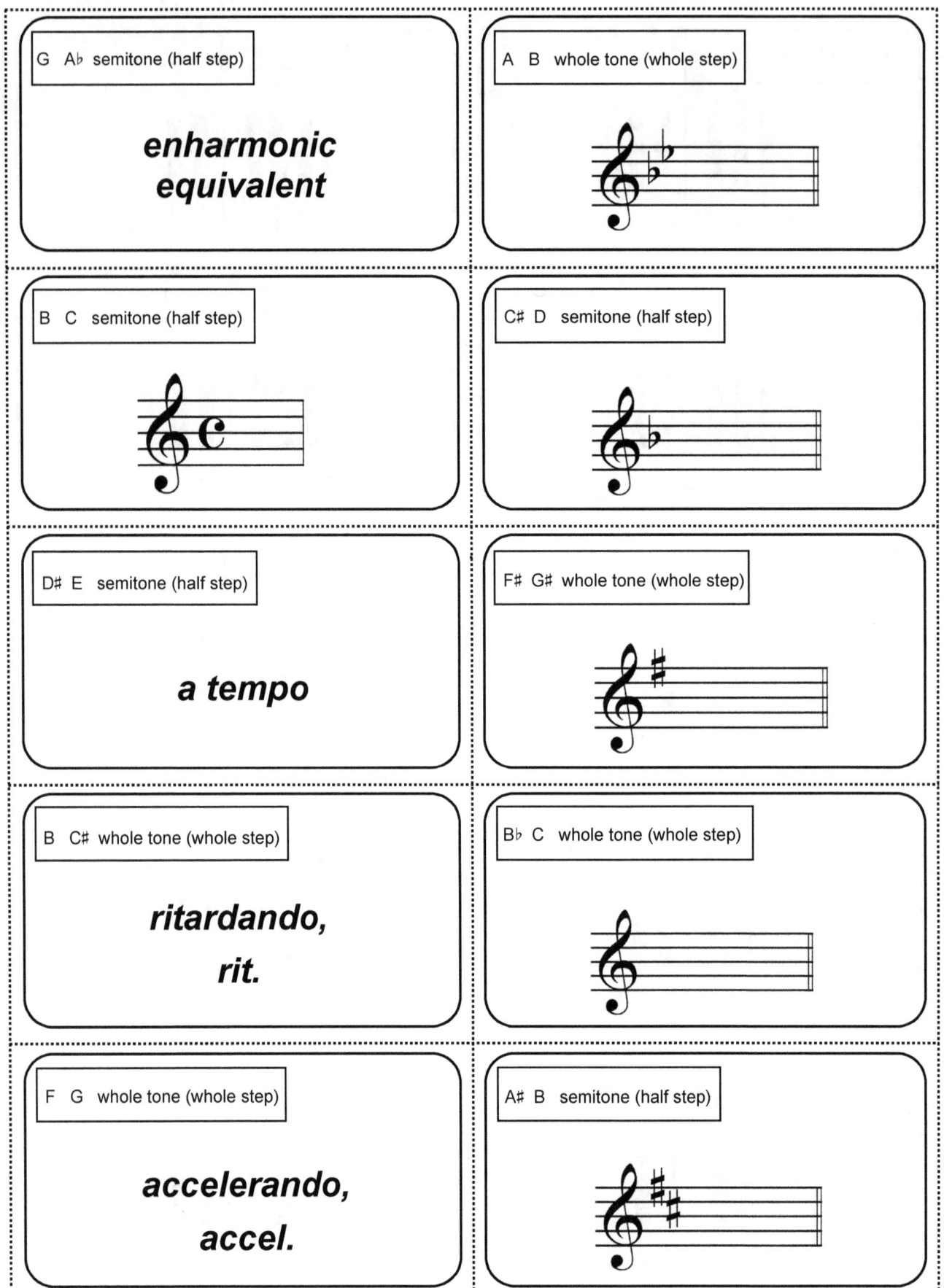

a minor melodic scale **Broken triad**	D Major scale
e minor harmonic scale **Solid (blocked) triad**	B♭ Major scale
b minor natural scale **natural minor scale**	C Major scale
d minor harmonic scale **harmonic minor scale**	F Major scale
g minor natural scale **melodic minor scale**	G Major scale

Go to: **UltimateMusicTheory.com** Learn Music Theory with a proven step-by-step system.

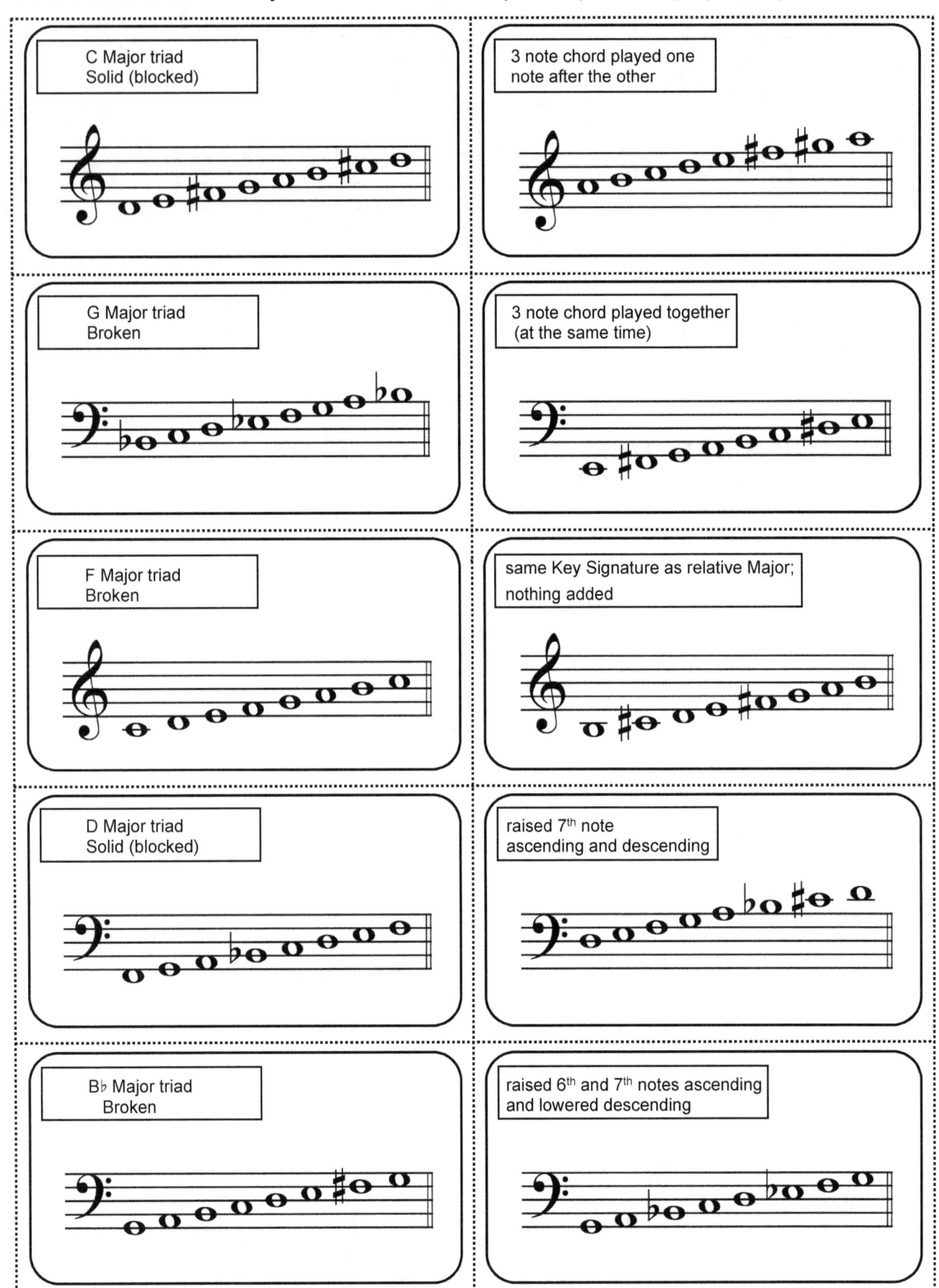

Ultimate Music Theory Ltd. © COPYRIGHT 2021 Gloryland Publishing. All Rights Reserved.

www.ingramcontent.com/pod-product-compliance
Lightning Source LLC
Chambersburg PA
CBHW060515300426
44112CB00017B/2679